ARNO⸜ P9-BIY-559
JUNE 11, 1990

Introduction
to the
CAUSA
Worldview

CAUSA International is based on the belief that positive
social change can only occur when God-accepting and
conscientious people are united upon common goals.
CAUSA, a non-profit organization, promotes an examination of values and a moral renaissance. To this end,
CAUSA conducts seminars for citizens who are concerned about their nations' well-being.

CAUSA International was founded in Washington, D.C.
in 1980 by the Reverend Sun Myung Moon.

The CAUSA Institute is an interdisciplinary research
and teaching center founded in New York for advanced
study on competing systems of thought and international
affairs in the twentieth century.

CAUSA Institute Publication 101
© 1985 by CAUSA International
401 Fifth Avenue
New York, New York 10016

Art Director, P.A. Beltrami
Third printing October, 1985
Produced by ACCORD, Inc.
Printed in the United States of America

CAUSA Institute
New York, New York

CONTENTS

Preface

This text presents an examination and critique of Marxist-Leninist ideology, a critique of confusion in the Western system of values, and a new worldview based on the affirmation of God. This new worldview, Godism, and these critiques were inspired by Reverend Sun Myung Moon, founder of CAUSA International.

Reverend Moon is calling for a worldwide ideological offensive to counter the global threat of communism. While all efforts made to oppose the advance of communism are commendable, the fact is that the West has been on the defensive too long. Anticommunism, being defensive in nature, will never bring a positive solution to the problems of communism. A strategy of victory over communism has been non-existent in the West, and the Free World has been on the retreat for nearly 70 years.

Communism is an ideology, a system of thought. It begins with certain beliefs, and builds upon these a philosophical system. It calls for commitment and provides a plan of action. It claims to be scientific, but appeals to the natural religious urge within every person. Communism promises the realization of the human dream, "utopia." Yet, after 70 years of rule, with virtually half of the world under its dominion, the communist utopia is nowhere in sight. Everywhere that communism has spread, unprecedented human misery is the result.

The reasons for this are manifold, but the central point emphasized by Reverend Moon is that communism will never work because it is based upon one fundamental error, *the denial of God*. The entire system of communist ideology begins with the assumption that *there is no God*. Marxist materialism and atheism begin from this point.

In 1848, Karl Marx and Friedrich Engels wrote the *Communist Manifesto*. Here was contained the essence of the communist program. They called for revolution and the destruction of all "bourgeois institutions," including the family. Their manifesto largely collected dust, however, until it became the tool which Lenin used in 1917 to take power in Russia. Since that time, the world has watched the unfolding of a nightmare. One nation after another has fallen into the hands of communism. Presently more than 1.5 billion people are forced to accept Marxism as their state ideology.

Communism, despite its obvious failures, continues to expand. Their goal is clearly world domination. Communist governments exercise a powerful monopoly of control over their people, effectively preventing any successful overthrow of the government. Then, massive military power is employed to threaten and bully the West to surrender helpless populations to the communist empire.

In nearly 70 years of application, Marxism-Leninism has proved to be the most barbaric and inhuman principle of government ever to come to power in history. This is a direct result of its belief in "no God." When there is no regard for God, there can be no basis for morality. Therefore, men can do anything without remorse. In its march to power, communism has destroyed more than 150,000,000 human lives. This number continues to increase at the rate of one every 15 seconds. Communism has become the funeral march of humanity. At the same time, communist ideologues proclaim that by the year 2000, the entire world will live under a communist utopia. The extinction of human freedom is a realistic possibility unless we do something now to turn the tide.

His personal intense suffering under communism led Reverend Moon to determine deeply to counter the relentless advance of communist ideology. Through extraordinary communion with God, he came to see clearly that there is no way we can eliminate communism if we do not confront it with a superior ideology or worldview. This worldview must begin with the idea of *God*. An affirmation of God's existence is the one way we can overcome communism. Reverend Moon believes fundamentally that just as light alone can overcome darkness, God alone can overcome godlessness.

Reverend Moon has developed a God-centered worldview, "Godism," as a winning solution to communism. Godism is effective in two ways:

(1) It carefully examines the ideology of communism, and exposes its lies and deception.

(2) It presents a counterproposal to communism. It offers a powerful logical and philosophical affirmation of the existence of God, appropriate for modern day human intellectual and spiritual development. By vividly presenting God and His purpose in creation and human history, Godism enlightens, inspires and motivates any man or woman of conscience. Godism represents a solution to communism from the roots.

Godism does not advocate maintaining the status quo. It calls for change in the West as well as the communist world. Under capitalism, there have been exploitation and severe economic inequalities in the third world. Exploitation results from a narrow and selfish perspective of value. It is the corruption in the West which allowed communism to come into being, and make its appeal for violent change. It is the corruption in the West which allows communism to portray itself as the liberator which will deliver developing nations from imperialist oppression. As long as we continue as we are in the West, we will never have any hope to see the end of communism.

Godism is like a two-edged sword. One edge cuts the

evil of communism, and the other edge cuts the corruption of the West. In this way, Western civilization can be restored to the God-centered tradition upon which true democracy and freedom can blossom.

Godism proposes a dramatic change in the West, and this can be achieved through a spiritual revolution in our free society. Selfishness can be eliminated, and the true revolution of man can be accomplished. Unless man changes, nothing changes, but once man changes, changed men and women can improve society and create a new moral world.

Godism is able to resolve confusion in the Western system of values. This is done by first providing an ideological framework for Western thought. Godism then reassures man of his purpose in life, and urges him to establish a harmonious relationship with his creator. Godism comes on the foundation of the Judeo-Christian tradition, which teaches that man is reconciled to God through the saving work of Christ, but at the same time, Godism is not incompatible with the other great faiths of the world, each of which stresses the need for the union of man with God. When the human heart and spirit are satisfied by God's love and truth, and when the practice of God's love has eliminated social injustice, then humanity will pass beyond the challenge of communism. There will be no room for communism in human life. Communism will totally lose its appeal.

Communism, based on an anti-God ideology, is an internationally organized and militant anti-religious movement. Religious people in the West, on the other hand, have been scattered and unmotivated up to now. More than this, the religious world has been weakened by division and petty infighting. This is a tragic situation. Unless God-loving people stand together on the front line and fight against the anti-religious force of communism, who will? Godism is a powerful unifying adhesive, able to bring God-loving people together. It is not based on doctrine, but rather on *common sense*. It therefore is able to bring together God-affirming and conscientious people beyond color or creed.

All mankind should be united, for we are all the children of God. Beyond religious, cultural and national differences, we are one family under one parent—God. We must defend our heritage from a common enemy. This is the basic motivation for the development of Godism. This is also the message which each CAUSA lecture and seminar strives to convey. Western civilization is ready to hear and embrace this message, and for this reason, CAUSA has realized phenomenal growth around the world.

The history of CAUSA is inseperable from the life and experiences of Reverend Moon. Reverend Moon was living in the southern part of Korea when the country was partitioned into a Soviet-controlled northern sector and a United States-controlled South. While multitudes of his fellow countrymen fled to the South, he felt called by God to journey north in 1946 to preach the Gospel in communist North Korea. For two years he was progressively harassed, beaten and tortured by the communist authorities as he worked to carry out his mission. As a result of his teaching of the Bible and vigorous propagation of God's message, he was finally charge with "spreading lies among the people" and sentenced to five years in a labor camp near Hungnam, North Korea.

The Hungnam camp was commonly known to be a death camp. It was intended to destroy opponents of the communist authorities through starvation and physical abuse. Most prisoners, tormented beyond human physical limitations, perished within months. Realizing that he could not survive through his own power, Reverend

Moon placed his life in the hands of God. Only with the help of God was he able to survive. In 1950, after nearly three years in Hungnam camp, Reverend Moon was liberated by advancing United Nations' troops led by General Douglas MacArthur.

As he resumed his ministry in the South, Reverend Moon felt strongly that he had been chosen by God to initiate a new way of fighting communism. He began to outline a system of thought of the highest dimension which would make clear the grave dangers of communist ideology and stimulate the God-affirming world to put an end to hypocrisy and live according to truths taught by the world's great religions. The worldview of Godism is the fruit of Reverend Moon's labors.

Reverend Moon founded the International Federation for Victory Over Communism in the early 1960's to teach Godism throughout Asia. The efforts of the IFVOC have met with great success, and IFVOC membership in Korea and Japan has grown to more than 7 millions persons in each country. However, Reverend Moon could see clearly that the most important nation in the struggle against communism is the United States. He felt called by God to come to America in 1971, and has been actively teaching this message here since that time.

In 1980, he founded CAUSA International to provide Latin Americans with an ideological framework in their struggle against communism. CAUSA chapters have now been initiated in more than 21 nations throughout South and Central America. Each year, a Pan-American Convention of CAUSA International brings major Latin American leaders together to coordinate programs of fighting communism and promoting social progress. CAUSA has now expanded beyond Latin America and become global in scope, being active in the U.S.A., Europe and Africa. CAUSA USA is headquartered in Washington, D.C., and has chapters throughout the 50 states.

Religious as well as political leaders are able to see that this movement can end the ideological confusion of the West, turn the tide of Western retreat, and provide the drive and determination to pursue the cause of freedom. CAUSA puts a sense of optimism and confidence into the air.

The work of these freedom-under-God organizations has been so effective that the Soviet Union has deemed it necessary to vehemently attack Reverend Moon and his work. In a recent issues of *Izvestia* (January 28, 1984), the Kremlin labelled Reverend Moon "The champion of anti-Sovietism." It is truly a testimony to the living God that a man who in 1950 was miraculously liberated from a communist death camp is today shaking the foundations of world communism, and worrying the Kremlin leadership.

The present text is intended to serve as a manual for those who wish to study Marxism-Leninism, its dangerous and destructive social implications, and the God-centered worldview absolutely essential to counter the advance of communism and stimulate a moral renaissance throughout the entire world. The initial work in elaborating Reverend Moon's thought into a critique of communism was undertaken by Dr. Sang Hun Lee, president of the Unification Thought Institute in Seoul, Korea. This text was authored by Dr. Bo Hi Pak, president of CAUSA International, Mr. Thomas Ward, executive vice-president of CAUSA International, and Mr/ William Lay, vice-president of CAUSA International and director of the CAUSA Institute, as a project of the CAUSA Institute.

May God bless you in your efforts to learn and to disseminate this vital message.

New York, New York
January, 1985

CAUSA International Conference

Opening Remarks

Dr. Bo Hi Pak
President of
CAUSA International

January 28, 1985
Washington D.C.

Distinguished Guests, Ladies and Gentlemen:

On behalf of CAUSA International, may I sincerely welcome all of you to this CAUSA leadership conference. I thank you for your deep interest in the CAUSA movement. You are not invited to this conference as an ordinary citizen. Instead you are chosen to come to this conference as distinguished leaders of America. Please accept my heartfelt congratulations for your service to God, country and freedom.

CAUSA is a new educational movement working on a global scale. We strongly oppose communism, and yet we do not consider ourselves to be merely anti-communist, simply because anti-communism is not enough. "Anti" is a defensive and passive expression. In any battle or war, you will never win victory with defense alone. We have been preaching anti-communism for 68 years, since the Bolshevik Revolution, and we are steadily losing ground. As long as we are anti-communist, we can only postpone the defeat at best. We will never have a chance to win. What we need is a positive solution to communism or a winning strategy. What we need is an ideological offensive. Our war against communism is primarily a war of ideas, a war of commitment. The battlefield of this war is the mind of man.

ideological offensive. Our war against communism is primarily a war of ideas, a war of commitment. The battlefield of this war is the mind of man.

In the next several days, we are going to discuss these very things: What are the problems facing us today? How can we work toward real solutions of these problems and avoid becoming victims of communism? How can we liberate the millions of people who have already been victimized by the communists? CAUSA is more than anti-communist. Nothing short of the victory over communism is CAUSA's goal.

As I said, CAUSA is a global movement. Yet, today we are putting our entire effort into the United States. Why? Because it is this nation, the United States of America, which holds the key to the future of the entire world. The United States is a young nation, and yet she is a great nation. But how has she achieved greatness? This greatness is not the result of her natural resources, or her geographic location. America has achieved greatness because of her faith in God and compassion toward the world.

Alexis de Tocqueville, the French political scientist and historian who visited America in the early 19th century, saw this very clearly. He said, "America is great because America is good and when America ceases to be good, she will cease to be great."

In what way has America been good? She is good because she has been a "Good Samaritan." The recent rescue of the tiny island of Grenada from the hands of Soviet-backed communists is an example of the United States being a Good Samaritan. The Washington Times proclaimed that accomplishment with an editorial entitled, "Grenada Libre."

Is it wrong to be looking forward to "Cuba Libre,"

"Nicaragua Libre," and ultimately, "Soviet Union Libre"? Many people in the United States would say that that is "nonsense." But when we think for a moment about God, the Creator with purpose, would He not think the same thing as we do? If God truly exists, is it not freedom to be His goal?

In recent years, however, we have seen this nation of America steadily losing faith in God and concern for the world. The Good Samaritan, the United States of America, is now fast becoming the "Levite" who passed by the wounded man in the Bible.

The Bible said, "The Levite passed on to the other side." But the irony is this: Today, the United States cannot pass to the other side of suffering neighbors in order to avoid the thieves because the thieves are after the United States. There is no way that the United States can flourish while the rest of the world perishes. The Free World has one common destiny. In order to have the United States survive, the Free World must survive. If the world goes, the United States goes. If the United States goes, of course, the world goes.

So we must live by one truth: United we stand, divided we fall. In order to have our Free World stand, the United States must be a "Good Samaritan" again. CAUSA wants to bring this new spirit to America.

Human freedom and democracy under God is precisely the goal of CAUSA. CAUSA promotes not only opposition to Communism, but liberation from, and of, communism. This "liberation movement" is gaining momentum, and Grenada is just the beginning. We want to continue to pursue the goal of freedom. This does not mean that the solutions will always be military, but it means that positive action and total commitment is absolutely necessary to stop the international lawlessness of communism.

The Origin of CAUSA

Let me now explain more about the history of CAUSA. The CAUSA movement began in Latin America through the inspiration and vision of the Reverend Sun Myung Moon. He initiated this movement in response to an acute and immediate need: The need to provide an ideological framework for Latin America in its struggle against communism.

C-A-U-S-A originally were the intitials of a very long name, Confederation of Associations for the Unity of the Societies of the Americas. At a recent seminar in the Dominican Republic, CAUSA was given a new name by one inspired participant. She said that CAUSA stood for, "Con amor y union, salvaremos America." This means, as many of you know, "With love and unity, we will save America." Yet CAUSA outgrew the Americas a long time ago. This movement is needed everywhere; Europe, Africa and Asia, etc.

As our work expanded beyond the Americas, we found that our old name was not international enough. So now we no longer keep the long name, but are still CAUSA—the Latin word for "cause." CAUSA stands for the first cause of the universe, God. The CAUSA movement, therefore, is the movement of God. CAUSA fights against all Godlessness. Therefore, our first enemy is Godless communism. CAUSA symbolizes the common cause and aspiration of all free men. CAUSA is a God-centered, humanitarian movement working against the worst inhumanity in history — international communism. Beyond this, CAUSA strives towards the ultimate realization of the human dream of the ideal society—the Kingdom of Heaven on earth. In contrast to communism, CAUSA upholds God as the source of man's freedom and creativity.

Communism: The Worst World Problem

What is the single worst problem which humanity faces today? In a recent issue of Commentary, French author Jean François Revel made this observation:

> "The closer we get to the end of this century, the more communist imperialism becomes the chief problem of our time. No other threat to the world freedom has endured as long.
>
> "A system that has grown so strong despite so many failings...must embody a principle of action and a concentration of power more effective than any mankind has ever known before. Communism and the Soviet empire are unprecedented in history."It is startling to compare communism with Christianity. Christ came 2,000 years ago and gave the world a powerful message of truth and love. Christianity has now become the world's largest religion and has been received by nearly one quarter of the world's population. But it took 2,000 years!

Communism, on the other hand, was only born in the last century, and yet it has come to enslave more people than are now Christians. During a short span of little more than half a century, Marxism-Leninism has spread like a forest fire. In this time, it has engulfed more than one and a half billion people, taking one nation after another, and spreading over the entire globe.

Will our children live in freedom, or will they live under a totalitarian system? No one knows. Yet, one thing is clear: The problem of communism is not something that someone else should worry about. It is my problem, and it is your problem. Our destiny and our children's well-being are at stake. Furthermore, it is God's problem. The very existence of God has been challenged.

Communism is an Ideology

To defeat communism, we must understand it. What is communism, anyway? Where does its power come from? Communism is more than a political system, more than a social system, and more than an economic system. Communism is an ideology, a system of thought.

Even though we know that communism is based on lies and deception, its false promises have the power to conquer a man's mind so completely that he would give his life for the victory of communism. It stems out of the power of faith, power of ideology. That power defeated the Free World in the Vietnam War. The outcome of the Vietnam War was not a military defeat. It was an ideological defeat. The communists assaulted America ideologically until she became confused and demoralized, and unable to carry on the fight.

The United States abandoned five billion dollars in weapons in South Vietnam. When there is no clear purpose and will to fight, five billion dollars worth of military armaments will not do any good.

In order to combat communism, we must fight with the same weapon which they use — ideology. A false ideology must be subjugated by a superior one. We must fight fire with fire. There is no other way we can fight.

Mr. David Satter, special correspondent to the Wall Street Journal and former Moscow correspondent of the Financial Times, wrote an article in the Wall Street Journal on May 21, 1983 entitled, "Soviet Threat Is One of Ideas More Than Arms." I quote from that article:

"As absurd as communist ideology may appear, it provides a consistent view of history to adherents and makes even the simplest citizen feel as though his life has meaning.

"Communism cannot be defeated militarily and, its adherents cannot be bribed into giving it up. It can be defeated in only one way: by being confronted with an idea that is better."

What is that better idea? Where can we find that

better idea? That is the question. People say, "Well, today we have democracy." But democracy is not an ideology, not a system of thought. Democracy is a system of government. "We have freedom," some say. Yet freedom is not an ideology either. It is a goal of ideology. Freedom is the fruit we enjoy when true democracy is practiced. Ironically, even Karl Marx started communism for the realization of freedom. Then what do we have to combat aggressive communism?

Certainly, we have Christianity and the other religions of the world. These religions are the God-accepting forces which oppose the God-denying forces of communism. But it is a painful reality that today's religions have demonstrated a lack of effectiveness in countering the spread of communism. One Christian nation after another has fallen into the hands of communism.

The Crisis of Religion

Today, clearly the religious world is in crisis. Religion seems to be unable to control the confusion of the world and elevate the human spirit. We can cite several causes for the collapse of the religious perspective, including the subtle instrusion of materialistic thought into all levels of society, as well as the subversion of the religious world by the forces of communism. But the greatest factor which is undermining the religious world today is the lack of a clear understanding of the reality of God.

The essential fact in our religious world today is that we are not sure about God. This is an honest statement. God has been progressively exluded from the life of modern-day man. Today, people are confused about the very purpose of God's creation, and thus man does not know what purpose he should live for. Out of this confusion, the "God is Dead" philosophy emerged, and Liberation

Theology became rampant in Latin America. Man is trying to take God's place, because he feels that God is either "dead" or helpless.

God or No God?

Today the struggle between communism and the Free World is really a struggle of ideas. It is boiling down to the question of God or no God.

If God does not exist, then communism may very well be correct. Once God is removed, communism does indeed offer a very convincing explanation of human life. However, if God truly exists, then there is no quesiton that communism is false. Communism is based on the very denial of God. Since two contradictory beliefs cannot both be true, then there must be a showdown. Who shall win? Communism? The Free World? No, one truth shall win. God or no God: One of the two must be a lie! Ultimately, lies will be defeated and truth shall prevail.

Crucial Questions

Therefore, today in the 20th century, now more than ever, the crucial question is the question of God's existence and nature. There are people today who are asking: Does God really exist? What is His purpose for creation? If God is of ultimate goodness, why does the survival of the fittest seem to prevail in our world? Why is there so much evil in our society, and why does evil seem to be winning? Unless reasonable and consistent answers are given to these questions, men of the modern age will not be willing to accept God as a reality.

The CAUSA Worldview

The CAUSA worldview is a philosophical framework that precisely deals with these very problems of the reality of God. The CAUSA worldview is a God-centered ideology which does two essential things: First, it totally exposes the lies and deceptions of communism. Second, it presents a clear counter-proposal to the communist view. The CAUSA worldview offers a complete solution to communism.

For CAUSA, this is the beginning point of the solution to world problems. We are beginning from the ground floor. From the recognition of the Absolute Being, we come to the awareness of absolute value. This vantage point can be called the absolute value perspective.

A Quiet Revolution

From the absolute value perspective, we can make the decisions which will lead us to genuine progress. When a person achieves this perspective his heart starts to change. Once man's heart changes, everything changes. Yet, this change cannot be forced. Only through an awakening into the absolute value perspective can you change man's heart. It is a quiet revolution, but a fundamental and most powerful revolution. This is the true revolution of man. This is the revolution that Jesus Christ brought to us 2,000 years ago. Now is the time to re-kindle that spiritual revolution here in America.

Communists' Revolution

Communism has been trying to bring about a revolution, too—a violent one—but without genuine success. Since 1917, and despite 68 years of total effort, the communist experiment has proven to be a bitter failure. According to the French magazine, Le Figaro, it has cost over 150 million human lives in the name of revolution and the "workers' paradise." Many people today say, "That paradise is lost." But we know that nothing was lost. That paradise never came in the first place. On the contrary, the Soviet economy is dying and corruption is rampant.

As a strategy for building a military empire, communism is successful in terms of improving the human condition, but communism is a miserable failure. Why is this?

There are two fundamental problems with communism. One, its ideology is rigid and not scientific. It is based on lies and false assumptions. To maintain it requires the constant generation of new lies and more lies. Whenever there are differences between the doctrine and reality, reality is denied and the doctirne is upheld. With this attitude, no progress can come.

Two, communism misses the target in its diagnosis of social evil. It is not the free market system or any economic system that is evil, as the communists believe, but rather it is a fundamental defect in man which is at fault. Communism destroys the system and sets up a new one, but the result is always worse. Why? A new system based on false assumptions and run by people with the same corrupt nature will not work.

A truly revolutionary change in society must come from the ground floor, the individual man. This is the root, and this is where the CAUSA worldview is addressing the problem.

God and 20th Century Logic

I must confess at this point, however, I know that it is not easy for us to speak about God when we are discussing economic and political problems. In fact, in many circles it is not fashionable to speak about God at all. Even as ministers, God may be a topic on Sunday but not from Monday to Saturday.

Instead, there has been a tendency toward a materialistc humanistic interpretation of human problems and goals. Many intellectuals have come to believe that God can be excluded from consideration when dealing with the world's problems. Obviously, CAUSA does not agree with that tendency. CAUSA believes in the God of seven days a week, 24 hours a day.

Accepting the Templeton Prize for Progress in Religion, Alexander Solzhenitsyn said bluntly, "If I were asked today to formulate as concisely possible, the main cause of the ruinous Russian revolution that swallowed up some 60 million of our people, I could not put it more accurately than to repeat: 'Men have forgotten God; that's why all this has happened.'"

This forsaking of God he identified as "the principal trait of the entire 20th century...[which] is being sucked into the vortex of atheism and self-destruction." It is one thing, he observed, that millions of human beings "have been corrupted and spiritually devastated by an officially imposed atheism," such as in the Soviet Union, and it is another that "the tide of secularism...has progressively inundated the West" so that "the concepts of good and evil have been ridiculed."

When you forsake God either by the name of communism or by secular humanism, the result will be the same: "self destruction." America and the Free World must awake now to this awesome truth, otherwise it will be too late. God or no God is the central issue. This is why the CAUSA movement is a new powerful voice. We brought down the question to a fundamental level: God or no God.

Dr. Kenneth Ryker, a distinquished educator, a man who has been an outstanding anti-communist for many years, testified after a recent CAUSA seminar in Washington D.C.:

"For the past twenty years, I have dedicated myself tire-
lessly to the battle against communism. I did so under
the banner of freedom. Yet, in spite of my efforts, we have
steadily been losing ground. Through this CAUSA seminar, I realized why freedom was not enough. To win this
battle, we must rally in proclaiming the existence of God."

During the next few days, we are going to talk about
"God" frequently and proudly. We feel easier on this one
because most of you are ministers. Yet, we speak of God
not from weakness, but from courage. When we speak
of God, we do so not out of ritual, but out of clear reason
based on 20th century science and logic, and with sin-
cerity and heart.

Furthermore, when we speak of God we are speaking
of the God of all religions and denominations. We examine God's existence and nature philosophically. We
affirm that the God of Judaism, Catholicism, Protestantism, Mormonism, the Unificationism and the God of
all religions are one and the same. Our purpose, then is
not to enter into theological debate, but instead to recognize the unifying factors of all religions with our fellow
man.

At this point, I want to make it absolutely clear that
CAUSA's purpose is not to change anyone's religion.
Although I am a member of the Unification Church, I
am not here to promote Unificiation Theology.

Instead, we are here to provide common ground for
unity. That common ground for unity is God. To know
about God more deeply is the only way we can unite.

When we recognize one common Father clearly and
unmistakenly, then we all naturally become true brothers and sisters.

CAUSA promotes a new way of fighting communism. We have been fighting communism in so many

ways—in a political way, social way, economic way or military way. None of these brought us victory yet. We must find a new way. That new way is the spiritual way.

We recognize communism as an evil religion or anti-God religion. You can only conquer it by spiritual power or by proclaiming the existence of God. Light alone overcomes darkness. God alone overcomes Godlessness.

In conclusion, CAUSA tries to bring together all God-accepting forces, transcendent of denomination and religion, to make one unified force. This force will be able to oppose the ungodly ideology of communism and work toward the establishment of a new, moral world. Fighting communism is the duty of God-loving people, whether you are white, black or yellow.

So, now you see, you have come to a very interesting seminar. There are thousands of seminars going on in our world, but you may not find anything like this anywhere else. If in these three days you feel that you are intellectually and spiritually enriched and inspired, then we have nothing more to ask.

Ladies and gentlemen, finally, I want to close my opening remarks by quoting Victor Hugo's historical utterances:

"More powerful than an invading army is an idea whose time has come."

I do believe CAUSA is an idea whose time has come. God bless you. Thank you very much.

COMMUNIST EXPANSIONISM AND THE WEST

We are living in the era of premeditation and the perfect crime. Our criminals are no longer helpless children who could plead love as their excuse. On the contrary, they are adults and they have a perfect alibi: philosophy, which can be used for every purpose — even for transforming murderers into judges.

Albert Camus[1]

I. Introduction

Nearly seventy years have passed since the Bolshevik Revolution. Marxism-Leninism has now entrenched itself in Europe, Asia, Africa and the Americas. Today approximately 39 percent of the world's surface and 42 percent of the world's population are in the hands of communism.[2] Especially in the Third World, Marx's world view continues to captivate the young, the idealistic and the socially concerned.

In these areas, there exist grave and persistent problems of corruption, greed and dictatorship. Many individuals have grown tired of seeking change through conventional means. They have turned to communism for solutions. Communism predicts a utopian future and an end to racism, social injustice and economic exploitation. These goals are to be accomplished through the application of the principles of Marx and Engels, as taught by Lenin, Mao and Castro.

Undoubtedly, a major reason for continued communist expansion stems from the West's ignorance of the true character of communism. Since the U.S. Senate's condemnation of Joseph McCarthy in 1954, anti-communists have rarely been taken seriously. They have been painted as "fascists" or "reactionaries" who seek only to maintain the status quo.

Yet, we must ask, what kind of liberation has communism brought? In Cuba, thousands of persons who opposed the policies of Fidel Castro are today languishing in prison. One out of every 10 Cubans has fled from Cuba. More than 10,000 young Cuban men have died on African soil while serving as surrogate troops in the service of Soviet imperialism. At the same time, Angolans and Ethiopians have been brought to Cuba to work in the sugar cane fields.

In Nicaragua today, we find a serious scarcity of goods. As early as 1981, real wages had decreased by 71 percent compared to the Somoza days. When people dare to differ with government policy, they are brutally punished. The Sandinistas have decimated the Miskito Indians. They have forced the closing of Jehovah Witness' Temples and Managua's Jewish Synagogue. They have likewise harassed Protestants as well as dissident Catholic priests, forcing many to leave the country.[3]

The Sandinistas promised the people free elections and democracy. Instead of an open society, however, the Sandinistas have enforced a policy which seriously curtailed freedom of the press, freedom of assembly and even freedom of religion. Originally the Sandinistas were to liberate the people from the cruel Somoza government. Today ironically the leaders of most of the local Sandinista Defense Committees are former Somocistas.[4] A saying has been popularized among disillusioned Nicaraguans: *"El frente y Somoza son la misma cosa."* (The Sandinistas and Somoza are the same thing.)

One is reminded of the words of the Cuban patriot José Martí, "To change masters is not to be free."

Over the past decade, however, an awakening has begun to occur in the West. A number of intellectuals have re-evaluated their Marxist concepts and found them lacking. Alarmed by the testimonies of Soviet dissidents such as Alexander Solzhenitsyn and Andrei Sakharov, as well as by Soviet incursions into Afghanistan and Poland, they have rejected Marxism. They warn that a new Holocaust is occurring not at Auschwitz but in the Gulag, in Phnom Penh, in Angola — *everywhere* communism has gained power.

Although we are witnessing this awakening, important political sectors as well as much of the media remain victims of the same methods which communists have used since the Bolshevik Revolution of 1917.

Communists advance their cause by focusing on the injustice of the present society within a target nation, whether it be Czar Nicholas' Russia, Somoza's Nicaragua, or the Philippines under Marcos. *By pointing out social injustice, they gain the support of the socially concerned in the West.*

The Western press has irresponsibly tended to join in attacking the status quo without seriously examining whether communist insurgents can bring a viable solution to social problems. Communists have successfully used this tactic over and over again. But once in power, they do not provide social justice. Instead, they silence the voices of opposition through totalitarian rule.

II. Nazism: a historical precedent

The West's persistent naivete toward Marxist-Leninist strategy closely resembles our blindness to Nazism some 40 years ago. At the end of World War I, Germany lay in shambles. Because of the draconian demands of the Treaty of Versailles, Germany confronted a huge war debt. When in 1923 the Weimar Republic could not meet payment of those debts, France claimed and occupied the Ruhr region of the country. Their nation divided, Germans felt abused, humiliated, and demoralized. In 1922, the value of the German mark fell from 162 to more than 7,000 per dollar. The following year, the rate became more than four million marks per dollar.[5] The rate eventually reached one trillion marks per dollar. Women, even children, resorted to prostitution as a means of survival. Everywhere German citizens began to denounce the deplorable living conditions of the Weimar Republic.

Adolf Hitler gained popular attention because he seemingly sympathized with the poor and victimized German people. He pointed out the ills, the shortcomings and the traitorous nature of the Weimar government. This drew the attention of the oppressed.

Hitler portrayed himself as a man of the people. Because of his dedication to his cause, he lived in a humble environment for years. Under difficult conditions, including imprisonment, he developed and propagated his ideology.

Regularly Hitler would awaken early in the morning and type out pamphlets, which he would then distribute on the street. When for the first time, he succeeded in gathering an audience of a hundred people, he interpreted this as an unqualified success.

Progressively, Hitler's influence grew both nationally and internationally. Many began to see Hitler as the one personality who could deliver Germany from a state of privation and open the way to a new and prosperous future. Growing support allowed Adolf Hitler to become the chancellor of Germany on January 30, 1933.

Concern about this development was expressed in various sectors. Some people warned that Hitler was violently anti-Semitic. Others maintained that Hitler wanted to destroy the Judeo-Christian tradition. Some saw Hitler as a warmonger, bent on avenging the bitter German defeat in World War I and the subsequent humiliation of Versailles.

Hitler, nevertheless, made certain declarations which seemed to allay those concerns. On February 2, 1933, *The New York Times* reported that Hitler had proclaimed that Christianity would be the basis of his government's moral conception.

As time went by, fears diminished. The West's attitude toward Hitler began to change. In a *New York Times* book review in 1935, we find the following observation:

> Hitler is doing much for Germany, his unification of the Germans... his training of the young, his creation of a Spartan state animated by patriotism, his curbing of parliamentary government so unsuited to the German character, his protection of the rights of private property are all good.

In England, the Prince of Wales who later became King Edward VIII, and after his abdication was known as the Duke of Windsor, called upon the British people to "stretch forth the hand of friendship to the Germans." In a speech delivered in Leipzig in 1937, he announced:

> I have travelled the world and my upbringing has made me familiar with the great achievements of mankind, but that which I have seen in Germany, I had hitherto believed to be impossible. It cannot be grasped and is a miracle; one can only begin to understand it when one realized that behind it all is one man and one will, Adolf Hitler.[6]

Similarly, newspaper magnate Viscount Rothermere wrote in his *Daily Mail* on September 24, 1930:

> I believe it would be a blunder for the British people

to take an attitude of hostility towards the Nazis
.... We must change our conception of Germany
.... The older generation of Germans were our
enemies. Must we make enemies of this younger
generation too?[7]

When fears had diminished, Hitler reintroduced military
conscription, and began to build an army of 36 divisions in
violation of the Treaty of Versailles. Hitler campaigned about
the need to reunite the German peoples. In the name of
expanding the German people's *Lebensraum* or living space,
he annexed the Sudetenland and eventually all of Czechoslovakia.

In the United States, reaction to Hitler closely paralleled
the current attitude towards Marxism-Leninism. Many people tried to ignore Hitler. Politicians spoke of the need for
solving domestic problems rather than worrying about Nazism.
University of Chicago president Robert Maynard Hutchins
declared in 1940, "It is easier to blame Hitler for our troubles
than to fight for democracy at home."[8]

When Hitler gave the order, however, his troops marched
through Poland, across Europe and into North Africa. Nazism
could no longer be ignored. Massive mobilization was
necessary. By the end, the human cost of World War II was
more than 50 million lives.

Yet that was only a part of the tragedy. When Allied
troops marched into Buchenwald, Dachau and Auschwitz,
they confirmed reports that additional millions of people had
been systematically murdered. Hitler's "final solution" dic-
tated that whoever was not part of the "select" Aryan race
could be abused or eliminated. Hitler's death camps were
responsible for the extermination of 6 to 12 million people.

What occurred in the case of Hitler is occurring today
with Marxism-Leninism. Citizens were dissatisfied with the
miserable conditions caused by the corruption and ineptitude
of the Weimar Republic. However, in their desperation to

solve these problems, they gravitated toward Hitler simply because he spoke out against the problem. People must have thought that because Hitler eloquently opposed the status quo, he also carried a solution, but they were mistaken.

III. Western naivete and communist expansion

Today, we face the same dilemma with respect to communism. In our desperation for change, many sympathize with Marxists because they criticize and attack the shortcomings of a presently existing government. Yet we fail to evaluate the implications of a Marxist-Leninist takeover. In fact, we live today in the midst of a new ideological deception. Like Nazism, communism promises justice and a better way of life. In reality, it exacerbates human misery and has provoked millions of senseless killings.

In order to gain power, Lenin denounced the corruption and the inability of the Kerensky government to respond to the needs of the Russian people. Lenin promised peace to the soldiers, land to the peasants and self-determination to the non-Russian minorities. Although he temporarily fulfilled the promise of land (to be reneged by Stalin), Lenin did not bring peace but a destructive civil war. He did not free the Russian minorities but created a new Russian empire. His reign brought terror by decree. He replaced the Czar's 15,000 secret policemen with a secret police force of 250,000. While he was in power, Lenin was responsible for the deaths of almost 2 million Soviet people.

Altogether, communism in the Soviet Union has provoked nearly 70 million senseless killings or approximately 1 million per year. In China, when Mao Tse Tung was able to occupy Tibet, his forces tortured Tibetan monks to death by pounding nails into their eyes. Mao's close associate, Lin Piao, admitted that 18 percent of the political prisoners in China had been executed. In total the Red Chinese murdered at least 67 million people.[9]

In Korea, there were over 3 million deaths due to communism. The Soviet invasion of Hungary in 1956 cost tens of thousands of lives. Events in Prague in 1968 led French new philosopher Bernard Henri Levy to refer to Marxism as "barbarism with a human face."

In Cambodia people were executed simply because they spoke English or French or had been teachers under the former government. For such "crimes," the Cambodians executed between 3 and 4 million of their countrymen. Since the fall of Saigon, a repressive communist government precipitated the deaths of at least 1 million Vietnamese.

According to the November 18, 1978, edition of the prestigious French magazine *Le Figaro*, communism has caused the deaths of 150 million people.

Human Cost of Communism

U.S.S.R.	70,000,000
China	67,000,000
Cambodia	3,000,000
Others	10,000,000
Total	**150,000,000**

In the West, adulation of communist leaders

USSR

Even as he initiated the Soviet terror, Lenin was proclaimed as a hero in the West. The same attitudes prevailed with regard to his successor, Stalin. In the December 4, 1930, issue of *The New York Times,* journalist Walter Duranty wrote of Stalin:

It is easy to speak admiringly of men who have proved their greatness by success, but Stalin has been tried

in the fires of prison, exile and disaster, of civil war
when at times his cause seemed desperate, of leadership challenged by men of greater mental agility, of
terrific material obstacles to his policies, and he has
come out stronger from each test of his strength. He
is veritably like steel, not rigid like iron, but resilient
and able to bend, as his modification of the agrarian
policy last March made clear.

The agrarian reform which Duranty commended eventually cost the lives of 7 million Ukrainians.

Cuba

When communism penetrated the Western hemisphere,
we find the same error. After his 1957 visit to Cuba, *New
York Times* reporter Herbert Matthews began to proclaim
the advent of a "modern day Bolivar" by the name of Fidel
Castro. We were assured by Matthews that Castro's only
desires for Cuba were democracy, peace and social justice.
Sympathy for Castro increased in the West. In commemoration of January 1, 1959, the day when Castro's troops marched
into Havana, *The New York Times* carried the following message in its editorial page:

One thing must be said. This is an acknowledgement
to an extraordinary young man, Fidel Castro. The
American people wish him good fortune. [10]

On January 4, 1959, Matthews also assured the American people that they need not worry about Che Guevara. He
described Guevara most favorably saying, "his voice is incredi-
bly low, and his smile unexpectedly gentle." [11]

In the same article, *The New York Times* quoted Guevara
as saying:

I have never been a communist. Dictators always say
that their enemies are communist, and it gave me
pain to be called an international communist all the
time. [12]

This was the same Guevara who had already written in

1957, "I belong, because of my ideological background, to that group which believes that the solution to the world's problems lies behind the Iron Curtain."[13]

Southeast Asia

Similarly, in our attempt to support a movement which criticized the status quo, we opened the way to Marxist-Leninist oppression in Southeast Asia.

In the 1960s during the Vietnam War, the Western press lambasted the corruption of the Diem, Ky and Thieu governments. The communists, by focusing their propaganda on this point, won a broad spectrum of public support, first among young people and then in the American society as a whole. The day after Saigon fell, *The New York Times* reported "The new South Vietnamese regime would follow a foreign policy of peace and nonalignment."[14]

Yet only a short time after the communist takeover, the Soviets began to use facilities constructed by the United States at Cam Ranh Bay for their own ships. This, plus the commissioning of Vietnamese workers to work on the Siberian pipeline, affirmed that another nation had been sovietized.

When Cambodia fell, a *New York Times* editorial lamented American involvement there:

> Must the futile battle for Phnom Penh now be dupli-
> cated at the far greater cost in lives, in a fight to the
> finish in Saigon? There is nothing in human power
> which can redeem the hundreds of deaths, the thou-
> sands of ruined lives, the tragic result of the last
> weeks around the Cambodian capital.[15]

The New York Times and others lamented hundreds of deaths, and yet we blindly opened the way for Pol Pot to come to power. Three to 4 million Cambodians perished after that nation fell into communism.

The Caribbean and Central America

When Maurice Bishop came to power in Grenada, *Time*

magazine exposed the alleged corruption of the former government of Eric Gairy, and assured its readers that Bishop was committed to "moderate socialist reform."[16] By December, however, there were over 1,000 Cuban troops in Grenada. With Soviet aid, Cubans began to build a huge airstrip capable of handling Soviet transport planes (en route to Central America) as well as MiG-23s. Grenada began to train its own security forces for use in what is now Marxist Surinam.

In Nicaragua, when the Sandinistas rose up against Somoza, they were heralded as "los muchachos" (the boys). We were told that we did not need to worry about communism. In this case, the revolution could be "Christianized" because of the considerable Church support for the FSLN (Sandinista Liberation Front). We had reports from *The Washington Post, The New York Times* and *Time* which constantly criticized the Somoza government, but failed to understand the character of the opposition. Finally *Time* proclaimed that the Nicaraguan junta had appointed a "15 member cabinet dominated by moderates."[17]

In a press conference on July 25, 1979, shortly after the Sandinista takeover, U.S. president Jimmy Carter declared, "I do not attribute at all the changes in Nicaragua to Cuba." *The New York Times* in an editorial referred to this as President Carter's "diplomatic highnote."[18] The United States granted large sums of aid to Nicaragua, believing that we would be able to counterbalance any radical elements of the revolution. A large portion of those funds were used to strengthen Nicaraguan communist security forces and to finance a propaganda effort thinly veiled as a literacy program. In the teachers' guide used in the literacy program, the first word that students learned was "revolution." The second word they learned was "liberation." Their first sentence was "Long live the Sandinista Liberation Front."[19] Eventually, all but the most stubborn Sandinista sympathizers came to the undeniable conclusion that another revolution had been betrayed.

> 2 — Leamos las palabras:
>
> ## la Revolución
>
> — Del texto de la oración anterior, saquemos las palabras "la Revolución" escribámoslas en el pizarrón y leámoslas.
>
> — Invitemos a los compañeros a leerlas con nosotros.
>
> — Aclaremos que esta forma de leer es sólo un reconocimiento de palabras, puesto que todavía no se han estudiado los sonidos que la forman.
>
> Señalemos las vocales y leámoslas.

Nicaragua is in the process of building a very professional army of 25,000 troops, and a militia of between 200,000 and 250,000. In Managua, Daniel Ortega speaks of a "revolution without borders." In the streets, Nicaraguan "turbas" (government agitators) shout *"Venció Nicaragua! El Salvador vencerá!"* (Nicaragua triumphed, El Salvador will win.)

The Peace Movement

While the communist strategy in Latin America hides behind the smokescreen of social justice, in Europe we see another kind of strategy. In Europe communists speak about peace. Time and again we find demonstrators emphasizing that the United States should not deploy Pershing IIs or cruise missiles.

Demonstrators maintain that the real culprit in the arms race is the U.S. and not the Soviet Union. But in the last 20 years, the West has shelved most major weapons development projects. Expenditures of the Soviet Union on strategic forces have been more than three times U.S. expenditures. While there has been incredible pressure on the West to disarm, the Soviets have updated and increased tenfold the size of their nuclear arsenal. Today, the USSR has a 3:1 overall superiority in the number of nuclear warheads. In all indexes of nuclear capability, the Soviets now hold commanding advantages that continue to grow.[20]

Coalition Governments

Today the communists are joined by the Western press in attacking El Salvador. We hear of government support of right-wing death squads. Meanwhile the communist left boycotts elections and demands a negotiated settlement. The left proposes a power-sharing coalition government.

Guillermo Ungo, strong man of the communist Democratic Revolutionary Front of El Salvador and a vice president of the Socialist International, recently stated, "The options are clear — a military or a political solution, intervention or power-sharing. The best option for El Salvador, and for the United States, is a broad-based coalition government that would achieve peace, lay the grounds for a democratic system and lead to free elections."

What is a "coalition government"? The *Soviet Encyclopedia* clearly defines coalition government in relation to the governments formed in Eastern Europe after World War II. A coalition government is referred to as a "people's democracy."

In a coalition government there are always two parts: communist and non-communist. The *Soviet Encyclopedia* explains that the communists should focus on the military and security posts rather than gaining the presidency or other prominent but powerless positions. In other words, let the communists take the posts of power. Once the communists have consolidated their power, they begin to use force to put pressure on the non-communists. Eventually non-communists will give up their positions because of such pressure.

Cuba and Nicaragua are examples of this process. It should be remembered that Fidel Castro did not start as the president of Cuba, but as minister of the army. Tomás Borge became the minister of interior and Humberto Ortega the minister of defense. They used people such as Alfonso Robelo and Violeta Chamorro as figureheads, but once communists gained control other coalition members were forced either to betray their principles or resign.

In Vietnam, Madame Binh was put forward as a figure-
head of democratic participation in government. Today Madame Binh plays no part in the Vietnamese government.

IV. Words and deeds

Some people say, however, that all of this is not real
communism. They maintain, for example, that Stalin took
communism and abused it. Revolutionaries often maintain,
"Here in our country, communism will be different. Here we
are going to build true Marxism. We are going to have what
has not existed anywhere else. We will build a just, Marxist
society."

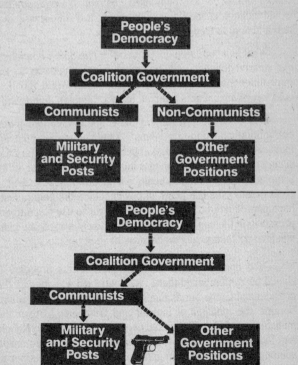

Yet every Marxist takeover has resulted in the same barbarism and economic failure.

We must learn the lesson of the Holocaust. Hitler's intentions were clearly expressed in *Mein Kampf*, but people either failed to read Hitler's works, or they did not take them seriously. What happened in Nazi Germany was an application of Hitler's world view. What happens in communist countries results from the application of Marxism-Leninism, just as it is described in works such as the *Communist Manifesto* and Lenin's *What Is to Be Done?*

What are the ideological and moral parameters of Marxism-Leninism? It would be naive to think that they are the same as our own. Commenting on this in Jeane Kirkpatrick's *The Strategy of Deception*, U.S. negotiator Charles Burton Marshall observed:

> In the language of game theory, communists and non-communists are like opponents playing different games by different rules on the same board. The United States, the nations of Western Europe, and many other countries are involved in a game which looks toward the resolution of conflict by the partial accommodation of the interests of all parties. The achievement of a stable equilibrium — called peace — is its goal. This game conceives the opponent as a fundamentally "reasonable man" with limited objectives, oriented to compromise, ready to discuss issues on their merits, to play by rules, and to obey the referee. Communist leaders, on the other hand, play a game which looks toward the resolution of conflict by the defeat and absorption of the enemy. This game conceives of the opponent as a mortal enemy, bent on annihilation, eternally aggressive and treacherous. The only rule of this game is the rule of the jungle: survival and victory by all available means. There is no referee. The world is the board. [21]

The communists do not act from a Judeo-Christian

perspective. Their moral system is different from our own. Vladimir Lenin contended that the communist should be ready to resort to "any trick, ruse or illegal method" in order to advance revolutionary objectives.

> **"From the point of view of communist morality, that which promotes the movement of society toward communism is moral."**
>
> **V.G. Afanasayev**
> *Marxist Philosophy*
> **USSR, Progress Publishers**

Commonly used expressions or terms with vague meaning for the West have clear and surprising definitions for communists. For example, according to Leninist thinking, "peaceful co-existence, is a revolutionary line, a revolutionary strategy. The purpose of the strategy of peaceful co-existence is to assure the conditions favorable to the victory of world socialism."[22]

The Soviets often speak of "peace", but what is the peace being addressed here? Lenin declared that "the policy of the Soviet Union is a policy of peace. It is merely another form under the present condition, to fight against capitalism."

For the Soviets, real peace can only come about when the entire world is communized. In 1930, three-time Lenin prize winner Dmitri Manuilski explained:

War unto the death is inevitable between communism and capitalism. At the present time, however, we are not strong enough to attack them. Our time will come within 20 or 30 years. In order to win we will need the surprise factor. We must put the bourgeoisie to sleep. For that reason we will begin the most spectacular peace movement that history has ever seen. We will make proposals, and concessions, as have never been seen. Because the capitalist nations are stupid and decadent, they will assist in their own destruction. They will do everything possible to have us as their friend. And as soon as they drop their guard, we will smash them with our closed fist. [23]

The Soviet view of detente was revealed in an exchange between Leonid Brezhnev and Walter Ulbricht, former chairman of the council of state of East Germany. Ulbricht felt that it was not wise to pursue a policy of detente. However, Brezhnev assured his other comrades:

Trust in us comrades, because by 1985, as a result of what we are accomplishing through detente, we will have accomplished a major part of our objective for Western Europe. By 1985 we will have consolidated our position. We will be ready to exert our will wherever we wish. [24]

In general, the Soviet strategy may be summarized as follows:

When weak, negotiate. When strong, attack.

> **"Trust in us comrades, because by 1985, as a result of what we are accomplishing through detente, we will...be ready to exert our will wherever we wish."**
>
> **Leonid Brezhnev to Walter Ulbricht of East Germany**

It was only when President Eisenhower secretly threatened the use of nuclear weapons in Korea that the North Koreans agreed to an armistice. When President Nixon renewed the bombing of Vietnam, the North Vietnamese agreed to "peace accords." Eight months after Nixon resigned from office, the North Vietnamese invaded and conquered the South.

Currently, the Soviets are insisting that space weapons be prohibited. This is directly linked to the fact that they have already developed a working anti-satellite system and laser technology, and fear the United States will catch up and overtake them. The Soviets were successful in negotiating a treaty in which the United States promised not to build effective defenses against ballistic missiles, the ABM Treaty of 1972. While the U.S. has until now honored this treaty, the Soviets have broken it. The existence of Soviet ABM radar as well as multiple violations of the SALT II Treaty have been disclosed and substantiated by the U.S. government.[25]

V. The Soviet Union's geopolitical objectives

The weakness of the West lies in its failure to recognize the ideological and global nature of the Soviet threat and develop an appropriate strategic response. Instead, we treat individual Soviet thrusts as isolated, regional events. We fail

to recognize that the Soviet Union is pursuing an international strategy to advance the communist cause.

Today the Soviets are dedicating considerable attention to the Caribbean region. This region is of great strategic importance. Juan Vives, a former member of Fidel Castro's secret police, writes in *The Masters of Cuba* that Stalin sent the co-founder of the KGB, Fabio Grobart, to Cuba in 1927 to pursue the eventual sovietization of Cuba. It was Grobart who recruited Fidel Castro, and later Grobart presided over the first congress of the Cuban Communist Party.[26]

Besides Cuba, now Nicaragua, Guyana and Surinam have fallen to communism. Today we find that El Salvador is tremendously threatened.

El Salvador is a densely populated nation. At the same time, it is a nation considered by many to have the hardest-working, most ambitious people of Central America. Armed with Marxist ideology, such people could feel ideologically justified about the need to expand their national territory.

We should recall that in 1821 Central America was one nation. For many people, a return to the former union remains an ideal.

With Nicaragua and El Salvador under their control, the communists could revive the call for a unified Central America

Military Forces in Central America

projected 250,000 troops			
currently 110,000 troops	12,000 troops	18,000 troops	
Sandinista Nicaragua	Samoza's Nicaragua	Honduras	Costa Rica no armed forces
Nicaragua		**Neighboring Countries**	

and they could proceed in their drive for the sovietization of Guatemala and Honduras. In that case, only "neutral" Costa Rica, a nation without an army, would remain. Costa Rica would be available whenever the Soviets should choose to act.

According to the most recent edition of *Defense and Foreign Affairs Handbook,* the Central American nations have the potential of forming an army of up to 3 million troops. Marxists could easily exploit the historical resentment of this region in order to create what could be a second Soviet proxy army. This is indeed alarming in light of the damage that Cuba, the first Soviet proxy, has done in Mozambique, Angola, Guinea-Bissau, Ethiopia, and Nicaragua.

By gaining control of the 20 million people of Central America, the communists would also gain access to the United States. They would, of course, have immediate access to the Panama Canal. Through MiG-23 bases in Central America and Cuba, they would be able to block the United States from shipping or receiving strategic goods via the Caribbean in case of war.

Communism has its eyes set on larger goals as well. Communists are already working to build a Hispanic separatist movement calling for the secession of Texas, Utah, California, Nevada, Arizona, and Colorado from the United States.[27]

The Soviets are also backing a "New Afrika" movement which calls for the secession from the United States of Mississippi, Louisiana, Alabama, Georgia, and South Carolina. Communists proclaim that through the secession of "Occupied Mexico," New Afrika and the Native American nations, they will "defeat U.S. imperialism."[28]

Shortly after World War II in an interview with U.S. reporter Richard C. Hottelet, Soviet chief negotiator Maximov Litivinov affirmed that genuine reconciliation between the USSR and the U.S. was absolutely impossible. When asked, "What would be the Soviet reaction if the West were to assent to all Soviet demands?" Litivinov responded that "it would lead to the West having to confront, after a period of time, the next series of demands."[29]

With this attitude, the communists will not be content until the United States has been sovietized.

VI. The need for a world view in the West

In 1975, the United States lost the war in Vietnam. Even though it may be painful, we must learn the lessons of that defeat. Today many people have fallen victim to the "Vietnam Syndrome," an almost paranoic reaction to even the thought of sending U.S. troops abroad. Yet we must understand why the lesson of Vietnam is so important to the communist strategy.

In 1967, Prensa Latina news service released a message from Che Guevara "from somewhere in the world to the Organization of Solidarity of the Peoples of Africa, Asia and Latin America." Guevara wrote:

> How close and bright would the future appear if two, three, many Vietnams, flowered on the face of the globe, with their quota of death and immense tragedies, with their daily heroism, with their repeated blows against imperialism, obliging it to disperse its forces under the lash of the growing hate of the people of the world![30]

Communist:
Cambodia
Vietnam
Laos
Guinea-Bissau
Sao Tome and Principe
Angola
Mozambique
Ethiopia
Afghanistan
Nicaragua
Cape Verde

Communist:
Cambodia
Vietnam
Laos
Guinea Bissau
Sao Tome and Principe
Angola
Mozambique
Ethiopia
Afghanistan
Nicaragua
Cape Verde

Wars:
Guatemala
El Salvador
Peru
Lebanon
Chad
Colombia

Communist:
Cambodia
Vietnam
Laos
Guinea Bissau
Sao Tome and Principe
Angola
Mozambique
Ethiopia
Afghanistan
Nicaragua
Cape Verde

Wars:
Guatemala
El Salvador
Peru
Lebanon
Chad
Colombia

Radical or
Uncertain:
Iran
Zimbabwe
Uganda
Sudan

Some politicians say, "No more Vietnams," but communists aim to create "one, two, three, many Vietnams." They believe it will drain the resources of the Free World, and more importantly, deplete our will to fight.

Why did the United States lose in Vietnam? We cannot say that it was a lack of weapons. The United States left $5 billion worth of stockpiled modern weapons when they abandoned Vietnam. The United States army was defeated by people who often fought with far more primitive weaponry.

Neither was it because of the economic conditions in Vietnam. For years after the fall of Saigon, tight controls

were kept on North Vietnamese wishing to visit Saigon, lest
they discover that actually, contrary to propaganda, South
Vietnam was far more advanced than the North.

It was not because of South Vietnamese political repression that we lost the war, either. Compared to other nations
in the region there was quite a bit of political freedom in
Vietnam.

Vietnam

1. **Weapons**
2. **Economic Development**
3. **Political Freedom**
4. **A Purpose to Fight**

Why was it then that the war was lost? Mao Tse Tung
once said, "Weapons are important, but they are not the
decisive factor. Man is the decisive factor." During the war in
Vietnam, the men of our nation lacked a purpose to fight. The
lyrics of a popular American song went:

And it's one, two, three. What are we fighting for?
Don't ask me, I don't give a damn. Next stop is
Vietnam.

This attitude stands in stark contrast to that of the
communists. When the Chinese communists occupied Peking
after years of battling the forces of Chiang Kai Shek, stories
began to appear about the attitude of Mao's soldiers. One
story concerned participants on the "long march" who had
nothing to eat.

Supposedly those soldiers went to Mao Tse Tung
explaining their situation. Mao replied, "Cook the leather of

your shoes and eat it." This is what they allegedly did.

When those troops finally marched victoriously into Peking, Mao gathered them and said, "Do not think that your lives will now be easier. They will not. But I promise you one thing. The lives of your children will be easier." What inspired people to live at such a level of sacrifice and commitment? What gave them that kind of determination? It was the Marxist ideology.

Marxist ideology gives a dream and the steps to realize that dream. Many people attribute the deaths and suffering of communism to Stalinism, but Lenin in *State and Revolution* used Marx's writings to prove that brutal "means" were ideologically necessary in order to achieve the "end." The "end" was the Marxist dream.

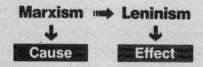

The Marxist dream has a mystical, almost religious quality. It has the ability to captivate people and to fill them with ideals and hopes of an almost religious character. In 1935, French writer André Gide, speaking of his experience with Marxism, said:

> My conversion is like a faith. All my being is directed to a single goal. In the deplorable state of the modern world, the plan of the Soviet Union seems to constitute the salvation of humanity.[31]

In his final letter to his parents before his death, Che Guevara communicated the same kind of ideal:

> My Marxism has taken root within me and been purified. I believe in armed struggle as the only solution to those who wish to liberate themselves, and I am faithful to my beliefs. [32]

Marxism and its promises have been able to ignite people throughout the world with the conviction that ultimately a good and ethical world will emerge if they are willing to fight and sacrifice today.

Conclusion

What are the real fruits of Marxism? Thousands of boat people. Millions who are starving. Ruthless murder.

Instead of apologizing before the world for the destruction of the unarmed civilian airliner KAL 007 in 1983, the Soviets arrogantly declared that their air space was "sacred" and decorated the pilot for his defense of the motherland.

When CAUSA members visited a refugee camp near the Nicaraguan border, one member of the delegation spoke with a peasant farmer who was 75 years old and had lived in a tiny village all his life. The man testified that when the Sandinistas took over, they began to force everyone in his village to go twice a week to a course in Marxism. This poor man did not understand anything. He attended the course once or twice and he did not want to attend any longer. Other people likewise did not want to go to the course. Then systematically the Sandinistas began to kill anyone who did not participate.

There can be no idyllic Marxist state, because the foundation of Marxism is itself a mandate to threaten, to abuse, and to destroy others. This is revealed when we study the Marxist ideology.

What is the fruit of Marxism? In *Forbes* magazine, December 6, 1982, it was indicated that in 66 years the Soviet Union

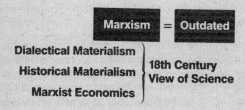

has realized "a long march to nowhere." It is CAUSA's conclusion that Marxism does not work because the ideological foundations of Marxism are false. Dialectical materialism, historical materialism, Marxist economic theories, and the Marxist theory of alienation are all founded in antiquated 17th and 18th century thought.

In the past, the West tried to deal with communism in different ways. We have pointed out their atrocities. We have spoken about the perverted personalities of certain communist leaders. However, today is a time to end communism.

The end will be realized by exposing and assailing communism's Achilles heel. The weakest point of communism is the ideology itself. After spending six years in the Soviet Union, American journalist David Satter made the following observations:

> As absurd as communist ideology may appear from the outside, it provides a consistent view of history to those who adhere to it and makes even the simplest citizen feel as though his life has meaning, thus fulfilling, albeit falsely, a basic spiritual need.

> It is, in fact, our failure to recognize the importance of ideology, rather than any military or economic weakness of the U.S., that is the reason the Soviet Union is now poised to spread its influence over ever larger areas of the developed and underdeveloped world.

> In an era without faith, communism has emerged as a powerful anti-faith, which renders irrelevant our accustomed frame of reference. It cannot be defeated militarily and its adherents cannot be bribed into giving it up. It can be defeated in only one way: by being confronted with an idea that is better.[33]

Marxism, based upon materialism, has been completely out of date since the turn of the century, due to the development and implications of such scientific advances as Einstein's view of matter as well as cybernetics.

In the 20th century, we are finding that science, instead of being the friend of Marxism, is the friend of the believer in God.

The 20th century is a time to launch an ideological offensive against Marxism. Likewise we must reflect on and re-evaluate the status of the Free World. What do we stand for? What do we want to accomplish? The implications of the Judeo-Christian world view are great. The ideal and the hopes that stem from that world view are compelling. Through an ideological offensive, CAUSA believes that we will see the decline and fall of communism and a reawakening of Western ideals.

As we have seen, the communist world has been successful in propagandizing about the injustices of the Free World. Foolishly, the Western press has often served as a tool to denounce these injustices without pointing out that communism has no solution to such problems. This naive policy has succeeded in turning the general population against certain governments and has left them with a blind spot as to what will follow once communism emerges.

The media has dedicated pages and pages to denouncing the Czar, Chiang Kai Shek, Diem, Lon Nol, Somoza, Batista and Gairy, but comparatively little was said about the atrocities of Castro, Stalin, Lenin, Pol Pot or Ortega.

In 1976, *The New York Times* dedicated four articles to the Cambodian holocaust and approximately 60 articles to human rights violations in Chile, yet for every person "missing" in Chile, 2,000 Cambodians were killed.

In response to this clear problem, CAUSA has two aims. First, we must recognize that communism is an ideological cousin to Nazism and that each is barbaric in form. Secondly, we must find a world view which can truly respond to the human condition.

Social ills + New World View = Better World

Forty years ago, the West learned its lesson when it tried to appease Hitler. The way to stop an aggressive force is through preparedness, not appeasement. CAUSA recognizes the need for a strong military posture, a superior ideology, and a moral commitment to the oppressed.

CHAPTER ONE NOTES

1. Albert Camus, *The Rebel*, New York, Vintage Books, 1956, p.3.

2. Georgi Arbatov, *The Soviet Viewpoint*, New York, Dodd, Mead and Company, 1983, p.25.

3. Humberto Belli, *Nicaragua: Christians Under Fire*, San José, Costa Rica, Instituto Puebla, 1982, pp.29-56.

4. Robert S. Leiken, "Nicaragua's Untold Stories," *The New Republic*, October 8, 1984, p.17.

5. *Encyclopedia Britannica*, Vol. 8, Chicago, Britannica, Inc., 1983, p.117. The mark eventually fell to 1 trillion marks per dollar.

6. James Pool and Suzanne Pool, *Who Financed Hitler?*, New York, The Dial Press, 1978, pp.314-318.

7. Ibid.

8. Herbert Philbrick, *I Led Three Lives*, Falls Church, Virginia, Capital Hill Press, 1973, p.36.

9. "Document: Les 150,000,000 morts du Communisme," *Le Figaro* (magazine), November 18, 1978.

10. *The New York Times*, January 2, 1959, p.24.

11. *The New York Times*, January 4, 1959, p.7.

12. Ibid.

13. See Carlos Franqui, *Family Portrait with Fidel*, New York, Random House, 1984.

14. *The New York Times*, May 1, 1975, p.1.

15. *The New York Times*, April 18, 1975, p.32.

16. *Time*, April 2, 1979.

17. *Time*, July 30, 1979, p.35.

18. *The New York Times*, July 27, 1979, p.A22.

19. *Cuaderno de Educación Sandinista*, Nicaragua, Ministerio de Educación, 1980, pp.19-21.

20. See remarks of William Van Cleave in *CAUSA International Seminar — The Nuclear Balance: Challenge and Response*, New York, CAUSA International, 1984.

21. *The Strategy of Deception*, Jeane Kirkpatrick, ed., London, Robert Hale, 1963, p.414.

22. Gyula Kallai, "Main Force of the Revolutionary Process," *World Marxist Review II* (November, 1972) quoted by Harvey and Miller, *Research Notes*, p.3.

23. Quoted by Joseph Kornpheder from a speech given by Manuilsky at the Lenin School of Peace in 1930.

24. N. Kagchenko, "Socialist Foreign Policy and the Restructuring of International Relations," *International Affairs*, April 1975.

25. See *Can America Catch Up?*, Washington, D.C., Committee on the Present Danger, 1984.

26. See Juan Vives, *Les Maitres de Cuba*, Paris, Robert Laffont, 1981.

27. *New York* (magazine), April 4, 1983.

28. Taken from a flyer for the New Afrika Movement announcing a meeting in the Ukrainian Labor Home, New York, July 15, 1983.

29. N.A. decimal files, 861.00/6-2146, quoted in Nicolai Tolstoy, *Stalin's Secret War*, New York, Holt, Rinehart and Winston, 1981.

30. *Che Guevara Speaks*, George Lavan, ed., New York, Pathfinder Press, 1980, p. 159.

31. *The God That Failed*, Richard Crossman, ed., New York, Harper and Row, 1949, p. 173.

32. *Che Guevara Speaks*, p. 142.

33. *The Wall Street Journal*, May 23, 1983.

MARXIST IDEOLOGY: OVERVIEW AND CRITIQUE

When we speak of Marxism today, we must bear in mind that there have been numerous divisions in the Marxist "family tree," particularly since the death of Marx's close follower, Friedrich Engels, in 1895. At that time, there was a dispute between the German Marxist, Eduard Bernstein, and the Russian Vladimir Ulyanov (Lenin). Bernstein criticized Marx's economic theories and advocated non-violent reforms leading to socialism. Lenin, meanwhile, defended Marx's economics while doing his own rewriting of other Marxist doctrines. He eventually claimed, for example, that the stage of capitalism might be by-passed altogether.

Karl Kautsky, who had supported Lenin in the dispute with Bernstein, later disagreed with him over the issue of party membership. (Lenin favored an exclusive party of professional revolutionaries.)

Lenin prevailed over Kautsky, but following Lenin's death there was another split between Trotsky, who advocated world-wide revolution, and Stalin, who held that the USSR must be strengthened and made a bulwark of communism before it could expand. Stalin prevailed, and Trotsky was later murdered while in exile.

When Stalin died, there was division between Mao Tse-Tung and Nikita Khrushchev. As a world figure, Mao would have been the natural successor to Stalin as communism's pre-eminent leader. Mao was the "older brother" of the communist world and had brought China into the communist camp. He was rebuffed by Khrushchev, however, and this was in part responsible for provoking the Sino-Soviet split.

This is by no means an exhaustive list of the divisions within Marxism, but it serves to illustrate why there are a number of differing interpretations of Marxist ideology today. The differences among them are primarily tactical in nature, however, concerning how most effectively to achieve the revolutionary transformation of the world. All forms of Marxism are based on the theories of Karl Marx (1818-1883), who together with Friedrich Engels co-authored the *Communist Manifesto* in 1848. No Marxist ideologue or scholar will deny the fundamental aspects of his theories. Marx is the forefather of all Marxisms, and whoever wants to understand them must begin with Marx.

As an overview and critique of basic Marxism, this chapter examines:

I) The person of Karl Marx, his environment and the trends of thought which influenced the development of his theories.

II) Basic Marxist doctrines, including the theory of human alienation.

III) The early chronological development of Marxism, up to the publication of the *Communist Manifesto*.

IV) The failure of Marxism to solve the problems of human alienation, that is, communism as a social failure.

V) The errors of Marxist doctrine in light of the CAUSA Worldview.

VI) Ideology in practice: Marxism and the CAUSA Worldview.

I. The person of Karl Marx and his environment

We find in the writings of Marx, the obvious spirit of rebellion against authority, particularly religious authority. In the introduction to his doctoral thesis, Marx honors Prometheus as the "most eminent saint and martyr in the philosophical calendar."

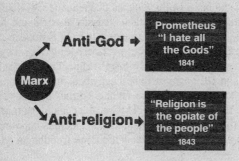

Prometheus, of course, is the mythological figure who stole fire from the gods and gave it to humankind. As a punishment, he was chained to a rock, and an eagle was sent every day to consume his liver, which grew back at night. He was then ordered by Zeus to repent, to which he replied, "I hate all the gods," and cried out that he would prefer to remain chained to the rock than serve the unjust gods. Marx echoed those very words in his doctoral dissertation.

Marx adopted Prometheus as the model of the philosopher in his challenge against the gods, and would later write that religion is the opiate of the people. Let us inquire into the

conditions and experiences which caused Karl Marx to adopt
this anti-religious perspective.

A. Influences on Marx's thought

1. The rise and suppression of liberalism

The French Revolution of 1789 and the Napoleonic wars
which followed introduced a new liberalism into Europe. After
a quarter century of tumult, Napoleon was finally defeated in
1814. When representatives of the victorious nations met in
Vienna, they were determined to restore the order which had
existed prior to 1789.

On the basis of the Council of Vienna (1814-1815), the
Quadruple Alliance of Britain, Prussia, Austria and Russia
was able for a time to reconstruct the old European order,
but liberal uprisings broke out with increasing frequency. The
reaction was often severe. British Parliament passed the harsh
Six Acts in 1819 against radical activities, and in France, the
aristocracy inaugurated the "White Terror" against republi-
cans. In the German Confederation, Austria's Metternich persuaded the Diet to adopt the Carlsbad Decrees imposing stiff
press censorship and curtailing academic freedom in August,
1819.

In 1832, in response to the activities of the radical student organizations known as Burshenschaften, Metternich
introduced into the federal Diet six articles reaffirming that all
power was in the hands of the princes and that parliaments
had no power to impede the prince's judgement.

With participation in government and free expression
denied, liberal and national aspiration broke out in the form of
revolutions in Europe in 1820 (Spain, Portugal, Italy), 1821
(Greece), 1825 (Russia) and 1830 (France, Belgium, Poland).
These were to be followed by another wave of revolutions in
1848-1849 in France, Italy, Germany and Austria.

2. The Industrial Revolution

Britain was the foremost commercial state at the outset of the 19th century, and it was here that the industrial revolution began, moving next to Belgium, northern France and eastward. As a result of industrialization, most people in the 18th and 19th centuries were able to live better than those of the 15th and 16th centuries. However, there was still a great deal of human suffering. Individuals and families were uprooted from villages, farms and feudal estates and concentrated in urban areas. Working conditions in factories and mills were often poor, and wages were low. Women and children were employed in factories, mines, shops and fields. Poor health conditions led to increased disease and a higher infant mortality rate for infants born to working mothers. As factory weaving replaced home industry, family unity suffered. This was aggravated by the extended work hours of both men and women.

Crime and prostitution increased. Rapid industrial growth caused fluctuations in employment and a consequent increase in unemployment and job insecurity. Historian Harold Perkin states that:

> In much larger towns of the new age, distress was more concentrated, more visible, more vociferous, and, since it affected much larger numbers of the potentially disaffected, more feared as the detonator of revolutionary explosions than in the old society, where the bread riot was less likely to trigger off political discontent. In the first half of the nineteenth century every major slump produced its wave of political protest, every major political crisis coincided with a period of marked distress.[1]

With improved economic mobility for many, there occurred a perceptible widening of the gap between the poorest and the richest elements of society. Additionally, as Perkins observes:

There was the increasing segregation of urban society into different streets, districts or suburbs according to income and status, which broke it down into isolated and mutually hostile classes.[2]

Nowhere was social dislocation and the sense of uncertainty more evident than in Germany where reforms in the years from 1807 to 1821 had altered the political and economic structure, but had been unable to establish a tradition of liberal government and national loyalty. The foundation of bourgeois consciousness and material prosperity upon which England and France had built their representative institutions was still lacking in the German Confederation at the time of the tremendous expansion of industry which took place between 1789 and 1848.

3. Conflict within Marx's family

Marx was born May 5, 1818 in Trier, in the German Rhineland, an area which had been annexed by France and held from 1795 to 1814. During this time period, the Rhineland had experienced economic, administrative and political reforms. The Rhineland was then occupied by Prussia as a result of the Council of Vienna.

It would be hard to find a more traditional Jewish lineage than that of Marx. However, his father, Heinrich Marx (1782-1838), converted to Christianity in 1816, probably to facilitate the advancement of his legal career. In 1824, he converted his children including Marx. However, Marx's mother, Henrietta (1787-1836), resisted the conversion. She did convert in 1825, but returned to Judaism after her husband's death.

Marx's family must have experienced a two-fold discrimination. On one hand, they were discriminated against by the Prussian society for being Jewish. On the other, they were looked down upon as apostate by the Jewish community.[3] In this situation, Marx may have had strong feelings of loneliness, alienation, inferiority, humiliation and defeat. Perhaps this lack of identity and self-assurance contributed to his transformation into an extremely rebellious and militant person, bitter toward the society around him.

These feelings would have been intensified by the oppressive actions of the Prussian government. However, very few of the leading radical intellectuals of that time had seriously suffered at the hands of the European authorities, and most of them (including Marx) appear never to have even been inside a factory. It was a new vision, rather than old grievances, which was the force behind their revolt.

Influences on Marx's Thought

4. Marx's personal break from God

In his early youth, Marx seemed to share his father's deistic views, although we find expressions of fervent Christian feelings as well. He wrote in an assignment submitted to the *Gymnasium* (secondary school):

> There stands man, the only being in nature which does not fulfill its purpose, the only member of the totality of creation which is not worthy of the God who created it. But that benign Creator could not hate His work; He wanted to raise it up to Him and He sent His Son, through whom He proclaimed to us: "Now ye are clean through the word which I have spoken unto you."

Then, when by union with Christ a more beautiful sun has risen for us, when we feel all our iniquity but at the same time rejoice over our redemption, we can for the first time love God, who previously appeared to us as an offended ruler but now appears as a forgiving father, as a kindly teacher.[5]

Perhaps it was a particular tragic or shameful event which shattered this Christian communion which the young Marx shared with God. It must have been something more abrupt and severe than a gradual diminishing of religious fervor, or a progressive estrangement from God, something more terrible and awful than doubt. The French writer Maurice Clavel speaks of a "counter-conversion" experienced by Marx. In the poem, "The Pale Maiden," Marx writes of one who has "lost heaven, this I know. My soul faithful to God was marked for Hell."[6]

Another poem suggests that after his break with God, Marx felt cursed for eternity:

So a god has snatched from me my all in the curse and rack of Destiny. All his worlds are gone beyond recall! Nothing but revenge is left to me![7]

It seems that Marx was unable to participate in the Christian experience of repentance. He eventually came to view God as the enemy of human progress, and committed himself to the elimination of religion. Later Marx would become an extremely militant atheist, regarding the Christian religion as "one of the most immoral there is."

B. Influential trends of thought

1. The influence of Hegel

In his university days, Marx was strongly influenced by the work of Georg Hegel (1770-1831), the most revered German philosopher of that time. Marx utilized the main themes of Hegel's thought, including development through contradiction (the dialectic), the eventual establishment of an ideal society, and the realization of freedom. Furthermore, he adopted Hegel's description of man as "alienated," and the solution of the problem of alienation came to be the apparent motivation of Marx's work.

a. Absolute idealism

Hegel's position on the ultimate nature of reality is known as "absolute idealism." This term has nothing to do with having lofty ideals or striving to be morally perfect. It refers to the philosophical position which says that it is ideas, or more broadly our minds, our thoughts and our consciousness, that constitute ultimate reality. (The opposed view is materialism, which contends that ultimate reality is material, while dualism states that both mind and matter are real).

b. God: Absolute Spirit

Hegel speaks of the *"Absoluter Geist,"* or Absolute Spirit. This is his description of God. It is certainly not an orthodox Christian view, although Hegel was a practicing Lutheran. Hegel sees God not as eternal and immutable, but as an essence that needs to manifest itself in the world, and, having made itself manifest, to perfect the world in order to perfect itself. Obviously, this view places a tremendous emphasis on the necessity of progress, for the onward movement of history is the path which God must take to achieve perfection.

c. Hegel's view of history: progress toward freedom

What is the goal which God seeks to attain, and how does God set about to achieve it? Hegel writes, "What the Spirit wants to achieve is its own conception." Simply put, it means that God is like a great intellect which seeks to think itself, a mind which seeks to know itself. This can be done by projecting itself into the created world, and knowing itself through this created world. The end point or culmination of this process can only be reached when a thinking and reasoning being is created through which the Absolute can know itself completely. For Hegel, this is possible through the human mind. However, it requires a totally free mind in a totally rational environment.

In elaborating his theory of history, Hegel introduced the notion of alienation. For Hegel, alienation occurs as the Absolute Spirit externalizes itself in the created world. That is, the Spirit becomes alienated temporarily in the process of creation. This alienation is resolved when the process of creation and history reaches its goal.

d. The goal of history

Hegel maintained that throughout history, all humanity was making its way towards the solution of alienation and the goal of freedom. In his *Philosophy of History*, he traces the progress of humankind toward realizing freedom and reason. Hegel speaks of the "oriental despot," such as the emperor of Persia, who experiences freedom while holding dominion over the people in his empire. This gives way to the Greek city states, where a few men enjoy freedom while keeping others as slaves.

Christianity, in Hegel's view, was important because it made men aware of their spiritual nature, and the Reformation was essential because it stressed that the individual could achieve salvation. The French revolution failed to liberate man, but Napoleon, greatly admired by Hegel, brought the concepts of personal freedom and the code of rights to Prussia, where the environment was prepared to receive them. On the soil of Prussia, then, the total freedom of man could be achieved. The means to this achievement would be the rational State, where the contradiction between individual interests and the collective interest would be resolved, bringing true freedom to everyone.

e. The dialectic of Hegel

Mention should also be made at this time of Hegel's view of the dialectical nature of the operation of the Absolute Spirit. In the dialectical movement as described by Hegel, the starting point is the thesis. The thesis shows itself to be incomplete or inconsistent, and it breaks down. It is replaced by the second stage, the antithesis.

The second stage also shows itself to be inadequate. Both the thesis and the antithesis are too one-sided. In a sense, they need each other. Thesis and antithesis are brought together and unified in a manner that preserves them in the third stage, the synthesis.

It will later be shown that the Hegelian dialectic is quite different from that of Marx. Hegel does not demand the destruction of one element by the other.

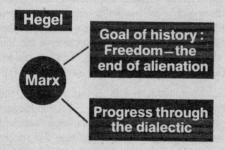

2. After Hegel: division into left and right

In the preface of his book, *The Philosophy of Law*, Hegel stated: "What is rational is actual, and what is actual is rational." After Hegel's death, those who considered themselves his followers split into two camps. The conservative, or Right Hegelians, put greater emphasis on the latter half of this statement, that "What is actual is rational." They reconciled his religious views with Protestant Christianity, and accepted the supportive view of the Prussian state. For them, since the Prussian government was actual, it was rational.

This orthodox school of Hegelianism produced no major thinkers, and after maintaining for some years the status of a semi-official philosophy in Berlin, it declined so rapidly that by the 1860's, Hegel's philosophy was totally out of fashion in Germany.

Left Hegelians, however, consisted of young men with radical leanings. They claimed that because he was too intent on showing that history matched his rational scheme, Hegel had failed to recognize the implications of his own basic ideas. By doing this, he produced merely a justification of the actual state of affairs. They felt that the task is not to *interpret history in a rational way*, but rather to *make history rational* by bringing, for example, new institutions into being which will be more rational than those already in place.

In considering Prussia, they saw a society filled with contradiction and injustice. They scorned the idea that this could be the fulfillment of the promise of Hegel's philosophy. In place of Hegel's predominantly speculative and theoretical attitude toward history and social life, they felt that a practical and revolutionary attitude was necessary.

It has been suggested by persons such as the Italian philosopher Benedetto Croce (1866-1952) that Hegel's philosophy represents a serious threat to religion because it seeks not to destroy religion, but to substitute itself for religion. The Left Hegelians appear to have pursued this objective, and progressively made their hostility toward religion more apparent. Among the most prominent of the Left Hegelians were Ludwig Feuerbach (1804-1872), Arnold Ruge (1802-1880), David Strauss (1808-1882) and of course, Karl Marx.

Marx came to the University of Berlin some six years after Hegel's death. He soon attached himself to the Young Hegelians (as the Left Hegelians came to be known) and joined in the prevailing criticism of religion. Bruno Bauer, a Young Hegelian lecturer in theology, espoused the idea that the Christian Gospels were not historically accurate, but were a fantasy related to men's emotional needs. He taught that a new social cataclysm "more tremendous" than the advent of Christianity was in the making. At one point, Marx and Bauer intended to collaborate in producing a periodical entitled "The

Archive of Atheism." This plan was abandoned when Bauer's political activism exceeded official University tolerance. He was dismissed from his post in 1839.

3. Feuerbach's critique of Hegel

The essence of Marxism is a transformation of Hegel's philosophy from idealism into materialism. That is to say, Marxist philosophy is the Hegelian scheme of history restated in explicitly materialistic, atheistic terms. Marx said that he found Hegel "standing on his head," and put him on his feet.

This transformation owes a great deal to the development of the anti-religious, anti-God trend which gained strength in the Enlightenment and reached a high point of expression in the thought of Ludwig Feuerbach.

The French philosophers of the Enlightenment challenged both religion as a social institution and the traditional view of God as a personal being able to intervene in man's life, accomplish miracles and guide the history of Providence.

Pierre Bayle, one of the pioneers of the Enlightenment, directed his attacks against religious constraints and dogmas. In his *Historical and Critical Dictionary*, which the 18th century philosophers used as a reference, he drew a systematic list of all the errors and crimes committed in the history of Western Christendom.

Voltaire's critique of religion was virulent and even sometimes vulgar. For him, religion automatically led to fanaticism. Instead of concentrating on other-worldly matters, people should seek happiness in this world.

Diderot's philosophy was materialistic and atheistic. For him, if God existed, evil would not exist. In his hedonistic vision, morality had nothing to do with religion. Good was associated with physical pleasure and evil with suffering.

D'Holbach was a fanatical enemy of religion. He saw in

religion — and especially in Christianity — the source of all human miseries.

Let us see how the anti-God thought was used to transform Hegel's philosophy into Marxism.

Hegel believed that although there is constant conflict between individuals in civil society, the State offers the possibility of resolving these through a higher form of unity. In other words, the State is able to mediate the disputes which might arise between the self-interested individuals in the society by calling them to participation in the political realm.

In the ultimate sense, this mediation is the result of the action of the Absolute, realizing itself dialectically in history. That is to say, according to Hegel, the complete freedom of man and the solution to selfish human conflicts would come about through the work of God, using the State as a means.

For the Left Hegelians, however, God does not exist. There must then be a different method to attain human freedom.

In trying to solve this problem, the most effective critique used against Hegel was that of Ludwig Feuerbach. Feuerbach had written *On Philosophy and Christianity* (1839) and *The Essence of Christianity* (1841), in which he criticized the Christian view of God and Hegel's view of the relationship between thinking and being.

Feuerbach prepared the way for revolutionary atheism by explaining religion, especially the Christian religion, in psychological terms. He inverted the Hegelian notion that God created man out of His spiritual need to overcome divine alienation. Feuerbach suggested that, on the contrary, man had created God out of man's material need to overcome human alienation. That is, faith in God owes its existence to the needy, miserable, battered state of the human psyche. In the early stages of development, human beings saw themselves as small and helpless in comparison to the forces of nature which threatened them and which they could not control. In this situation, people created the myth of a benevolent power behind the universe: God.

Feuerbach contended that the God of Christianity is an illusion. He claimed that God is not the creator of man, but rather it is man who has created "God." To create God, man has projected his own nature into an imaginary being. Spirit, according to Feuerbach, is the product of matter, and God is simply the objectification of the essence of man.

Concerning God, Feuerbach wrote:

> (God) is... the human nature (human reason, feeling, love, will) purified, freed from the limits of the individual man, made objective... The divine being is nothing else than the human being.[8]

Having created God, man is then oppressed by his creation:

> Religion is the separation of man from himself: he sets God over against himself as an opposed being.[9]

Feuerbach stressed that the confusion in society can be settled by denying God and improving human relationships. He exalted human virtues such as love, friendship, and compassion, and did not advocate violence.

Ludwig Feuerbach
(1804–1872)
The Essence of Christianity—1841

Man created God

"The Divine Being is nothing else than the human being"

In addition to this, in *Preliminary Theses for a Reform of
Christianity* (1843), Feuerbach elaborated a general critique
of Hegel's idealism. Feuerbach said that in dealing with
"thought" and "being," Hegel had reversed the positions of
subject and predicate. To correct this, it is necessary to make
Hegel's subject into the predicate and Hegel's predicate into
the subject. For Hegel, thought is subject and being is
predicate. For Feuerbach, "being must be subject and thinking must be predicate."

Reading Feuerbach gave great satisfaction and hope to
Marx. Concerning Marx's jubilation upon encountering
Feuerbach, Engels later wrote:

> One must himself have experienced the liberating
> effect of this book to get an idea of it. Enthusiasm
> was general, we all became at once Feuerbachians.
> How enthusiastically Marx greeted the new concep-
> tion and how he was greatly influenced by it in spite of
> critical reservations may also be noted in *The Holy
> Family.*[10]

Marx himself later confessed to a "love of Feuerbach," a
sentiment he rarely expressed, so enthused was he that his
philosophical way had been cleared.[11]

In essence, Feuerbach allowed Marx to substitute materialism for idealism while retaining a monistic, deterministic
view of history. (Monism is the view that all of reality is
composed of one substance. For Hegel, this substance was
"idea." For the Marxists, this substance is "matter.")

Feuerbach may be regarded philosophically as an atheist
and materialist. Marx utilized these elements of Feuerbach's
critique of Hegel, but later criticized Feuerbach's humanism.
Feuerbach believed that people could be exhorted to be good,
that they could be inspired to change themselves. Marx said
that people and circumstances could only be changed through
revolution.

In his *Theses on Feuerbach* (1845), Marx would write, "He does not grasp the significance of 'revolutionary', of 'practical-critical', activity."

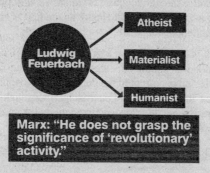

4. The socialists and Hess

During this time, many conscientious thinkers expressed deep sympathy for the laborers and criticized the magnates of business who appeared to be interested only in material gain. Pointing out the immorality of exploitation and suppression, they appealed to the conscience and humanitarian feelings of those in positions of power. Robert Owen (1771-1858), Claude-Henri Saint-Simon (1760-1835) and Charles Fourier (1772-1837) were among those who took this approach, believing that change could come through the power of reason and morality.

The influence of these ideas on Marx may have been considerable. Marx's native town of Trier had been a center of the new Saint-Simonian teaching.[12] In particular, Marx grafted certain key Saint-Simonian beliefs onto his Hegelian view of history: the liberating potential of the Industrial Revolution, the need for a "scientific" analysis of society by classes, and the historical destiny of "the poorest and most numerous class."

Another important influence in the development of Marxism is Moses Hess, an older member of the Young Hegelians who became known in the circle as the "communist rabbi." Hess was the originator of the German philosophical communism that Engels described in an article of 1843 as the inevitable outcome of the development of German philosophy. Engels expressly acknowledged that Hess was the first of their group to reach communism by the "philosophical path."

Hess was a correspondent for the *Rheinische Zeitung* when Marx was editor. He was an enthusiastic disciple of Feuerbach, and constructed the doctrine of philosophical communism as an extension of Feuerbach's "humanism," enlarging on the theme that "productive activity" is the essential attribute of the human species.

Hess studied extensively the contemporary literature on socialism and communism, of which France in those days was the primary source. In particular, he was impressed by Proudhon's *What is Property?*, published in 1840. Proudhon anticipated Marx in calling the capital-labor relation an exploitation of man by man, and decried the right of the owner of capital goods to employ the labor of others to augment his own wealth. This he called "property" in his noted aphorism, "property is theft."

Probably because Proudhon had vaguely outlined the idea of incorporating communism into Hegel's philosophy of history, Hess regarded Proudhon as the most philosophical of all the French communist writers. Marx and Engels came to share the same view. Prior to Marx's move to Paris, Hess was the main link between Marx and the French socialists and communists.

II. Marx's earliest writings and the theory of alienation

A. Marx's doctoral thesis and earliest writings

In 1841, Marx submitted a doctoral thesis to the University of Jena. His topic was the difference between the materialism of Epicurus and that of Democritus. In this study he

favored the former because it allowed for an energizing principle in matter. If matter were auto-dynamic, it would do away
with the need for a Creator. In the introduction to this thesis,
Marx wrote:

> Philosophy makes no secret of it. The proclamation
> of Prometheus — in one word, I detest all the gods
> — is her own profession, her own slogan against all
> the gods of heaven and earth who do not recognize
> man's self-consciousness as the highest divinity. There
> shall be no other beside it.[13]

B. Marx as editor of the Rheinische Zeitung

When Marx finished his studies at the University of Jena
in 1841, he was forced to abandon his hopes for an academic
career due to his association with Bauer and others. Hoping
to be married, he began to write for the newly-founded liberal
newspaper known as the *Rheinische Zeitung*. This paper had
been founded in that year by followers of Ruge as a direct
challenge to the conservative *Kölnische Zeitung*. When the
editor resigned in 1842, Marx took over that position, and he
consistently involved the paper in various political and social
causes.

Several incidents are noteworthy. In a controversy with
the *Allgemeine Ausberger Zeitung*, Marx showed that he had
not yet subscribed to the communist cause. He declared
editorially that communism was "only a dogmatic abstraction
... a particularly one-sided application of the socialist
principle." He also wrote that "*The Rheinische Zeitung* ...
does not admit that communist ideas in their present form
possess even theoretical reality, and ... still less ... practical realization."[14] Later, Marx would reminisce that he then
knew very little about the matter, writing "... my previous
studies did not permit me even to venture any judgement on
the content of the French theories."[15]

Marx also plunged into the dispute regarding the deliber-
ations of the *Rheinisch Landtag* (Rhineland Assembly) on thefts

of wood from the forests. In October 1842, the Assembly promised to revise the law, but in the end only protected the interests of the forest owners. Indignant, Marx wrote that the rights of the trees were placed above the rights of the peasants.

In the closing months of 1842, Marx began to investigate the contemporary French literature on socialism and communism. With the exception of Proudhon, writers on this subject were largely concerned with sketching designs of future communist organizations of society. Marx dismissed them as "utopians." He rejected the notion that the future could be designed, and maintained instead that a new world could be discovered *through the merciless criticism of everything existing.*

In 1843, Marx resigned his post at the *Rheinische Zeitung* in the face of increasing governmental pressures. He married Jenny von Westphalen (1814-1881) in June, and withdrew to his mother-in-law's house in Bad Kreuznach to think out the basics of his philosophy. It was here that he wrote out many pages of notes of his critique of Hegel (compiled as "Contribution to a Critique of Hegel's Philosophy of Law"), and began to assemble two articles entitled "On the Jewish Question," and "Contribution to a Critique of Hegel's Philosophy of Law, Introduction."

In October he left for Paris with Jenny, who was three months pregnant, to collaborate with Ruge in publishing a revolutionary periodical called the "German-French Annals" (*Deutsch-Französische Jahrbücher*).

Jenny Marx was to serve her husband with extraordinary devotion until the end of her life. It appears that Marx, however, never assumed the responsibilities which a husband normally assumes as the head of a family. His wife and children lived in constant poverty and several of his children perished at early ages.

C. The fundamental doctrines of Marxism

The beginning of Marxism

a. Alienation and liberation defined

In the earliest writings of Marx, we find that he redefines the Hegelian usage of "alienation" and "liberation." For Hegel, alienation was a period in the development of the Absolute Spirit in which the Spirit failed to recognize the external world as part of itself. For Marx, following the line of Feuerbach, alienation means that man is cut off from reality, and therefore develops religion as a substitute for relations with the real world.

> It (religion) is the fantastic realization of the human being inasmuch as the human being possesses no true reality. [16]

Liberated man, then, is man cut off from the fictitious "God" and returned to relation with reality.

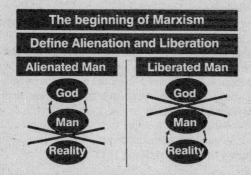

b. The ultimate source of alienation

Marx asserts, however, that religious alienation is not the fundamental form of alienation. Beneath religion is the state, and beneath the state is society. Finally, Marx came to contend that the basis of society itself is the economic structure.

Ultimately, Marx would hold that it is economic alienation, especially in the form of its manifestation as private property, which gives rise to the notion of God and religious alienation. Liberation must begin with the destruction of private property. Destroying the basis of alienation, according to Marx, will eliminate the belief in God altogether.

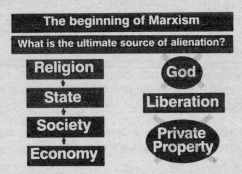

As we study the early formulation of Marx's thought, we come to realize that by the end of 1843, he had already arrived at his basic conclusions regarding the human situation. Contrary to Hegel, who considered that problems due to selfish individualism in civil society will be overcome by means of the state, Marx considered that the state was depriving man of his original nature.

D. Marx's life and writings: 1843

We can observe the development of Marx's critique of Hegel's philosophy in the latter part of 1843. In the collection of writings entitled *A Contribution to the Critique of Hegel's Philosophy of Law* (August 1843), he called for the abolition of the State. Two months later, in the text *On the Jewish Question* (October 1843), he maintained that overcoming the disorder of civil society will be achieved when men restore their original status of "species-being."

In this text, Marx describes man as he is encountered in present reality as follows:

> ... man in his uncivilized, unsocial form, man in his fortuitous existence, man just as he is, man as he *has been corrupted by the whole organization of our society*, who has *lost himself, been alienated*, and handed over to the rule of inhuman conditions and elements—in short, man who is not yet a *real species-being*. (emphasis added)[17]

Implicit in such a view is the notion that there is some original nature of man, and that this original nature has been "corrupted," "lost," and "alienated." This view, of course, is familiar in the religious tradition as the concept of the fall of man. That is, human beings are endowed by God with an original nature. However, they have lost this nature, or fail to manifest this nature, due to their separation from God through the fall of man.

The fall of man, or loss of the human essence, is quite comprehensible in the religious framework. Its appearance in a rigorously materialistic ideology, however, is difficult to reconcile. Marx states that "the whole organization of our

Alienation

Religious view	Marxist view
Fall of man	Alienation
Separation from God	Economic process

society" has "corrupted" man, caused him to lose himself and dehumanized him.

Species-essence refers to the essential qualities of a human being. It is these qualities which set a human being apart from any other species. In the CAUSA worldview, the term "original human nature" is used to refer to the nature with which God has endowed man. According to Marx, then, this original nature, or species-essence, has been lost.

How can the original species-essence be recovered? The method would depend on how the species-essence was lost. Feuerbach had said that man has an essential nature which is different than animals. Man has the qualities of reason, emotion, love and will. However, by objectifying this essence and making it a "God," man has made himself powerless. Belief in God, in Feuerbach's view, destroys the essence of man. Accordingly, the recovery of the lost human nature can only come about when man denies God and reclaims from Him the human essence.

Marx's view, however, is different:

> the existence of religion is the existence of a defect, the source of this defect can only be sought in the nature of the state itself. We no longer regard religion as the *cause*, but only as the *manifestation* ... [18]

> religion in itself is without content, it owes its being not to heaven but to the earth, and with the abolition of distorted reality, of which it is the *theory*, it will collapse of itself. [19]

Thus, the elimination of the defect which is religion is impossible without the elimination of the *cause* for that defect. The emancipation of man and the recuperation of his species-essence will be possible, says Marx, when the conflict between the individual (who is concerned about *himself*) and the citizen (who is concerned about *society*) is resolved.

Only when the real individual man re-absorbs in himself the abstract citizen, and as an individual human being has become a *species-being* in his everyday life... only then will human emancipation have been accomplished.[20]

This conflict will finally be resolved when "huckstering" is done away with:

Once society has succeeded in abolishing... huckstering and its preconditions... the conflict between man's individual-sensuous existence and his species-existence has been abolished.[21]

In *Contribution to a Critique of Hegel's Philosophy of Law, Introduction*, December 1843, Marx eventually came to the conclusion that the fundamental way to settle the problem of the alienation of man is the "negation of private property."

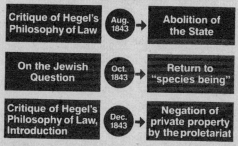

Marx's Life and Writings: 1843

Critique of Hegel's Philosophy of Law	Aug. 1843	→	Abolition of the State
On the Jewish Question	Oct. 1843	→	Return to "species being"
Critique of Hegel's Philosophy of Law, Introduction	Dec. 1843	→	Negation of private property by the proletariat

It should be recalled that although Marx at first accepted Feuerbach's materialism and humanism (in the sense of emphasis on self-realization through reason) with enthusiasm, he later abandoned humanism and utilized only materialism in prescribing a solution to alienation. He further declared that he would turn from the "criticism of heaven" to the "criticism of earth," by which he meant that he would deal with law and politics (and later, economics) rather than religion and theology.

Furthermore, in the latter months of 1843, Marx had

altered his view that "the liberation of man must be accomplished by the hands of actual man in civil society." He began to insist instead that the lost essence of humanity could be recaptured by "the proletariat's negation of private property." He not only decided upon the overthrow of the capitalist system as his goal, but also portrayed the proletariat as the only force having the power to bring about a revolution.

The sociologist and legal theorist Lorenz von Stein had introduced French socialism and communism to Prussia in 1842 with his text *The Socialism and Communism of Today's France*. Von Stein, a conservative Hegelian, had been investigating socialist movements under the instructions of the Prussian government, which was interested in subversive activity among German workers in Paris. He was anti-socialist and regarded the class hierarchy as a precondition of organized society. His book, however, which contained a large amount of information, was widely known in radical circles in Germany. He described the proletariat as a major political force in modern society—a united body awakened under the purpose of the negation of private property. It appears that Marx borrowed that concept intact.

E. Marx's life and writings: 1844

Marx studied economics in Paris from November 1843 to February 1845. Using Engel's *Outline of a Critique of Political Economy* as a guide, he investigated the works of Smith, Ricardo, Say, Sismondi and others. The three manuscripts which he compiled during this period were later published as the *Economic and Philosophic Manuscripts of 1844*. In these manuscripts, Marx begins the transformation of his philosophical view of alienation into a materialistic and dialectical point of view.

The main points which Marx came to espouse after studying economics while in Paris were: first, that in capitalist society the worker has become a commodity and, second, that capitalist society thrives only by exploiting the worker.

Thus, regardless of however hard the worker may work, all the product of his labor will be plundered, so that the worker becomes all the poorer the more wealth he produces.

Marx claimed that as a result of the dehumanizing system of capitalism, and in particular the loss of the product of the worker's labor, both capitalist and worker are estranged from their human nature:

> The propertied class and the class of the proletariat present the same human self-estrangement. But the former class feels at ease and strengthened in this self-estrangement, it recognizes estrangement as its own power and has in it the semblance of a human existence. [22]

Neither one leads a life of fulfillment, but the capitalist maintains the semblance of a human existence. The lost human nature of both must be recovered. How to recover this lost nature depends on how it has been lost. According to Marx, how has alienation come about?

Marx writes: "How does it happen, we ask now, that man alienates his labor?" He then says that this question must be transformed into "a question regarding the relationship between alienated labor and the process of development of mankind." That is, the Marxist view of alienation is based on Marx's view of the development of man.

1. The Marxist view of man

The Marxist view of alienation revolves around the concept of "labor." To understand the central importance of labor to Marx, we need to consider the French biologist Jean Lamarck's theory of the origin of the species as well as Engels' discussion of the role of labor in the development of man.

a. Lamarckism

Lamarckism is a theory of evolution asserting that environmental changes cause structural changes in animals and plants that are transmitted to offspring. This is known as the inheritance of acquired characteristics. According to Lamarckism a new species comes about through (1) interaction with a changing environment, which produces (2) physiological changes in the organism. These can then be (3) passed on to the offspring. Through a succession of generations, a new species is produced.

For example, a monkey climbs in trees and gathers food. By doing so (interacting with its environment), the physiology of the animal is modified. In this case, the central nervous system and the muscles of the limbs become more developed. When the next generation of monkeys is born, these physiological variations will be present. After many generations, a new species of monkey can be observed.

b. Engel's discussion of the development of man

Engels applied the ideas of Lamarckism to a theory of human development. In "The part played by labor in the transition from ape to man," Engels characterizes man as a highly developed animal which has evolved as a consequence of interaction with its material environment. This interaction has taken the specific form of labor. Through labor, man has developed the ability to communicate and the capacity of reason. The ape became man through labor, and it is labor which distinguishes man from ape. (For Feuerbach, reason, love and will are the essence of man, but for Marx, the essential factor is the ability to labor.)

In Marxian theory, labor even replaces God as the creator of humankind. Engels wrote that: "Labor ... is the prime basic condition for all human existence, and this is to such an extent that, in a sense, we have to say that labor created man himself."[23]

2. Labor and alienation

Because he viewed man as being fundamentally a laboring animal, Marx concluded that alienation must be a problem in

Engels: The origin of man

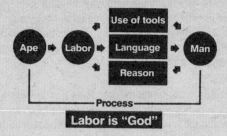

human labor-centered relations. In *Economic and Philosophic Manuscripts of 1844*, he described four types of alienation.

a. Types of alienation

(1) *Alienation of the laborer from the product of his labor.*

Under the capitalist system, whatever the laborer produces is immediately taken from him and becomes the property of the capitalist who contributed no value to its production. When the products of labor are taken, they become "an alien object" from which the worker is estranged.

Marx's types of alienation

(2) *Alienation of the laborer from his labor.*

The capitalist takes away the products of labor from the worker. The worker is left with only his labor itself, which he must sell in order to survive. He must work day after day in a factory, completely without dignity. The worker does not know his identity or his true value. Everything about himself which is important is lost.

In this situation, the worker finds that the more that he works, the richer the capitalist becomes. Since the products of his labor are expropriated by the capitalist, the more he pours out his blood and sweat, the more the capitalist benefits, entrenching himself in a position of dominance, and reinforcing the entire capitalist system.

labour for the worker... is not his own, but someone else's...[24]

(3) *Alienation of the human species.*

According to Engels, the human species is characterized by the mastery of its environment: "The animal merely *uses* its environment and brings about changes in it simply by his presence; man by his changes makes it serve his ends, *masters* it."[25]

Under the capitalist system, however, labor has become "a material power above us, growing out of our control, thwarting our expectations, bringing to naught our calculations."[26]

Man's species-essence refers to the free and conscious activity of production, which distinguishes man from an animal directed only by its physical instincts and producing only what it or its offspring directly require.

"Man" is man acting in freedom upon the objective world, specifically, engaging in the free activity of creation. Because the worker is alienated from his labor, however, labor has been reduced to merely the means of satisfying the desire to maintain one's physical existence, and labor no longer exists as a free conscious activity.

For the worker, labor is reduced to merely the means of sustaining one's physical existence. For the capitalist, labor is the commodity which he must buy in order to produce profit. They have both lost the basis of their humanity.

3 Alienation of the human species

Product of labor

Labor is what makes man

Labor

Deprived of species-essence of man

(4) *Alienation of man from man.*

In the de-humanized world of capitalism, laborers are not free in their human relationships. How can they be? They are not human. They do not experience joy among themselves, nor do they discover love and understanding.

b. The root of alienation: private ownership of property

Marx had already singled out the "division of labor" as the major cause of man's "loss of himself," in *"Debatte uber*

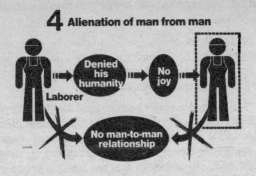

4 Alienation of man from man

die Pressefreiheit," from *Rheinische Zeitung* of May, 1842. For Marx, however, division of labor and the private ownership of property are one and the same.

> Division of labour and private property are, moreover, identical expressions: in one the same thing is affirmed with reference to activity as is affirmed in the other with reference to the product of activity.[27]

Thus, Marx holds that private property is the consequence of alienated labor, but it is also the means by which labor alienates itself. He called it the "realization of this alienation."

c. The solution to alienation: communism

By 1844, Marx began to advocate communism—"the positive abolition of private property and therefore the real appropriation of the human essence by and for man"—as the solution to alienation.

Although in Marx's writings the exact cause and effect relationship between alienation and private property seems to be somewhat unclear, Marx assures us that when private ownership has been abolished, the human condition will change:

The abolition of private property is therefore the complete emancipation of all human senses and qualities.[28]

Marx claimed that the elimination of private property is the basis for recovering the species-essence of man and ending his alienation.

III. The development of Marxism

A. Early communism

Although theories of communal societies date from antiquity, communism as a class-conscious revolutionary movement originated in France in the second half of the 1830's. Following the suppression of a workers' revolt in Lyon in 1834, a small number of leaders went underground and began to develop increasingly radical programs. The resulting secret "Society of Flowers" of 1836-38 has been called the first communist society.

Attempts were soon made to make explicit a communist viewpoint. The radical socialist Etienne Cabet presented his secularized *Communist Credo* in 1841. Theodore Dezamy challenged Cabet's moralistic credo with a version based on the radical Enlightenment model of a rational "code" in the *Code de la Communaute* of 1842, which featured an extended discussion of the rationality and inevitability of social revolution as opposed to the compromises of reformist politics. Dezamy insisted that a communist revolution must immediately confiscate all property and money. Furthermore, he argued that a materialist and atheist worldview must supplant Catholicism for the "universal well-being." Karl Marx was an admirer of Dezamy, and like other radical foreign intellectuals in Paris in 1844, was attracted and inspired by his arrest and trial.

The term communism was popularized in England by John Goodwin Barmby. Barmby founded a Communist Propaganda Society and published *The Communist Chronicle*. In

March 1842, he set forth the first communist theory of history: a scheme based on four ages of humanity (an early pastoral stage, "paradization," which leads through feudalization and civilization to "communization").

B. Marx's life and writings: 1845

Marx had been introduced to his life-long collaborator, Friedrich Engels, in 1843. In 1844-1845, Marx and Engels together produced *The Holy Family*. They criticized the Hegelians and held up as a model the recently suppressed German worker's movement led by Wilhelm Weitling in Switzerland. Marx wrote, "Ideas can accomplish absolutely nothing. To become real, ideas require men who apply a practical force."[29] (Two years later, Marx denounced Weitling's Christianized communism.)

Marx was expelled from France by the government of Guizot, and left for Brussels on February 5, 1845. That year in Belgium, he renounced his Prussian nationality.

Soon after he arrived in Brussels in 1845, Marx wrote *Theses on Feuerbach*, parting completely from the humanism of Feuerbach. It was at this time that he emphasized that revolution was the only way to change circumstances and human beings. "The coincidence of the changing of circumstances and of human activity or self-change can be conceived and rationally understood only as *revolutionary practice*."[30]

C. Marx's life and writings: 1846

He then began the writing of *The German Ideology* with Engels, who had emigrated to Brussels, and finished by May of the next year. This text contained the most complete exposition of their materialistic conception of history, concluding that a violent communist revolution was necessary. From this time, however, the theme of recovery of the alienated human nature was scarcely mentioned. The materialist conception of history holds that material conditions determine historical development: "The nature of individuals thus depends on the material conditions which determine their production." Furthermore, history procedes in a deterministic way, as these conditions are "conditions independent of their will."[31]

Whereas other socialists offered revolutionary ideas, Marx provided a revolutionary ideology, emphasizing the destiny of the proletariat and the necessity of dictatorship, and casting his beliefs in terminology that would appear to be scientific. He further engaged in a series of polemical attacks against his would-be allies, trying to carve out for himself a pre-eminent position in the revolutionary socialist movement not unlike the dominion which Hegel had exercised in the German academic world.

Marx employed the term "utopian" to describe all socialists who did not share his views. Utopianism meant un-scientific socialism, and Marxism, through constant repetition, came to mean "scientific socialism."

D. Marx's life and writings: 1847

In Brussels, Marx worked through his Communist Correspondence Committee, an organization of about fifteen German writers and typesetters. The first foreign allies of the committee were two Chartist internationalists who formed an affiliated London Correspondence Committee in March, 1846. In the summer of 1846, Marx and Engels sought allies in the League of the Just, a group of German emigres in London. In October 1846, Engels defined the aim of the communists as support of the proletariat against the bourgeoisie through a violent democratic revolution that would end private property and establish a community of goods.

Marx used the early part of 1847 to write his polemical *The Poverty of Philosophy*, directed against Pierre Proudhon, a well-known rival of Marx. Marx wrote, "It is only in an order of things in which there are no more classes, and class antagonisms, that *social evolutions* will cease to be *political revolutions*."[32]

E. The Communist Manifesto

Up to this point, Marx had generated a body of writings demanding violence against the existing order, but there was no specific plan of action. In the summer of 1847, however, the League (now the League of Communists) requested Marx and Engels to draw up a summary of the communist position on social and political questions. They responded by writing the *Communist Manifesto* in February 1848.

In the *Communist Manifesto*, Marx and Engels exalt the role of class struggle in human history. They insist on the abolition of private property through violent revolution, and criticize all previous forms of socialism. The *Communist Manifesto* concludes by declaring that the task of all communists is revolution: "The communists openly declare that their ends can be attained only by the forcible overthrow of all existing social conditions." The *Communist Manifesto* also summarized the task of communism as follows:

> In this sense, the theory of the communists may be summed up in the single sentence: Abolition of private property.[33]

F. The Marxist program to solve alienation

By the time of the publication of the *Communist Manifesto*, Marxism had taken shape as a program of action with a promised result: the solution of human alienation. (The solution to alienation is expressed in various ways in Marx's writings. In *The German Ideology*, for example, he writes of mankind "ridding itself of the muck of ages" and becoming fit to "found society anew.")

This solution is to be brought about by the abolition of "bourgeois private property." Bourgeois property is described in the *Communist Manifesto* as the "most complete expression of the system of producing and appropriating products that is based on class antagonisms, on the exploitation of the many by the few."[34] Marx goes on to say that this will require the elimination of the bourgeois himself. "This person must, indeed, be swept out of the way, and made impossible."[35]

The class which is designated to carry out this process is the proletariat, "the class of modern wage-labourers who, having no means of production of their own, are reduced to selling their labour power in order to live."[36] The proletariat will "wrest" all instruments of production from the bourgeoisie and concentrate all power into its own hands, organizing itself as the ruling class until all classes can be eliminated.

The method of seizing power is to be violent revolution.

> The Communists disdain to conceal their views and aims. They openly declare that their ends can be attained only by the forcible overthrow of all existing social conditions.[37]

Marx opposed attempting a peaceful process to achieve the elimination of private property. He also opposed any appeal to human sympathies or morality. He saw that previous attempts to realize ideal socialist communities always failed, and he laid the blame for their failures on lack of philosophy and a disregard for the vital role of mass violence.

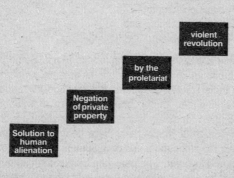

G. Marxism as a philosophical weapon

For the communist revolution to be successful, it is necessary to mobilize and motivate the workers to make revolution. To do this, Marx, Lenin and other Marxists have molded a formidable "philosophical weapon."

Marx himself referred to his writings in this way when he wrote, "As philosophy finds its material weapons in the proletariat, so the proletariat finds its spiritual weapons in philosophy."[38]

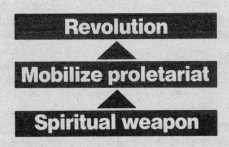

Marxism has been highly successful as a revolutionary ideology. It has set forth a system of beliefs, which provides:

1. A basic philosophy,
2. Hope and a vision, and
3. A plan of action.

There are many ways to approach Marx. Some people approach him as an economist, others as a philosopher, others as a social scientist. But clearly Marx considered himself to be the engineer, the architect of a spiritual weapon, the architect of an ideology designed to bring about revolution. Since the death of Marx, there have been others who have taken over the refinement and development of this philosophical weapon. However, Marxism-Leninism today can be properly understood as an ideological tool to bring about revolution.

There are three major components of this tool, each with its own function and purpose.

One is the economic theories, which are contained in *Das Kapital* and certain other minor texts. These theories intend to prove that capitalism requires exploitation, that you cannot have capitalism, or the private ownership of the means of production, without having exploitation. Marx went to great lengths to argue this through his theory of surplus value. This theory argues that the problem is not a few greedy capitalists, or some kind of selfishness in the capitalist world, or some misplaced values. The problem is capital. Capital, capitalism and the capitalists must be destroyed.

The second element of this weapon is dialectical materialism. Dialectical materialism was developed after Marx, in what is called the scholastic period of Marxism. It attempts in an organized, systematic way to destroy the fundamental ethics of religion, particularly Christianity. This is done first of all by undermining belief in God. That is the materialism aspect. If there is no God behind the Ten Commandments and the other ethical and moral guidelines which religion puts forth, then we must look in the universe around us to learn our ethics and morality. Dialectical materialism proceeds to argue that the morality of the universe is the morality of struggle, conflict and destruction. This is how progress occurs. Therefore dialectical materialism becomes a tremendous justification for murder, used today in communist countries.

The final component is historical materialism, the application of the dialectic to history. Historical materialism has a very important role. In the early years of Christianity, the Christians lived with the feeling that at any moment Christ might return and the world may end. This apocalyptic feeling gave fervor to early Christianity. Communism also shares that kind of apocalyptic vision. Historical materialism teaches people that we are now in the last days of history; we are at the great turning point. The entire history up to this point is just pre-history, and we are going to begin history when we begin communism. Furthermore it argues that communism is a historical inevitability. You can try to stop it, you can destroy yourself trying to stop it, but you cannot stop communism. This idea is widely accepted in the United States today. There are many people who somehow feel that communism is inevitable for Latin America or other parts of the world, and there is nothing we can do to stop this. In that sense, historical materialism has successfully propagated the idea that communism is the inevitable future.

Together, these elements comprise a very powerful philosophical weapon.

H. Marxist theory and practice

Marxism in theory says that private property and property relationships encourage belief in God and religion. They are not the source of belief in God; however, they encourage it, they institutionalize it, and therefore they increase human alienation. Then, if private property relationships can be destroyed, the belief in God will soon vanish. This has been the official doctrine of the Soviet Union. Once the means of production have been seized, it is only a question of time before the human situation is completely solved.

It must of course be pointed out that we do not find Marxism in practice as such. Marxism is too utopian to even practice. It is too unrealistic to even apply. It is only after the modifications of Lenin that Marxism became practicable. Marx-

ism in practice is always Marxism-Leninism, the communism of today. Marxism-Leninism has successfully provoked a series of revolutions beginning in 1917 and lasting up until the present day. Let us ask the question then, Does communism solve alienation? Once you have taken away the means of production from private ownership, is the human problem solved?

In practice, private property cannot be abolished, but human freedom can be destroyed. This is communism in the Soviet Union today. God has been replaced by the totalitarian state, and the result is greater alienation.

One individual who was ignited and inspired by Marxist-Leninist rhetoric was the French writer Andre Gide. Prior to his visit to the USSR in 1938, Gide wrote:

> My conversion is like a faith; all my being goes toward a single goal. In the deplorable state of anxiety of the modern world, the plan of the Soviet Union seems to me to constitute the salvation of mankind.[39]

After visiting the USSR, however, Gide wrote in disillusionment:

> The disappearance of capitalism in Soviet Russia has not brought freedom of the Soviet worker. It is essen-

tial that the proletariat abroad should realize this fully
... It was precisely in order to find none of the
poverty that I went to the Soviet Union, but poverty
there is frowned upon ... one might imagine that it
was indelicate and criminal ... it does not arouse pity
or charity ... only contempt.

Those who parade themselves so proudly are
those whose prosperity has been bought at the price
of this infinite poverty...[40]

IV. Communism as a social failure

The *Communist Manifesto* has been invoked to justify
various revolutionary efforts since its writing, and a communist state was born in 1917. Since then, scores of countries
have fallen under communist control. It must be said that
Marxist theory has been given ample time to prove itself.
Looking at the record, Marxism clearly has not provided the
means to solve the problem of alienation.

In 1960, Nikita Khruschev promised his people that by
the year 1980, the communist ideal state would exist in the
Soviet Union. This is clearly not the case. Soviet apologists
argue that the Soviet Union is still in the transition stage
moving toward true communism. If so, then some progress
toward the goal should be evident. When we survey the four
areas of human alienation mentioned by Marx in his Paris
Manuscripts, however, we see that progress toward their
solution has not been made.

*a) Marx spoke about the alienation of the laborer from the
product of his labor.* Has the laborer under Marxism come to
be the owner of what he produces?

He has not.

Soviet workers are supposedly working for the state,
and the state is supposedly taking care of the workers in an
optimum fashion. Yet Soviet workers today are not advancing

toward an optimum life, they are struggling to survive.

The average salary of a Moscow laborer is 171 rubles per month, yet the necessary salary for subsistence of an average family is 210 rubles.[41]

Outside of Moscow, the situation is far more severe. Former Soviet official Ilja Zemtsov describes abject poverty in outlying parts of the USSR such as Azerbaijian in his text *La corruption en Union soviétique*.

In spite of this, according to Michael Voslensky's, *La Nomenklatura*, a certain group lives quite well in the Soviet Union. They enjoy the newest products from Europe, Japan and the United States. Their children attend private schools. They are the new Soviet super-elite.

Marshall I. Goldman, associate director of the Russian Research Center of Harvard University, in his text, *USSR in Crisis*, points out that Russia was formerly the world's largest exporter of grain. Under communism it is forced to supplement its failing grain production with imports. He also notes that various indicators of prosperity, such as the annual growth rate of GNP, show that the Soviet economy is less and less prosperous each year.[42]

Untrue to its promises, a Marxist economy is not able to put wealth into the hands of the workers. Ironically, this has given rise to a vast (and illegal) system of free enterprise in the USSR. Soviet citizens engage in activities such as manufacturing, buying, selling, transportation, etc., clandestinely. This black market, or "second economy" may total as much as 25% of the national GNP.[43] Without this clandestine "capitalist" activity, the Soviet society would be unable to sustain itself at the present levels.

The Soviet worker's contempt for the product of his labor is evidenced by the shoddy quality of the goods he produces. Soviet citizens will always try to avoid purchasing goods manufactured in the USSR.[44]

The rigid, often senseless dictates of the Soviet central

economic planning system provide another factor which alienates the Soviet worker from the product of his labor. Michael
Binyon writes, "For almost every factory, fulfilling the Plan is
the only criterion, and quality control is lost in the scramble
to turn out the requisite number of products... Russians try
to avoid buying things made at the end of the month as they
are bound to be faulty."[45]

This confusing and contradictory situation creates what
may be called the most alienating working conditions in history.

1. Alienation of the laborer from the product of his labor

Is the Soviet worker the owner of what he produces?

—A new elite
—Widespread poverty
—Underground free market system

*b) Marx spoke about the alienation of the laborer from his
labor.* Does the Soviet laborer find fulfillment and satisfaction
in his labor?

He does not. From 20%-30% of the Soviet workers
leave their jobs each year, often taking as much as a month to
register at a new work place, and several more months to
conform to the norms of labor output at their new job.[46] In
the United States, 12% of workers quit their jobs each year.[47]

Absenteeism and alcoholism are two chronic and unsolved
labor problems in the communist system. There are frequent
campaigns in the Soviet Union to rid the economy of the
severe problem of alcoholism.

When Yuri Andropov, and later Konstantin Chernenko,
took over leadership of the USSR, one of their major concerns was to institute new means of combatting absenteeism,

and the disregard for work, officially called "lack of labor discipline."

In spite of this, the regime stubbornly resists offering material incentives to its workers. The failure of the communist system to generate wealth and offer its people incentives to work has given rise to the expression, "They pretend to pay us and we pretend to work."[48]

Expressions of worker discontent are supressed. Union organizers are frequently imprisoned or given "psychiatric treatment."

Kevin Klose writes in *Russia and the Russians* of the case of Vasilyevich Nikitin, a worker who criticized poor conditions in his mine, and was sent to the psychiatric hospital in Dnepropetrovsk in 1972.

Of all the many drugs administered at Dnepropetrovsk to impose discipline, sulfazine stood at the pinnacle of pain. Originally used more than fifty years earlier to treat malaria by inducing a high fever (giving sulfazine its oddly sinister classification as a "pyrogenic"), the concoction had been used intermittently in European and American mental hospitals in the 1920's and 1930's to treat some kinds of extreme and chronic schizophrenia. Despite its bizarre power to subdue even a violent person by inducing high fever, nausea, mental disorientation, and severe muscle spasms, most Western psychiatrists found that sulfazine had no therapeutic value and discontinued its use.

These were the qualities that made it so attractive to the MVD doctors at Dnepropetrovsk. "People injected with sulfazine were groaning, sighing with pain, cursing the psychiatrists and Soviet power, cursing with everything in their hearts," Alexei told us. "People go into horrible convulsions and get completely disoriented. Their body temperature rises to 40 degrees centigrade almost instantly, and the pain is so intense they cannot move from their beds for three days. Sulfazine is simply a way to destroy a man completely. If they torture you and break your arms, there is a certain specific pain and you can somehow stand it. But sulfazine is like a drill boring into your body that gets worse and worse until it's more than you can stand. It's impossible to endure. It is worse than torture, because, sometimes, torture may end. But this kind of torture may continue for years.

Sulfazine normally was "prescribed" in a "course" of injections of increasing strength over a period that might last up to two months. The mixture caused a violent, long-term reaction in the muscles at the site of the injection, normally the buttocks. Within hours after the first shot, the pain was so excruciating that a victim could not sit down and was forced to lie on his stomach to sleep. He could not lift his legs, which meant that some men were trapped by the maze of bed frames in Nikitin's ward, unable to propel themselves to toilet or dining hall. They languished in misery, dependent upon the whims of the orderlies or the compassion of other inmates for food and companionship. The stench from their suffering hung in the air.[49]

Once again, we are forced to conclude that communism increases alienation.

c) What can be said about the alienation of the human species? Is the original nature of man being expressed in the USSR? References avowing that this is not the case are plentiful.

Konstantin Simis, formerly a defense attorney in the Soviet Union, writes about an underground free enterprise economy which is flourishing in the Soviet Union. This economy, without which the country could not survive, has the side effect of making everyone a criminal for engaging in activities

2. Alienation of the laborer from his labor

Does the Soviet worker derive joy and satisfaction from his work?

—Forced labor
—Meaningless quotas
—Widespread sabotage
—Suppression of labor disatisfaction

which are normal affairs of life in the free world, such as manufacturing, buying and selling.

Simis describes the widespread corruption which has come about as a result:

> The corruption that has rotted the ruling apparat of the country has had the terrible effect of eating away the morals not only of the people who give or receive bribes, but also of the innocent, those who have not been party to corruption but who have merely been living in an atmosphere of corruption and have been forced to breathe its tainted air.[50]

> And now, finishing this book, I ask myself: What next? What is the future of the country? And I answer my own question with bitterness: The Soviet government, Soviet society, cannot rid itself of corruption as long as it remains Soviet. It is as simple as that.[51]

The Soviet woman has an average of eight abortions during her life, and many have as many as fifteen.[52]

Perhaps the most significant factor inhibiting the development of the original human nature among the populations of the communist world is the systematic indoctrination in what is known as "scientific atheism". This doctrine, based on the dialectical materialism of Marx and Engels and taught daily from elementary school on up, seeks to convince the populace that there is no God or eternal life, and that humans have no moral laws higher than those laid down by the communist party. Domestic publication or entry into the country of any literature or materials that have a theme proclaiming faith in God or a higher spirituality are meticulously searched out and destroyed.[53]

The individual searching for his true human nature could encounter no greater governmental interference and repression than in the Soviet communist system.

3. Alienation of the human species

Does man find his true human nature in the Soviet system?

—Widespread corruption

d) *Finally, has Marxism solved the alienation of man from man?* Are the worker-citizens of the USSR able to establish fulfilling human relationships?

Sadly, they are not. It is known that fulfilling human relationships require an environment of trust and honesty. Yet, communist regimes encourage their citizens to monitor each other for total ideological loyalty, and inform on those who are suspected of holding ideas different from those of the Party. This can only foster the greatest degree of distrust among the people.

By preserving the caste-like distinction of the ruling elite and their multitude of special priviledges, the communist system actually foments hatred towards those in position of authority.

Furthermore, Marxism cannot resolve the problem of racism. Former Black Panther Eldridge Cleaver tells of the racist attitudes in Cuba, as does Anthony Bryant, author of *Hijack*. Says Bryant, "The racism in Cuba is more intense than the racism in the United States. I was told that I was not black; I was mulatto. I then came to realize that there is a rigid system of racial castes. Racism has become a part of the communist structure."[54]

The intense animosity between the Soviet Union and Communist China is a further affirmation of the fact that communism has not been able to resolve the problem of racial discrimination.

Communism claims to build a unified society of brotherhood by removing the barriers of nationalism. However, the Soviet Union provides a clear example of national supremacy in the policy of Russification of the 100 or more non-Russian nationalities.

The mass exodus of refugees from any nation unlucky enough to fall under Communist control seems to testify that nowhere is man less able to express his original nature than under the stifling burden of Communism. It is said that when the Berlin wall was constructed on the night of August 12, 1961, behind every worker was a soldier with a gun, and behind every soldier with a gun was another soldier with another gun.

The wall today is far more than the barbed wire barrier strung in 1961. Today's "wall" consists of 850 miles of fortifications surrounding the city of West Berlin. A giant wall is backed by minefields, anti-tank traps, sand pits and automatic rifle traps, and is guarded by dogs and machine gunners in elevated outposts.[55]

The Western side of the wall is spotted with white crosses which mark where freedom-seeking persons were killed trying to cross. The wall was called an "anti-facist protective rampart" by the East Germans when it was built, but no facist has ever been shot trying to enter East Germany. No one can visit the wall of Berlin without being profoundly saddened to think of the giant prison which is the communist world.

The case of the Vietnamese boat people is most poignant. The Vietnamese people have suffered centuries of domination and exploitation, yet they refused to abandon their native soil—until the arrival of communism. Now they are willing to risk death and tragedy at sea, with no guarantee of acceptance by the free world, to escape from their communist oppressors.

4. Alienation of man from man

> Are the citizen-workers of the Soviet Union able to establish fulfilling and joyful human relationships?

—Constant surveillance
—Elitism
—Racism
—Nationalism
—Mass exodus

Marxism does not solve alienation

When we look at the Soviet Union and other Communist countries, we are led to conclude that Marxism does not solve the problems of alienation. It worsens them. Ironically, the very conditions condemned by Marx and Engels in the *Communist Manifesto* have reached their greatest expression in the Soviet Union.

V. Why communism does not solve alienation: the errors of Marxism

Communism as it is practiced today does not solve alienation. It leads instead to anti-democratic totalitarian dictatorships. It promotes atheism and stifles the spirituality of its citizens. It creates economic systems which are not self-sufficient and depend upon a stolen technology as well as that bought with credits from the Western world. It dehumanizes further the frustrated workers and peasants of the world who have turned to it for help, or who have had it foisted upon them by militant political factions which have gained power in their countries.

Why is communism such a social failure and such a real and continuing threat to freedom in the world?

There are those who hold that communism today is a "betrayal" or "distortion" of Marxism. It seems that they wish to absolve Marx of responsibility for the actions of those who claim to follow him. Often, they would also have us try again to carry out the Marxist program hoping for a different result.

We will take the position that it is meaningless to speak of whether the communism of today is a "betrayal" of Marx. Our purpose is not to establish the "guilt" of Karl Marx. Rather than affix guilt, the point for us will be to see what are the elements in Marxism which have allowed the communism of today to come about. It is the thought of Marx which has served as the base for today's Marxism-Leninism. In this section we will discuss the flaws of Marxism which gave rise to the communism of today.

Why communism does not solve alienation

1. Not scientific

2. Not true

Four fundamental errors

A. The unscientific formulation of Marxism

It is often thought that Marx arrived at his conclusions after a scientific inquiry into the functioning of the capitalist system, but we can clearly see that this is not the case.

Rather than an inquiring scientific mind, a Marxist must have a great deal of blind faith. That is, there are a number of key assertions in Marxism which cannot be arrived at by science and reason alone. How did Marx arrive at the conclusion that mankind could be liberated by abolishing private property? How did he know that the proletariat would carry out this liberation? How could he prove, by science or history, that the human species-essence would emerge after private property had been abolished? Needless to say, he merely "believed" these things, and his followers are called upon to believe them as well.

This is contrary to the scientific method. In general, a scientist may formulate a hypothesis and seek to verify it through experiment and observation. However, he must be prepared to yield his hypothesis to whatever lessons those experiments and observations may teach him. Marx was unwilling to do this. In preparing revisions of *Capital*, for example, as Bertram Wolfe has pointed out, he disingeniously ignored updated statistics which disproved his predictions of the impoverishment of the worker.[56]

Marx did not relocate in Paris and later in London to carry out a scientific investigation. He went to study economics in order to learn how that area of study could be used to support revolution, the Marxist solution for human alienation.

In the introduction to his *A Contribution to the Critique of Political Economy*, Marx reminisced that soon after he arrived in Paris in 1844, he had already come to the conclusion that the materialistic relations of production are the foundation of legal and political forms. This is the basic premise of the materialist view of history, historical materialism. Declared Marx:

The general conclusion at which I arrived and which, once reached, continued to serve as the guiding thread in my studies, may be briefly summed up as follows: In the social production which men carry on, they enter into definite relations that are indispensible and independent of their will; these relations of production correspond to a definite stage of development of their material powers of production. The sum total of these relations of production constitutes the economic structure of society—the real foundation, on which rise legal and political superstructures and to which correspond definite forms of social consciousness. [57]

Marx wrote *A Contribution to the Critique of Hegel's Philosophy of Law, Introduction* when he was being introduced to economics and revolutionary socialism by Moses Hess. Nevertheless, he set as his goal the overthrow of the capitalist system by the proletariat. Subjective and emotional factors appear to have been of major influence in his conclusions.

Marx resigned from the *Rheinische Zeitung* under duress: strict censorship and pressure from the Prussian government. He harbored hostility towards that government, and expressed it in his writings. In *A Contribution to the Critique of Hegel's Philosophy of Law, Introduction*, he writes:

War on the German conditions! By all means! They are below the level of history, beneath any criticism, but they are still an object of criticism, like the criminal who is below the level of humanity but still an object for the executioner... (The object of the criticism) is not to refute but to exterminate ... Its essential sentiment is indignation, its essential activity is denunciation. [58]

In this situation, Karl Marx assembled a program to strike back at what he perceived to be his enemies and the enemies of human progress. He did so from the philosophical elements available to him at that time. Marx borrowed Hegel's dialectic of "thesis-antithesis-synthesis" and applied it materialistically to civil society. In this way he concluded that private property (the thesis) must be "negated." In *The Holy Family* (Feb. 1845), Marx sets private property and the proletariat against one another as thesis and antithesis:

> Private property as private property, as wealth, is compelled to maintain itself, and thereby its opposite, the proletariat, in existence... The proletariat, on the contrary, is compelled as proletariat to abolish itself and thereby its opposite, private property, which determines its existence and makes it proletariat.[59]

When Marx used the ideas of other thinkers, he revised them as necessary to fit his needs. In invoking the dialectic, for example, he completely altered the Hegelian meaning of the terms "opposites," "contradiction" and "negation." Marx also took elements of Feuerbach's materialism, but criticized Feuerbach for appealing to the human conscience.

Of course, not all truth has come to humanity through science. However, Marx and Engels emphatically ridicule non-scientific methods of knowledge, such as religious revelation. Then they proceed not merely to go outside of the scientific method in making their theories, but also to take great pains to conceal what they were doing. They speak incessantly about "scientific socialism," but were anything but scientific. In the same way, communists since Marx and Engels have masqueraded as scientists even while they cling to an outdated scientism.

B. The unscientific application of Marxism

The scientific method requires that one first develop a hypothesis and then subject that hypothesis to experiment. Although it may be said that experiments cannot conclusively "prove" that a hypothesis is true, it is usually possible after conducting experiments to determine whether it is beneficial to keep working with the hypothesis or not.

If Marxism were to be applied scientifically, it would be seen that the Marxist theories of (a) materialism, (b) alienation, (c) dialectics and (d) communism are so many hypotheses. Seventy years of application constitute the communist experiment, and the scientific verdict is clearly that Marxism is not valid.

C. The nature of ideology

Marxism is an ideology. By that we mean that it is a perspective of the universe and history based upon certain beliefs or basic tenets of faith. Upon these is constructed a philosophy.

At this point we wish to discuss what are those basic tenets of Marxist faith. We will then oppose them with basic beliefs of a God-affirming view, which we call Godism. In the sections which follow, we will elaborate the philosophical implications of Godism, and we will see the contrast between Marxism and Godism in practice.

D. The four fundamental errors of Marxism

The ultimate problem with Marxism is not that it is not scientific, but rather that it is not true. We can summarize the faulty premises of Marxist doctrine as four fundamental errors.

First error

Marx: No God

CAUSA Worldview:

God

Absolute values
Morality
Ethics

1. First Error: According to Marx, there is no God

Marxist materialism asserts that the universe is matter in motion and this matter has always existed. Marx denies the possibility that God created the universe.

The universe is seen to be an uncaused phenomenon. There is no ultimate first cause, but simply a succession of "contingent" causes and effects. There is no source of absolute values, morality, right and wrong, or good and evil.

Critique:

Marxism claims that it observes the "real" world without making false premises. Nevertheless, the denial of God is the first premise of dialectical materialism. Dialectical materialism denies God and then attributes to matter the qualities of God necessary to provide a semblance of explanation for the origin of the universe.

CAUSA Worldview: God exists

We observe in the universe a progression of beings of increasing complexity, differentiation and order. These pass from particles to atoms, molecules, plants, animals and human beings. How can this increasing order and complexity be explained?

To one who is only familiar with the laws of chemistry

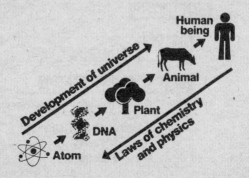

and physics, this progress would seem to be impossible without some miraculous intervention.

In order to explain this phenomenon, theories of evolution have been advanced. Like many other scientific theories, theories of evolution attempt to show that the observable phenomena of the world are not "miraculous" but "natural." These theories are interesting and stimulating, and are able to explain convincingly the mechanics of the development of life forms from an external point of view. They are limited by the very nature of scientific inquiry, however, and can never deal with a more fundamental question for which the human mind seeks an answer: Why did this process occur?

If there is an answer to this question, the answer can only come from God. Marxism in the guise of a science denies that there is any answer to this question. Marxism as a pseudo-religion, however, has its own eschatology and makes its own appeal to the religious nature of man, encouraging him to give his life to fulfill the great purpose of establishing an ideal world. The very drive of communists to build their ideal testifies to man's need for purpose.

It is only by openly examining the question of God's purpose of creation that we can come to achieve an understanding of absolute values, morality and ethics.

Supplement: There is logical, scientific and experiential evidence that God exists.

1. Logic: proofs of God

In his 800 page bestseller entitled *Does God Exist?*, German theologian Hans Küng writes:

> Proofs of God today have lost much of their force but little of their fascination. They continue to exercise a silent, secret fascination on thinking people. Does God exist? It must be possible to prove this. There must be a proof that is irrefutable, rational, obvious to everyone.[60]

Traditionally, the most common proofs for God's existence are the cosmological and teleological proofs. The cosmological argument says that the creation and maintenance of the universe requires a powerful and intelligent God. This was the proof for the existence of the divine used by Plato and Aristotle and further elaborated upon by Aquinas. William Paley stated it most simply, as follows: "If a watch requires a watchmaker, then our complex world necessitates a divine creator."

In a 1948 radio debate with Bertrand Russell, the Jesuit theologian F. C. Copleston used the cosmological argument to prove God's existence. According to Copleston, God exists, and His existence can be proved philosophically. We know that none of the material objects in the world are self-caused. Therefore, they must have an external reason for being. Since we cannot imagine an infinity of independent beings, there must be a prime mover and first cause, God.

Numerous scientists have accepted this cosmological proof: astronomers like Sir James Jeans, physicists like Sir Arthur Eddington, biologists like Alister Hardy and paleontologists like Teilhard de Chardin. According to them, our universe is so complicated, so intricate, that it had to be made by a superhuman intelligence, which we call God. Mere chance cannot explain our kind of world. As the philosopher Michael Polanyi put it, no monkey can produce a play like "Hamlet" by pounding on a typewriter at random. Neither can mere chance have caused our world.

The teleological proof of God is built on the notion that creation exhibits purposiveness. Man-made objects do not come into existence without a purpose of manufacture. In addition, things in nature have small-scale purposes, and these point to an all-inclusive cosmic design. (When we encounter part of our anatomy which seems to lack purpose—the appendix, for example—we are puzzled.)

Stanley Jaki, a priest and scientist, maintained that science itself has been successful because it has taken as its basic operating assumption the Christian belief that there is a rational plan to all of nature.

A recent approach to proofs of the existence of God views them as inductive, rather than deductive arguments, and assesses them according to the logic of Confirmation Theory. Richard Swinburne, in his book on this topic, explains that while the validity of inductive arguments cannot be judged in the same way as deductive arguments, nevertheless there are clear standards for judging inductive arguments to be correct or incorrect.

A correct inductive argument is one whose premises support its conclusion, i.e., make it more likely than not (or more likely than some other hypothesis). According to a theorem of Confirmation Theory, a hypothesis is valid when particular evidence is more probable under that hypothesis than it would be, given another hypothesis.

The postulation of an omnipotent, omniscient, all-benevolent God as the creator of the universe is an extremely simple hypothesis, which by the normal standards of judgement of scientific hypothesis gives it an advantage over competing hypotheses, such as that: 1) the universe is caused by a being lacking God's infinite properties; or 2) the universe has no cause or explanation. For example, with regard to the cosmological argument, Swinburne says there is quite a chance that if there is a God He will make something like our finite and complex universe. It is very unlikely that a universe would exist uncaused, but rather more likely that God would exist uncaused. The existence of the universe is strange and puzzling, but can be made comprehensible if we suppose that it is divinely created. This supposition postulates a simpler explanation than does the supposition of the existence of an uncaused universe, and that is a ground for believing the former hypothesis to be true.[61]

It should be understood that until now, proofs of God's existence have been countered by various counter-arguments. Still, when all the discussion is weighed, we must conclude with Küng:

The question 'Does God exist?' can now be answered by a clear and convinced Yes, justifiable at the bar of critical reason.[62]

2. Science: The threshold of proof

Arguments for the existence of God are greatly benefitted by the results of modern scientific research. Significant areas include particle physics, thermodynamics of systems, genetics, evolutionary theory, cosmology and molecular biology.

In evolutionary theory, for example, a revolution similar to that of 20th century physics may be in the making. At the turn of the century, physics was thought to be complete. The great British physicist Rutherford, when still a student, was advised to choose another field because there was little left to be done in physics. Today, evolutionary theory, based upon Darwinism, seems to have answered most questions. Still, certain problem areas remain, such as the mechanism of new species formation. Additional work in this area may cause a dramatic opening of the field.

With regard to Marxism, Engels' discussion of the origin of man is based on Lamarckism, a theory which has been discredited by modern scientific research. No case whatever is known of the inheritance of any modified character by the effect of the environment or the use or disuse of organs. As Gregor Mendel has shown, characters are controlled by

Theories of evolution

Lamarckism
Inheritance of acquired characteristics

Darwinism
Random mutation
Natural Selection

Still being evaluated

genes. Modifications in offspring are generally the result of modification in the genetic code.

Marxists since Engels have tried to disavow the dependence of the Marxist view of man on Lamarckism. Nevertheless, it is difficult to explain the central importance of labor in human evolution by means other than Lamarckism.

It might be said that Marx admired Darwin greatly for emphasizing the role of conflict in nature. However, the Marxist view of man cannot be easily reconciled with Darwin.

The presently accepted theory of evolution involves Mendelian genetics and the Darwinian principle of natural selection. This theory is still being evaluated by scientists. Nevertheless, the question of why genetic modifications themselves occur is beyond the scope of biology. The CAUSA view does not specify the mechanism of the development of the human form, but deals with the question why. Human beings are created as the children of a loving, parental Creator. It is reasonable to believe that the Creator acted with purpose through natural mechanisms. God may have used natural selection in the process of creation.

Many of the pioneers in the area of modern biology and evolutionary theory today question some of the basic assumptions which are popularly accepted by the scientific community, and often taught in schools as seeming facts. Albert Szent-Gyoergyi, twice winner of the Nobel prize, having devoted his life to reading "in the book of creation," writes:

> This brings me to the problem on which I plan to spend the next fifty years of my research. The problem is this: most biological reactions are chain reactions. To interact in a chain, these precisely built molecules must fit together most precisely, as the cog-wheels of a Swiss watch do. But if this is so, then how can such a system develop at all? For if any one of the very specific cogswheel in these chains is changed, then the whole system must simply become

inoperative. Saying that it can be improved by random mutation of one link sounds to me like saying that you could improve a Swiss watch by dropping it and thus bending one of its wheels or axles. To get a better watch, all the wheels must be changed simultaneously to make a good fit again.[63]

In the field of cosmology, additional scientific work seems to point in the direction of a willful and intelligent first cause.

As a materialist, Marx could only assert that the universe exists. He could not explain the origin of the universe and its purpose of existence. In spite of this, as Kolakowski points out, in his texts on the dialectic Engels rejected the possibility of uncaused phenomena, and:

asserted that matter by its very nature tends to evolve higher forms of Being in the manner observable on earth. He does not explain, however, in what way the higher forms are potentially contained in the elementary attributes of matter.[64]

Why does he not consider more carefully the lawful relationship which exists between cause and effect? Science indeed holds that nothing occurs by accident. Without understanding God, the Creator of the universe, we cannot fully understand reality.

3. Experience: the ultimate personal determinant

People are believers, probably more than anything else because of their personal experiences, which defy simple description and characterization. Experiences of love, hope and penetrating insight have kindled the faith of the great saints and enlightened ones, and have been shared by millions of people everywhere.

Experiences of disillusionment, frustration, hatred, tragedy, and injustice may intensify a person's faith, or they may destroy it. When the faith in God is gone, and particularly when it is replaced by the faith in no-God, then the construction of the Marxist worldview can begin.

2. Second Error: According to Marx, alienation is an economic problem

We have seen that Marx diagnosed the cause of human alienation as division of labor or its counterpart, private property. The solution, said Marx, is the forcible elimination of private property by communism.

Second error

Marx: Alienation is an economic problem

CAUSA Worldview:

Alienation begins with separation from God

Critique:

Communism, the forcible elimination of private property, does nothing to solve alienation. Marx's theory is false, as 70 years of communism in the Soviet Union have shown. Contrary to what Marx predicted, communism increases alienation.

CAUSA can agree with Karl Marx on one thing, however, that human beings are indeed alienated. The grave error of Marx was in failing to understand the true cause of human alienation.

CAUSA Worldview: Alienation begins with separation from God

Men and women are created by God and are endowed by God with their original nature. The Judeo-Christian tradition is correct, however, in its belief that man has fallen away from God. This is the beginning point of human alienation. Through the fall of man, man has become estranged from his own original nature. In this way, he has become estranged from God, from his fellow man, and from the world around him.

Human nature is spiritual and physical

In the CAUSA Worldview, the economic behavior of men is seen as only one dimension of human life. In fact, although important, it is secondary to the spiritual dimension, the inner man. Man's economic behavior is governed and controlled by the inner man or the spiritual dimension.

Scientists often treat mystical phenomena with contemptuous disregard. Nevertheless, the phenomena are there. Throughout history, we find things like divinations, inspirations, demonical possession, apparitions, trances, ecstasies, miraculous healings, and occult powers. These occurances cannot be explained by a materialistic ideology, but they must be reckoned with for a satisfactory world view to emerge.

In spite of the tremendous diversity of religious teachings about life after death, the common point is that man has an eternal spiritual aspect. From Plato and the early Greeks, through Jesus and Paul, through most African and Oriental cultures, to spiritualists of the twentieth century, a belief in some kind of survival of bodily death has been unequivocally affirmed.

Certainly testimony to the existence of a spirit world permeates the Bible. Prophets such as Ezekiel and Isaiah testify to powerful spiritual visions, as does the writer of the book of Revelations. In the Gospels, angels speak (Lk. 1:28) and on the Mount of Transfiguration, Jesus talks with the long-dead Moses and Elijah.

Today perhaps the most dramatic testimony to the existence of the spiritual dimension comes from those who have had what are commonly called "near death" experiences. These individuals, who were pronounced clinically dead but who were later revived, recall vivid and strikingly similar experiences while they were "dead." Books such as Dr. Raymond Moody's *Life after Life*, tell of these experiences.

The CAUSA Worldview holds that even during the physical lifetime, we are existing in the two realms of the material and the spiritual. In this view, "death" means the separation of the eternal spiritual self from the temporal physical self which has served as a vehicle for the development and maturation of the spirit.

Is such a view reasonable and believable? The prominent American pragmatist William James in his essay, "The Will to Believe," examines some of the factors which determine whether something is "believable," and concludes that many reasonable assertions are considered unbelievable just because they are extraordinary and new.[65]

A novel assertion which appears in the realm of science is often the target of ridicule until the scientific society can reconcile itself to the fact that this new view is superior to preceeding views. This occured when Copernicus introduced his view of the solar system, when Darwin wrote about evolution and when Einstein proposed the theory of relativity.

As additional evidence is gathered regarding the spiritual aspect of the human being, it is likely that we shall be faced more and more with the reasonableness of belief in the eternal life.

The discoveries of modern science lend credit to this prospect. Whereas in prior times scientists thought of the material world as constructed of solid though minute blocks of matter, they now believe this is not the case. What we think of as the material world seems to consist of invisible patterns of energy. As Professor Raynor C. Johnson of the University of Melbourne has pointed out:

> The world of hills and rocks, tables and chairs is for the ordinary unreflective man the one real world. There may have been some excuse for the materialis-

tic philosophy of the nineteenth century which supported this, but the discoveries of the modern physics ... have undermined that outlook. The solidity of the material world has proved illusory...[66]

It seems that a similar realization prompted Einstein to remark that his work involved the discovery of where matter ended and spirit began.

The physical lifetime is the opportunity for spiritual development

It appears that the development of one's spiritual character is dependent on several factors. Among them are the quality of love and guidance which he receives from his parents and parental figures, and the quality of his physical actions. If a person, for example, uses his physical lifetime to carry out small-minded and selfish actions, such as stealing and exploiting, he will need to rectify such matters in order to mature spiritually.

A difference between heaven and hell has been suggested by the 17th century Swedish scientist, Emmanuel Swedenborg, who in his later years had an extended series of experiences in and with the spirit world. Swedenborg describes the distinction:

The attitude that causes a drift toward heaven is a feeling that there is a higher power... (and in the striving) to relate to it. This same spirit of humility and respect for the greatness of creation goes with an effort to be with others and to be of some use. By this a person faces toward heaven... The opposite attitude is to put down creation and elevate the self. The one bound for hell serves himself first, last and foremost. By this he is cut off from the opening-out possibilities of heaven and becomes enclosed in concerns for himself over and above others.[67]

If indeed our spirit selves grow in conjunction with our physical bodies, then our experiences of love, beauty and joy on earth condition our ability to experience these qualities in the eternal world. The quality of eternal life would then be determined by the degree of love which we had experienced on earth. The most profound experiences of love must take place in the family, thus the family unit is the basic element in the fabric of a moral society.

Present reality is "fallen reality"

Although created with extraordinary capabilities, man became separated from God and suffered the loss of his own divine nature. This is the doctrine of the fall of man, accepted by most religions. For this to have occurred implies that God must have granted freedom and responsibility to human beings and determined not to intervene in a way that would destroy human responsibility or violate human freedom.

The belief in the fall of man also has profound and far-reaching implications. If God is a being of love and emotion, as Christian scripture teaches, then God must be deeply grieving following the loss of the intimate love relationship with His children. Furthermore, human beings will never be able to satisfy themselves until they are able to restore their fundamental relationship with their Creator and Parent, God.

How will this relationship be restored? To answer this question will take us into the realm of highly specific theologies. Certainly the Christian religion believes that salvation occurs

Concept of the Fall of man

Original	Fallen	Restored
God	God	God
Man	Man	Man

through Christ. The Jewish religion believes the same, although particulars are different. In fact, most of the world's religions speak of some messianic figure. For Christians, Christ is the Messiah who has come for all the world. All religious people of the world, then are potentially able to unite on the basis of our common understanding of the need for salvation in Christ.

The concept of the fall of man is vitally important for the God-centered world view. We must explain two paradoxical truths: God is good, and the world is a place of suffering. Clearly, only by some concept of the fall of man can these two be reconciled.

Belief in the fall of man also offers a tremendous hope. If God created with an original ideal, and the suffering and evil in the world today are the result of man's separation from the ideal, then there is the possibility of ending the suffering and evil if the original ideal of God can be restored. That is, there is the promise of salvation for man.

In the twentieth century, the idea of a human fall has encountered no little skepticism. Challenges to the scriptural view have come from those who state that if we are to be scientific, we have to give up the notion of original sin, the historicity of Adam and Eve, and the concept of the fall. Biology, they maintain, suggests that man has not fallen from

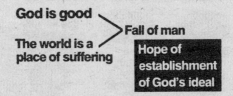

Why is the concept of the Fall important?

God is good

The world is a place of suffering

Fall of man

Hope of establishment of God's ideal

a state of supernatural bliss. Quite the opposite; originally we were animals without a conscience. Very slowly, man evolved to the primitive stage of society. Morality at this level meant obedience to external norms sanctioned by custom and enforced by the tribe. More recently, man has recognized the dignity of the individual, endowed with personal rights and responsibilities.

Another approach, taken by the well-known psychologist Rollo May, holds that the Eden story describes the coming of age of every individual, involving an inevitable loss of innocence and the painful dawning of self-awareness symbolized by eating from the Tree of the Knowledge of Good and Evil.

With regard to these views, we note that even evolutionism cannot exclude the possibility of divine creation and a distinct starting point of human life. Then, we are left with the key question of whether God created or not. If God created, and He is a God of goodness and love who would not will His children to suffer, then a real, historical fall of man *must* have occurred.

Whatever view of the fall we may accept, we must deal squarely with the fact that evil is real, and immorality is highly destructive. Abstract and symbolic interpretations of the fall fail to explain how men and women became estranged from God, and how evil came into the world.

3. Third Error: According to Marx, conflict brings progress

Marxism is based upon the dialectical model of thesis in contradiction and conflict with antithesis.

The belief that contradiction is the means toward progress is in fact a doctrinal part of Soviet policy today. For example, General Leksei A. Yepishev, chief of the Main Political Administration of the Armed Forces, writes describing the operation of the dialectic on a global level, "The dialectics of the present epoch is such that the historical confrontation between the two social systems, between the forces of progress and reaction, is taking place in the conditions of the growing superiority of the socialist community and the revolutionary forces over imperialism, over the forces of reaction and war."[68]

When the dialectic is made into a law of nature and society, then progress can only come through opposition and conflict. When Marx spoke of the struggle between contradictory elements, he made it clear that he meant overthrow or extermination. The law of the dialectic inevitably became a justification for barbarism, because killing ceases to be a crime. For this reason, the record of communism is a history of murder. Murder being the inexorable law of progress, it continues long after the revolution is finished.

Third error

Marx:

Progress through conflict

CAUSA Worldview:

Progress through cooperation

Critique:

Dialectical materialism will be comprehensively critiqued in Chapter 3. At this point, let us simply note that conflict does not bring progress. Conflict may be necessary, but progress itself can only be realized through cooperation.

CAUSA Worldview: Progress occurs through cooperation

In contrast to the Marxist dialectic, the CAUSA worldview affirms that the law of progress in nature and society is that of giving and receiving in relationships of mutual cooperation.

How is an atom formed? First there must be some purpose which brings the elemental parts together into relationship. Clearly, this would be the purpose of forming an atom. Centering on this purpose, the proton and electron interrelate in the positions of subject and object. Through their mutual interaction, the atom is formed and the purpose is fulfilled.

Every creation in the universe is formed from the union of paired subject and object elements which share a common purpose and are pursuing mutual benefit. The complementary relationship between the two provides the energy for existence, action, multiplication and progress.

The law of cooperation is in operation from the smallest levels of particles, such as the proton and electron, to the highest level of creation, human life. In human society, husband and wife form a reciprocal relationship where the giving and receiving of love fulfills their happiness and multiplies children. Ultimately, even the relationship between God and man conforms to this law. In this case, God is the subject, and all men and women are the objects forming reciprocal relation-

How is an atom formed?

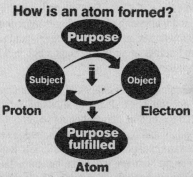

ships with Him. This fulfills the joy and satisfaction of God which is the purpose of creation, and also fulfills the joy, satisfaction, and eternal life of man.

Supplement: The growth process and its social implications

Human beings and the societies which they compose are not static, but appear instead to be always changing and developing. How do these changes occur? What is the dynamic of change and growth in the individual and in society?

According to the Marxist doctrine of historical materialism, productive forces are continuously being developed. At a certain point, the progress of productive forces is opposed by the production relations and revolution occurs. Through revolutionary leaps, changes occur in social organizations and in individuals.

It can be said that Marxism does not enlarge upon the concept of growth. It is not clear, for example, what are the dynamics of the progress of production forces. Neither is it explained how a person grows to maturity. Nor is it clear how a social stage grows to maturity, except that it is assumed that some internal dialectic is in operation.

This is a serious shortcoming. Marxist ideology offers no guidelines whatsoever for the maturation of societies to the point when they can achieve functional democracy. It merely calls for revolution. The religious tradition, on the other hand, is a wellspring of rich thought regarding the process of the growth and purpose of creation, and personality, character and spirit, in all the various ways in which these terms are understood.

The Hebraic scriptures speak of the command of God to man to be fruitful (Gen 1:28), a blessing which may be interpreted to mean that human beings are endowed by God with the freedom and responsibility to pursue their individual growth. Even the creation story itself is a clear indication that nothing enters into mature existence instantly, but all things must pass through periods of growth. The universe, in this case, is depicted as passing through a creation period of six "days."

For Christians, spiritual growth is closely linked with the two great commandments to love God and love one's fellow man. In loving God first, the vertical pillar of the spiritual life is established, and from this vertical foundation, the Christian reaches out to extend the love of God to others.

In this century, the religious view has further been enriched by the observations of social scientists and psychologists, particularly those who stand upon the religious foundation.

Victor Frankl, for example, in developing his method of Logotherapy, speaks of three fundamental assumptions underlying his work. (1) Freedom of Will, (2) Will to Meaning, and (3) Meaning of Life. Frankl believes that man is first of all free, and as a free being he is inclined by his nature to pursue meaning. Engaged in the pursuit, he finds that life is indeed filled with potential meaning. Frankl writes:

Life can be made meaningful (1) by what we *give* to the world in terms of our creation; (2) by what we *take* from the world in terms of our experience; and (3) by the stand we take toward the world, that is to say, by the attitude we choose toward suffering. (emphasis added)[69]

M. Scott Peck, in his work *The Road Less Travelled*, discusses his view of life as the process of growing spiritually. After years of successful counselling, Peck has come to believe that this growth comes through the grace of God coupled with the utmost continuous efforts of the individual.

It is widely accepted today that one's early experiences within his family are profoundly influential in determining his future psychological health and wholeness. The diverse relations of the family also provide the natural ground for ongoing growth in the dynamics of love. Specifically, we may identify three basic expressions of love that develop progressively in the family: passive, mutual and unconditional. When, for example, a person is a child, he experiences love passively as he receives love and care from his parents.

In relationships with brothers and sisters the individual is called to know love in a different way, through mutual exchange. The mutual exchange of love finds its most complete expression in the relationship between husband and wife. Finally, in becoming a parent, one is called upon to express unconditional love towards his children.

In a sense, the family is the only institution created by God. Clearly, the family is created to be the school of love, where each person may come to full maturity in his capacity for love. Since God's love is expressed primarily through human beings, the family appears to be the basis for the fullest knowledge of God, thus reaffirming the sacredness of marriage.

Further social implications

While Marxism intensifies grievances and urges the immediate violent expression of accusations, the understanding of the growth process tempers and influences our responses to social injustices.

For example, we are coming to realize that deviant human behavior is often symptomatic of immaturity of character, and cannot simply be corrected by force or reprogramming, but rather by creating environments and providing the spiritual enrichment which allow natural maturation to take place. It was discovered in the United States, for example, that racism could not be legislated away. In families and communities, however, where people have been able to feel to the depths of their own hearts that all men and women are children of God, racial prejudices may diminish and disappear.

On a socio-political level, we would like to see genuine and healthy democracy flourishing in all parts of the world. We find in certain areas, however, there is a tendency toward corruption, inefficiency and authoritarianism. Such situations are not only unfortunate in themselves, but they are also fertile grounds for totalitarianism to be established through communist revolution. Here again, legislation, aid, bullying, etc., on the part of the United States or any other nation are not the complete solution.

We need to recognize that a natural growth process has to occur, and the conditions have to be created for that growth to occur. Part of the communist strategy for the take-over of such areas seems to be to create situations where the process of spiritual growth is hindered or blocked.

4. Fourth Error: According to Marx, history is a series of class struggles, leading to communism

Marx greatly misunderstood human history. He saw it as a succession of class struggles. By applying the dialectic to history from its imagined beginnings, he developed historical materialism.

Marx maintained that at the beginning of history there existed a primitive communal society where everyone lived in harmony without private possessions. With the emergence of slaves and slave masters, this communal society became a slave society, and class struggle began. Transition from one stage of social organization to another can only be made through violence.

Fourth error

Marx: **Class struggle**
             Communism

CAUSA Worldview:

Struggle of good and evil
Good and moral world

The final struggle will occur between the proletariat and the bourgeoisie, and this will give rise to socialism. Socialism, said Marx, will tremendously increase human productivity, so that eventually distribution of goods will be based solely on need, and this will be communism.

Critique:

Contrary to this observation, peaceful transitions from one stage to another are possible. In the case of the Meiji empire of Japan, for example, the transition was made from feudalism to a modern industrial society through cooperation between the heads of state and the people. There was no violent revolution.

Furthermore, there were many wars in history that had nothing to do with class struggle. The struggle that is occurring in Ireland today has its roots in religious differences. Canada is experiencing division due to differences in languages and culture.

By viewing all struggles as class struggles, Marxist thinkers have consistently misunderstood the nature of conflicts. During the first World War, Lenin urged the workers of Russia, Germany, France and England not to fight. He believed that the most important basis for unity and solidarity was class. Lenin failed to understand that there are many things more powerful than class. Love of country is one of these. In spite of all of Lenin's pleas, the workers chose to go and fight for their nations.

Furthermore, we find that Marx only applied his dialectical law selectively. If the dialectic is the basis of all behavior, there should be no exceptions. If all of history is a manifestation of its functioning, then how can communist society be the ultimate stage? Why will the progression of societies stop at that point?

Finally, what is communism? If communism means Marxism-Leninism as it is applied today, then it is a dismal social failure. If communism refers to the world which comes at the end of history as Marx imagined it, then it is a myth.

CAUSA Worldview: Struggle of good and evil

The ultimate cause of struggle in this world stems from the internal struggle that exists in man. As great political and ethical philosophers from Plato until today have noted, this is a struggle between virtue and vice, selfishness and unselfishness. This struggle is manifested externally on the levels of society, nation, and world as a struggle between good and evil.

There is no doubt that there have been tremendous struggles throughout history. These struggles came about because selfishness and evil have become part of man's nature, and they will continue until the original good nature of human beings is completely restored.

Selfishness is not the natural desire of men and women to seek for their self-benefit. It is rather the perversion of that desire which results from a narrow view of what is beneficial. Life involves a succession of decisions and choices. Selfishness means making a bad choice. The selfish person loses greater benefit by seeking after smaller value. Selfishness is the lack of a proper perspective of value.

Selfishness manifests itself in such social ills as racism, corruption, abuse of the environment and exploitation. Of

Racism

Corruption

Selfishness

Abuse of the environment

Exploitation

course, these are the very things which Marxists cry out against, but Marxism does not have the power to stop these social ills, because it does not have the power to reach into the human heart and solve the problem of selfishness. Selfishness can only be solved by elevating the human perspective towards the absolute perspective of value centered on God.

This cannot be done through class struggle. Each person must conquer selfishness and evil in his own daily life. This is only possible if man can find God and find eternal value in relationship with Him. Men and women must establish appropriate relationships with God and with their fellow human beings.

It is CAUSA's view that humankind has hope because the original human nature is good. When one changes his priority of values, establishing the proper relationship with God, this will permanently solve the problem of alienation. From that point, there shall be no more war and conflict. Human beings and the universe will progress according to the original pattern of giving and receiving in mutual cooperation.

History is moving toward the establishment of a good and moral world

Religions which attempt to deal with history become involved in the concept of the providence of God. Providence may generally be considered as God's continuing relationship to our world. It is the means God uses to guide humans to fulfill their own potentialities, as well as realize God's plan for creation.

Finally, God remains sovereign. In spite of our real but limited freedoms, He is still the ultimate master of our destiny. Furthermore, God's purpose for creation must remain unchanging. If God created men and women and the entire universe with a good purpose, then certainly this good purpose must come to pass.

As Toynbee has written, the destiny of mankind must be sainthood, not only for a select few, but for everyone. In such a world, families, societies and nations would live in conformity with the divine will and realizing the purpose which God had in creating. This purpose would then remain as the ultimate goal of human history.

VI. Ideology in practice: Marxism and the CAUSA Worldview

Marxism served as the basis for the development of the communism of today. Today's communism is Marxism in practice. Let us examine once more the tenets of Marxism so as to see how this barbaric practice is encouraged and justified.

Marxism	
Belief	**Practice**
No God	Nihilism
Alienation	Resentment
Dialectic	Hatred
Communism	Totalitarian State

A. The practical application of Marxist philosophy

1. Marxism denies God.

What does that mean in practice? It does not necessarily mean anything, but it can mean a variety of things. It removes the basis for ethics and morality; it removes the basis for absolute value; and it opens the way for barbarism.

2. Marxism says that men are alienated by their economic environment, that the problem is private property, and that the solution is communism.

This idea is being advanced with great vigor throughout

the world. What effect does this have on people? What effect does this have on human emotion? People tend to be emotional rather than rational, and the view that they are being oppressed and alienated sharpens human resentment and prepares people to more effectively participate in revolution.

3. Marxism says that contradiction brings progress.

Marxism in practice means confrontation and conflict.

4. Marxism says that communism is the goal.

But when this goal is reached in practice, it is the totalitarian state. God is denied. Atheism becomes the state religion. Property is contraband. Everyone becomes a criminal. Everyone has crimes to hide and fears surveillance, which is everywhere. This is communism.

In conclusion, the essence of Marxism is an apologetic for murder. The French "new philosopher" André Glucksmann once said:

> I do not believe in God, but after reading about the Gulag, I have come to the conclusion that the Devil must exist.[70]

Indeed, Marxism resembles evil incarnate. It represents evil of a dimension which human history has never before seen.

B. The practical applications of the CAUSA Worldview

We shall close this chapter by introducing Godism, a God-affirming worldview formulated as a response to Marxism and the confusion in the West which has allowed Marxism to emerge and continue. Godism begins with the affirmation of God, and goes on to examine some of the implications of this. The motivation behind developing and formulating Godism, is that it can serve as a unifying factor among conscientious people and God-affirming people. It tends to avoid particular theological positions and emphasizes shared values. The basic notions of this worldview and their implications can be summarized as follows.

CAUSA Worldview

Belief	Practice
God	Love
Fall of man	Responsibility
Mutual interaction	Cooperation
God's ideal	Good and moral world

1. God exists.

The belief in God calls for a certain human response. That response is to meet situations and to meet one another with love. The notion, for example, that every human being is a child of God implies that everyone is brother and sister to everyone else, and this calls for loving interrelations between people.

2. Man has fallen away from God.

Human beings should enjoy an intimate and close relationship with their creator, and yet, something has taken place so that this relationship is not realized. There are many different interpretations of the fall, but we need not limit ourselves to a particular view to see how vital the concept is.

The solution to the human situation is salvation and restoration to God. Therefore, each human being is encouraged to take responsibility for this restoration process. No matter what situation one may find himself in, hate and resentment are not the way out. Destruction is not the solution. The way out is the path of responsibility and restoring the damaged relationship between God and man.

This view calls upon individuals to take responsibility to reestablish their relationship with the Creator and live in a proper way.

3. Human happiness and progress come about through the mutual interaction of giving and receiving.

Progress can only come through cooperation. Men and women must build common bases. Shared beliefs must be identified and built upon. The exchange of selfless love brings the highest good and benefit for one's eternal well-being.

4. History moves toward the fulfillment of God's ideal.

Therefore, we must assume our positions in a good and moral world. The importance of the physical life in the process of spiritual development means that we must practice morality and bring about justice in our lifetimes.

Conclusion: Two paths

All conscientious people are seeking for justice and well-being. We have spoken about the importance of *ideology* in choosing a path to that end. Ideology gives rise to *praxis*, and praxis in turn brings about a certain *process*. In the case of communism, the communist ideology gives rise to violent revolution with the goal of changing the structure of society.

Beneath ideology, however, is the crucial realm of faith. Communism demands faith that there is no God.

Communism does not bring about justice and well-being. The problem is at the very root—the denial of God. We must begin our quest for justice and well-being by affirming the existence of God. This will serve as the foundation for a God-affirming worldview—Godism—which gives rise to an internal revolution of heart. The goal of this revolution is to change the quality of human relations within existing social structures.

In reality, there is only one path to fulfill the purpose of creation given by God. This path is the path of Godism.

CHAPTER TWO NOTES

1. Harold Perkin, *The Origins of Modern English Society 1780-1880*, London, Routledge and Kegan Paul, 1969, p.164.
2. Perkin, p.163.
3. Wataru Hiromatsu, *On Young Marx*, Tokyo, Heibonsha Press, p.15.
4. James H. Billington, *Fire in the Minds of Men*, New York, Basic Books, 1980, p.232.
5. Karl Marx and Frederick Engels, *Collected Works*, Moscow, Progress Publishers, 1975, (Hereafter referred to as MECW) Vol.I, pp.637-8.
6. Ibid., p.613.
7. Ibid., p.563.
8. Ludwig Feuerbach, *The Essence of Christianity*, New York, Harper Torchbooks, 1957, p.14, as quoted by Sang Hun Lee in *The End of Communism*, unpublished manuscript.
9. Ludwig Feuerbach, *Works*, by Friedrich Jodl, Stuttgart, 1959-1960, Vol.VI, p.41, as quoted by Frederick Copleston, *A History of Philosophy*, Garden City, New York, Image Books, Vol.7, Part II, p.64.
10. Frederick Engels, "Ludwig Feuerbach and the End of Classical German Philosophy," *Selected Books*, Moscow, Progress Publishers, 1970, Vol.3, p.354.
11. Billington, p.267.
12. Billington, p.268.
13. As quoted in Peter Singer, *Marx*, Oxford, Oxford University Press, 1980, pp.14-15.
14. MECW, Vol.1, p.220.
15. Karl Marx, *A Contribution to the Critique of Political Economy*, Marx and Engels, Selected Works, 3 vols., Moscow, Progress Publishers, 1969, Vol.1, p.502.
16. Marx, *A Contribution to the Critique of Hegel's Philosophy of Law, Introduction*, as quoted in Melvin Rader, *Marx's Interpretation of History*, Oxford, Oxford University Press, p.50.
17. Marx, *On the Jewish Question*, MECW, Vol.3, p.159.
18. Ibid., p.151.
19. Marx, Letter to Ruge, November 30, 1842, MECW, Vol.1, p.395.
20. Marx, *On the Jewish Question*, MECW, Vol.3, p.168.
21. Ibid., p. 174.
22. Marx and Engels, *The Holy Family*, MECW, Vol.4, p.36.
23. Engels, "The Part Played by Labor in the Transition Ape to Man," in *The Origin of the Family, Private Property, and the State*, International Publishers, New York, 1972, p.251.
24. Marx, *Economic and Philosophic Manuscripts of 1844*, MECW, Vol.3, p.274.
25. Engels, "The Part Played by Labor . . . ," p.260.
26. Marx and Engels, *The German Ideology*, MECW, Vol.5, p.47.
27. Ibid., p.46.
28. Marx, *Economic and Philosophic Manuscripts of 1844*, MECW, Vol.3, p.300.
29. Marx and Engels, *The Holy Family*, quoted in David McLellan, *The Thought of Karl Marx*, New York, Harper Torchbooks, 1974, p.32.
30. Marx, "Theses on Feuerbach," MECW, Vol.5, p.4.
31. Marx and Engels, *The German Ideology*, quoted in David McLellan, p.35.
32. Marx, *The Poverty of Philosophy*, quoted in David McLellan, p.39.
33. Marx and Engels, *Manifesto of the Communist Party*, MECW, Vol.6, p.498.

34. Ibid.

35. Ibid., p.500.

36. Ibid., p.482. (Note by Engels to the English edition of 1888.)

37. Ibid., p.519.

38. Marx, *Contribution to a Critique of Hegel's Philosophy of Law, Introduction*, MECW, Vol.3, p.187.

39. Andre Gide, cited in *The God that Failed*, Richard Crossman, ed., New York, Harper and Brothers, 1949, p.173.

40. Ibid., p.183.

41. Lawrence Minard and James Michaels, "Why workers won't work in the Soviet Union," *Forbes*, December 6, 1982, p.141.

42. Marshall Goldman, *USSR in Crisis*, New York, Norton, 1983, pp.2, 47.

43. Gregory Grossman, "The Second Economy of the USSR," *Problems of Communism*, Sept-Oct 1977, p.25.

44. Hedrick Smith, *The Russians*, New York, Valentine Books, 1976, pp.81-82.

45. Michael Binyon, *Life in Russia*, New York, Pantheon Books, 1983, pp.16-17.

46. Ibid., p.24.

47. U.S. Dept. of Labor, *Turnover Statistics*, Feb. 1982.

48. Minard and Michaels, *Forbes*, p.138.

49. Kevin Klose, *Russia and the Russians*, New York, Norton, 1984, pp.80-81.

50. Konstantin Simis, *USSR: The Corrupt Society*, New York, Simon and Schuster, 1982, p.248.

51. Ibid., p.300.

52. Binyon, p.39.

53. For a survey of this subject, see James Thrower, *Marxist-Leninist "Scientific Atheism" and the Study of Religion and Atheism in the USSR*, Berlin and New York, Mouton, 1983, 500p.

54. From a videotaped interview distributed by Freedom Press, Oklahoma City.

55. East German authorities have announced that minefields and automatic rifle traps will no longer be maintained surrounding the city of West Berlin, but will still be used along the frontier between East and West Germanies.

56. Leszek Kolakowski, *Main Currents of Marxism*, 3 Vols., trans. by P.S. Falla, New York, Oxford University Press, 1978, Vol.1, p.290.

57. Marx, "A Contribution to the Critique of Political Economy," from *Marx and Engels, Basic Writings on Politics and Philosophy*, Lewis Feuer, ed., New York, Anchor Books, 1959, p.43.

58. Marx, *A Contribution to the Critique of Hegel's Philosophy of Law, Introduction*, MECW, Vol.3, p.177.

59. Marx and Engels, *The Holy Family*, MECW, Vol.4, p.36.

60. Hans Küng, *Does God Exist?*, New York, Vintage Books, 1981, p.529.

61. The above discussion draws heavily from Young Oon Kim, *An Introduction to Theology*, New York, The Holy Spirit Association for the Unification of World Christianity, 1983, pp.25-30. In her text, Dr. Kim cites Richard Swinburne, *The Existence of God*, Oxford, Clarendon Press, 1979.

62. Küng, p.702.

63. Albert Szent-Gyoergyi, "Drive in Living Matter to Perfect Itself," *Synthesis*, No.1, 1976, p.18.

64. Kolakowski, p.384.

65. William James, "The Will to Believe," in *Pragmatism and Other Essays*, New

York, Washington Square Press, 1963, pp. 193-213.

66. Raynor C. Johnson, *The Imprisoned Splendor*, New York, Harper and Row, 1953, pp. 297-298.

67. Summarized in W. Van Dusen, *The Presence of Other Worlds*, New York, Harper and Row, 1974, p. 76.

68. A. A. Yepishev, *Some Aspects of Party-Political Work in the Soviet Armed Forces*, Moscow, Progress Publishers, 1975, pp. 5-6, quoted in R. Judson Mitchell, *Ideology of a Superpower*, Stanford, Hoover Institution Press, 1982, p. 9.

69. Victor Frankl, *Psychotherapy and Existentialism*, New York, Simon and Schuster, p. 24.

70. Maurice Clavel, *Deux Siecles chez Lucifer*, Paris, Seuil, 1978, p. 18.

DIALECTICAL AND HISTORICAL MATERIALISM

> Marx is the personification of revolution. After his early conversion to communism, he never swerved from his devotion to the revolutionary cause... Because of his intransigent attitude and unrivaled influence, he is the pre-eminent symbol of the revolutionist. Only Lenin rivals him in this respect. [1]

Leszek Kolakowski begins his comprehensive study, *Main Currents of Marxism*, by stating that Karl Marx was a German philosopher. It would seem that this is a simple fact which cannot be argued, but actually it is very misleading. We will not be able to understand Marx if we try to think of him only as a philosopher. Marxism is not so much a method of increasing our understanding as it is a concerted attempt to bring about what Karl Marx felt had to occur: a revolution that would destroy the entire society in which he lived. From the point that this conclusion became fixed in the mind of Marx, we might say that he ceased to be a philosopher, German or otherwise, and he became instead an engineer of ideas, an architect of an ideology.

Marx summed up his view of philosophy as practice when he wrote, as one of his theses on Feuerbach, "The philosophers have only *interpreted* the world in various ways; the point however is to *change* it."

In this section, we will examine the fundamental concepts of Marxist philosophical materialism as well as the materialist view of history, historical materialism. Our treatment of this extensive subject will be brief, but we hope to show how a simple model of development was applied to society and history to produce a powerful pseudo-religion, which, for all its shortcomings and inconsistencies, is having a tremendous impact on our world.

The metaphysics of Marxism have come to be known as dialectical materialism. Dialectical materialism is the way Marxists view the world. Although Marx and Engels did not coin this term, they did lay down the essential principles which are held today. The term "dialectical materialism" was erroneously attributed to Marx and Engels by Lenin, but was probably first used to describe the Marxist world view by the Russian Menshevik Georgy Plekhanov in 1891. Engels did initiate the term "historical materialism" to refer to the Marxist view of society and history, also known as the materialist view of history.

I. Materialism and idealism

A. "Two great camps"

> The great basic question of all philosophy, especially of modern philosophy, is that concerning the relation of thinking and being... that question, in relation to the Church, was sharpened into this: "Did God create the world or has the world been in existence eternally?" The answers which the philosophers gave to this question split them into two great camps.

> Engels, *Ludwig Feuerbach* (1888)[2]

According to Engels, there are two great camps in philosophy. Every philosopher must fall into one or the other. One is idealism. The school of idealism, according to Engels, holds that the mind or idea is essence, and that matter is derived from that.

On the other hand, said Engels, the school of materialism holds that matter is the essential substance, and the phenomenon of mind comes from and is a reflection of matter. According to Engels, a thinker must belong to one camp or the other, and this division has characterized the history of philosophy.

Furthermore, in the Marxist view, idealists are those who defend the status quo, whereas the materialist philosophers are in the vanguard of revolutionary change. They constitute the camp of progress, which is trying to alter, change and improve the human situation. Marxists see themselves within this camp.

We will return to the doctrine of "two great camps" at the conclusion of this chapter.

B. Materialism as a trend in philosophy

Dialectical materialism is one particular species of materialism. There are two main contentions held by materialism:

a. The world consists of material particles (or more generally, physical entities) that interact.

b. Regarding immaterial or apparently immaterial entities, such as the human mind, either: (i) these do not exist; (ii) these are in fact material things, or the motions of material things; or, (iii) as Marxism contends, these cannot exist independently but are wholly dependent upon material processes. That is, they are by-products of matter and they cannot exist apart from matter. Matter is primary to "spirit." "Mind" is a by-product of the brain.

C. Materialism before Marx

Dialectical materialism developed from the criticism of other trends in materialism, particularly mechanistic materialism and Feuerbach's materialism.

1. Mechanistic materialism

Renaissance and post-Renaissance science conceived of the universe as an extremely elaborate machine. Once this machine was set in motion, all future circumstances were determined. The dynamics and mechanics of that age were reflected in its dominant philosophy, mechanistic materialism, which originated during the Renaissance of the 14th century and reached its height during the 17th and 18th centuries. In the deistic view pioneered by Newton and Descartes, once God set a certain process in motion, there could be nothing but change of pace, or increase and/or decrease, in regularly determined cycles.

Because it characterized each person as an essential part of the whole, mechanistic materialism was employed by thinkers of the French Revolution to argue in favor of the rights of the individual. For Marx's purposes, however, strictly mechanistic materialism would prove unsuitable. He criticized it for not being rigorously materialistic. Ultimately it leads back to idealism because it fails to provide an atheistic explanation for the origin of the universe. If the universe is like a complex "machine," its existence seems to suggest that there is a Creator, a First Cause, who created the universe and set it in motion.

Furthermore, this materialism fails to explain the appearance and development of new beings and new qualities in the universe. It offers only a static view.[3]

(In general, Marxist materialists today follow the pattern of Lenin and do not deal with a scientific description of matter. They hold instead the philosophical definition, that matter is objective reality, and has motion as its attribute. This, they feel, exempts them from dealing with the scientific reality of matter, although it may be argued that it really only evades the question.)

2. Feuerbach and the origin of God

Religious practices have been part of human life since well before recorded history. Nevertheless, the Renaissance brought with it a great wave of rebellion against Church authority. This worked to discredit belief in God as well.

Strong expressions of anti-religious rebellion are found throughout Marx's work. In particular, he seems to have been greatly influenced by the work of the German philosopher, Ludwig Feuerbach.

Feuerbach speculated as to how religion or belief in God had come about. He asserted that God is a projection of what human beings themselves would like to be. We would like to be all-powerful; we would like to be totally good; we would like to be omniscient. We have projected these desires into an imaginary being which he called "God." For Feuerbach, the divine being is nothing more than a projection of the human being into a concept. Ironically, this concept has come to oppress its own creator, man. Feuerbach believed that human liberation would result from destroying the concept of God and destroying religion, thus recovering the human nature.

Although at first inspired by Feuerbach's humanism, Marx later found fault with it. He said that Feuerbach lapsed back into idealism in calling for a human-centered religious solution. Feuerbach felt that the solution to man's problems would come through exalting human love and human virtues. This was not satisfactory for Marx, because it did not promote a solution on a strictly material level. He criticized Feuerbach, calling him "a materialist below, but an idealist above."

Marx thus had to continue in his efforts to create an absolute materialism, a materialism that made no recourse to idealism or to God. As we noted in Chapter 2, Marx found the philosophical device to make his materialism absolute in the idealistic philosophy of Georg Hegel. This device is the dialectic.

It is the dialectic which distinguishes Marxist materialism from all others and gives ideological power to the call for revolution, class struggle and the inevitability of communism. For the most part, this chapter will be devoted to a discussion of the dialectic.

II. The dialectic

A. The dialectic of Hegel

Although the roots of the dialectic lie in antiquity, it was Johann Fichte (1762-1814) who set forth the general scheme of what has come to be known as the Hegelian dialectic. Fichte identified three basic propositions of philosophy in the positions of thesis, antithesis and synthesis which resolved themselves dialectically. Apparent contradictions, he held, are resolved by making mutual compatibility become evident. "All contradictions are reconciled by determining more clearly the contradictory propositions."[4]

Hegel carried the dialectical method even further. He envisioned the dialectic as the general law penetrating the entire world. He formulated it as the law of development of

Hegel's dialectic

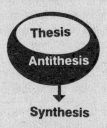

Thesis

Antithesis

Synthesis

thinking and applied it also to the development of nature and society, envisioning the synthesis of all opposites as the culmination of history. This mechanism was of tremendous interest to Marx. When removed from its idealistic framework, the dialectic seemed to represent a process through which the *simple* could proceed to the *complex* without any higher cause. That is, it seemed to be a self-energizing principle.

Hegel was concerned with the development of the Mind. He used the German word "Geist" which is sometimes translated as Mind or Spirit but can probably best be understood as God. He was concerned with how and why God created, and he put great emphasis on human intellectual development.

Marx severely criticized Hegel's philosophy in general, but one part that he utilized was the dialectic itself. He took the Hegelian dialectic and transferred it to his materialistic framework. In this way, he believed that he had constructed a rigorous materialism that needed no reference or recourse to God.

The Hegelian dialectic describes every entity as a thesis which contains within itself its own opposite or contradiction, the antithesis. Through the contradictory relationship between thesis and antithesis, new development occurs. The synthesis is formed, and a step forward is taken in development and in history.

Marx made certain crucial modifications in the Hegelian dialectic and then used it in his analysis of capitalistic society. He later expanded that analysis to examine all of history.

B. The Marxist dialectic

Marx himself did not elaborate his metaphysics. It was Engels who articulated exactly what the Marxist dialectic is and exactly what are its rules. In his texts, *Anti-Dühring* and *Dialectics of Nature*, we find three laws of the Marxist dialectic.

1. Three laws

a. The first law concerns relationship. This is the law of

The Marxist dialectic
(According to Engels)

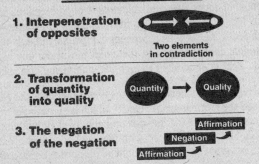

1. Interpenetration of opposites

Two elements in contradiction

2. Transformation of quantity into quality

Quantity → Quality

3. The negation of the negation

Affirmation

Negation

Affirmation

interpenetration of opposites. This law is listed second in Engels' text, but we treat it first because it is most fundamental. Marxists usually describe the interpenetration of opposites as the most important of the three main laws. According to Lenin it is the "kernel" of dialectics.

According to this law, every entity is composed of two sub-entities which are fundamentally contradictory to one another. In the Marxist dialectic, cooperation is something transitory; contradiction is fundamental. Every entity in the universe is formed through a temporary union of fundamentally opposite and contradictory elements. "It is contradiction, the conflict of opposites that is the main source of development of matter and consciousness."[5]

b. The second law concerns the process of development. This is the law of transformation of quantity into quality and vice versa. The law states that every kind of change in the universe—every process of development—is first of all a change in quantity. At some point that change in quantity transforms itself into a change in quality. In other words, there is first a change in amount or degree (quantity), and then a transformation, usually abrupt, which produces a change in shape or form (quality).

A Soviet handbook on Marxist philosophy describes it as follows:

> As soon as these limits are overstepped... the seemingly inessential quantitative changes inevitably bring about a radical qualitative transformation: quantity passes into quality.[6]

> Quantitative changes are relatively slow and continuous, while qualitative transformations are discontinuous.[7]

c. The third law is the negation of the negation. According to this law, every entity exists first of all as an affirmation, then is negated (produces its own negation), and the negation is negated again. This yields the affirmation, multiplied manyfold, on a higher plane of development.[8]

> The term "negation" was introduced in philosophy by Hegel, but he invested it with an idealist meaning.... Marx and Engels preserved the term "negation" but interpreted it in a materialist way.[9]

2. How the laws are used

As far as Marxists are concerned, these laws are not just for the purpose of theoretical discussion. Each law is making a point, and is used to justify a certain practice.

The interpenetration of opposites is used as a justification and explanation for continuous class struggle. It holds that society is composed of contradictory classes, and that only through their struggle can progress come about.

The law of transformation of quantity into quality is used to reinforce the notion that revolution is essential. There can be no gradual change. There can be no gradual socialization through democratic means. There must be revolution and the destruction of society.

The negation of negation becomes the backbone of the

Marxist view of history. This view holds that just as primitive man lived communally, the negation of the negation will cause man to return to communism at the close of a long process of historical development.

3. An example of the three laws in operation: the egg

To illustrate these laws, we can apply them to something in nature. The chicken egg is used in the Soviet school system to teach dialectical materialism, and appears also in communist literature distributed in the United States.

The chicken egg may be said to consist of two components: the shell and the embryo. The shell would be the thesis (in Hegel's terminology) or the affirmation (in Marx's terminology), and the embryo contained within the shell would be the antithesis or negation. According to Marxist dialectic, these two elements exist in contradiction. They experience a temporary union, but they are fundamentally contradictory to one another and cannot coexist indefinitely.

The dialectic applied to an example of development:

The egg

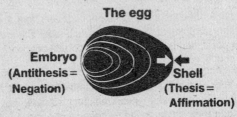

Embryo (Antithesis = Negation)   **Shell (Thesis = Affirmation)**

Development begins as a change in quantity: the size of the embryo increases. The embryo grows until a point is reached where the contradiction between it and the shell becomes acute. At this point the embryo violently breaks the shell apart and destroys it. Something qualitatively different then emerges, a chick. The change in quantity has been transformed into a change in quality.

Furthermore, if we look at the life cycle of the chicken, it would seem to provide an example of how the negation of the negation operates. In this case, the chicken itself is the affirmation. At some point in its life cycle it is negated to produce the egg, and the egg is once again negated to produce again the affirmation, presumably on a higher level of evolutionary development. In other words, the process keeps repeating, and as it does, progress occurs. In this case, the species is continuously evolving and advancing.

The egg is destroyed

Chick

C. The application of the laws of the dialectic to society

Though our treatment of the chicken egg may appear elementary, Marx applied this type of analysis to society. This is most extensively described in *The German Ideology*, written by Marx and Engels.

1. The general Marxist view of social change

According to Marx, society is like the egg. The larger whole is the society itself, but within that society, in the position of the embryo, is an *oppressed* class which eventually becomes the majority class. In the case of the capitalist society, the oppressed class is the working class, or the proletariat.

How does development occur? How is the situation brought to the point of revolution? Marx spoke about the development of productive forces. Briefly, productive forces are the tools, techniques and raw materials used in production, as well as the workers' labor power itself. Marx said that the tools and skills of the laborers are constantly developing. The development of productive forces is like the motor power behind historical social development. The development of these productive forces is analogous to the growth of the embryo within the egg.

The point is reached, however, where production relations become a "fetter" or barrier to the continued development of the productive forces. The capitalist society itself becomes a barrier to the continued development of productive forces. Revolution must then take place.

In the words of one Marxist writer:

> The shell of the egg is destroyed and replaced by its opposite, the chicken; the shell of the capitalist society is ruptured by the proletarian revolution and a new society begins to be created.

> An egg, while containing a developing chicken, remains an egg—a hard, white shell surrounding an embryo. Capitalist society, while containing elements of future socialist society ... which continually struggle within and against the dominant capitalist framework, is still nevertheless capitalist society.[10]

Marx argued that the conditions of the proletariat would become increasingly intolerable, and this class would be driven to revolution. We have noted in chapter two that Marx was willing to ignore the improvement in the workers' situation within his own lifetime.

> It is clear, however, that Marx was determined to find in capitalism a relentless tendency to degrade the worker, and that he resisted facts which indicated that the worker was getting better off. Bertram Wolfe has pointed out that in the first edition of *Capital* various

statistics are brought down to 1865 or 1866, but those for the movement of wages stop at 1850; in the second edition (1873) the statistics are brought up to date, again with the exception of those on wages, which had failed to bear out the impoverishment theory.[11]

In defiance of the facts, Marx claimed that the misery of the working class would increase to intolerable levels. In obedience to dialectical laws, a quantitative change would be occurring. The quantitative increase of the working class occurs in the sense that as the number of workers increases, the percentage of people in society who are workers increases, and the misery and poverty of the workers increase. The contradiction between the working class and the capitalist society becomes acute, and affirmation and negation no longer can coexist.

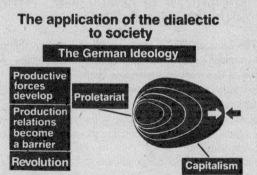

The application of the dialectic to society

The German Ideology

Productive forces develop — Proletariat

Production relations become a barrier

Revolution

Capitalism

D. Socialist revolution

From that situation of acute contradiction, socialism is born. In order for socialism to emerge and be consolidated, capitalism must be destroyed. According to dialectical analysis, if progress is to occur, there must be violence. The nature of the human being, the worker, is contradictory to the capitalist system. Since the capitalist system cannot be changed, it must be destroyed.

The application of the dialectic to society

The German Ideology

Productive forces develop

Production relations become a barrier

Revolution

Capitalism is destroyed

Socialism

In Marx's model, socialist revolution destroys the capitalist society and socialism is born.

III. The process of development: critique of the Marxist dialectic

The Marxist view stresses conflicts between the interests of various groups. We have discussed the results of the practice of this view in a previous chapter. In contrast, the CAUSA view stresses the possibilities of mutual benefit in the relations between the various groups within society, including social or economic classes. We will review the three laws of the Marxist dialectic and criticize them in the light of the CAUSA Worldview.

A. Law 1: Relationship

Marxism

The first law has to do with the nature of relationships. According to the Marxist view, thesis and antithesis oppose one another and generate the synthesis.

1. There is no mention of purpose to bring elements into a relationship.

2. This relationship may be characterized as a subject-subject relationship. Subject refers to the part which initiates and object to the part which responds. In the Marxist view, there is no initiation-response, there is struggle. Two subject elements are each trying to dominate the other. This may be called a zero-sum struggle. There is no mutual benefit possible. One has to destroy the other in order to progress.

3. Contradiction is the essence of this relationship. According to this concept, progress is brought about when one party of the relationship destroys the other party. Biologically, for an individual to be successful, it must dominate and hopefully destroy other individuals. For one species to succeed, it must destroy competing species. In human life, if there is a dispute between a labor union and the management, for example, the management must be destroyed. If there is a dispute between the people and government of some particular nation, one party has to destroy the other. This is the practical application of the dialectic. The only way for progress to occur is when one party forces its will or its program on the other and destroys that party.

Godism

Marxism presents an explanation of conflict, but does not examine the process of development itself. The CAUSA

Law 1	Relationship
Marxism	**CAUSA Worldview**

Marxism	CAUSA Worldview
Thesis ↔ Antithesis ↓ Synthesis	God Subject ⇄ Object Union
1. No Purpose	1. Purpose
2. Subject → ← Subject	2. Subject ⇄ Object
3. Contradiction Destruction	3. Correlation Construction

Worldview is an alternative view of progress. Because it is a God-centered worldview, it may be called Godism in contrast to Marxism.

1. We begin by asserting that beings do not come into relationship at all unless there is a common purpose to bring them together.

2. The primary interaction necessary to bring about development and progress is not the subject/subject interaction. Rather, it is subject/object interaction: mutual exchange between subject and object elements centered on a common purpose. This can also be called the action of giving and receiving. A common purpose (perceived mutual benefit) brings the two elements into relationship, giving and receiving brings them into unity, and when they unite, the purpose is fulfilled (mutual benefit is realized). The purpose may be simply the enrichment of the relationship or it may be a new creation.

This general law holds on all levels. Proton and electron come together to form atoms; pistil and stamen come together to form a seed. We see that this law is even in operation in a CAUSA conference. Unless we have some common purpose, we cannot hold a conference. As much as we share common concerns for freedom and democracy, that is how productive our conference can be.

Even the egg which we referred to earlier is an example of this relationship. In the case of the egg, the purpose is the development of the chick. All of the elements will function together to serve this purpose. The embryo is in the subject position, and the shell is in the object position to the embryo. The shell is actually serving the embryo. It protects the embryo until development is completed and the chick is ready to emerge. At that point it offers almost no resistance, and it is very easy for the chick to peck its way out of the shell.

Repulsion

When there is no common purpose, repulsion occurs.

Repulsion is associated with subject/subject interactions. When two subjects approach each other, two protons for example, they tend to experience a force of repulsion. This is a secondary phenomenon which occurs to support the primary phenomenon of interaction. By repelling each other, the protons are able to attract electrons and form atoms.

Repulsion

Secondary phenomenon

On a physical level, if all matter attracted itself, we might imagine that the universe would condense to a "point" and space would not exist as we know it. On the level of plants and animals, we can easily see that repulsion behavior is necessary to ensure optimum distribution of individuals for survival and reproduction. Male deer will fight and relocate themselves in order that each is able to secure a mate and territory for feeding.

On a human level, it is quite apparent that individuals are not attracted by mutual relationships if they do not feel that some mutual benefit will come about.

3. The essence of relationship in this model is correlation, a basis for construction.

Summary

The Marxist model can be called a three-position model. The important first position of purpose is excluded. It is natural that Marx wanted to exclude the position of purpose, because the question of purpose must ultimately lead to the question of God, and God's overall purpose of creation. In order to formulate an atheistic model, Marx had to exclude considerations of purpose.

The model of Godism can be called a four-position model, with the topmost position being that of purpose and ultimately of God.

Predator and prey: Hierarchy of purpose in the universe

One may think at this point, "That is very nice, but I am familiar with another kind of world out there. There is the question of predator and prey." The world of nature seems to be the world where one little fish gets eaten by a bigger fish, and that bigger fish gets eaten by a bigger fish. How can we explain the phenomenon of predator and prey?

This is certainly not a trivial question. Darwin himself declared that it was the existence of suffering in the animal realm which caused him to deny the existence of God. A God-affirming view must deal with this particular question.

In general, the CAUSA Worldview speaks of a hierarchy of purpose in the universe. The highest creation of God is the human being. In the Judeo-Christian tradition, human beings are identified as the *children* of God. The most essential purpose of creation is for the creator to express His character into human beings, His children, with whom He is

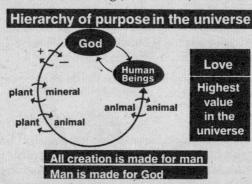

Hierarchy of purpose in the universe

God

Human Beings

+ −

plant | mineral

plant | animal

animal | animal

Love

Highest value in the universe

All creation is made for man
Man is made for God

able to enjoy a relationship of love. The entire universe, then, exists in order to support this fundamental and central relationship.

A variety of interactions occur in the physical world in order to support human life. We know that plants consume minerals. Animals consume plants. Animals consume other animals. These are all necessary in order to sustain a physical realm for the purpose of maintaining human life. All of creation exists for human beings, and human beings exist for God.

The highest value in the universe is love. People exist in order to have a loving relationship with God and with one another. They can also share their love with the created world. Satisfaction and joy are experienced on all levels of creation when human beings fulfill their purpose and enter into loving relationship with God.

B. Law 2: Change

The second law of dialectical materialism treats the process of change. This law holds that change is first of all change in quantity, which later becomes change in quality. This usually takes place through an abrupt transformation.

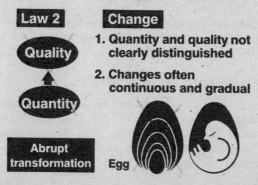

Law 2 Change

Quality

Quantity

Abrupt transformation

1. Quantity and quality not clearly distinguished
2. Changes often continuous and gradual

Egg

The error in this law is twofold. First, quantity and quality themselves cannot be clearly distinguished.

Secondly, changes are often continuous and gradual, not necessarily abrupt.

In the example of the chicken, if quantity changed first, then we would expect the embryo to merely get bigger and bigger until it finally breaks the shell. As the shell is being broken, the embryo would transform into a chick. In fact, what is happening inside the egg is a *simultaneous* change of quality and quantity. There is a complex series of chemical and biological interactions occurring within the egg as the embryo develops into the chick. After 21 days incubation, a developed chick exists within the shell.

In the same way, social reforms may occur gradually. There have been many labor reform laws enacted since the time of Marx which have produced a working environment far different from that which he described.

Interpreted less rigidly than the Soviet version, this law becomes meaningless. If a thing keeps changing in one direction, it will eventually become something different than what it was to begin with. This is hardly a useful insight. Even this assertion is neutralized by some Marxist texts which hedge by saying, "quantitative and qualitative are thus interconnected and influence one another."[12]

Although Marxist literature is replete with dialectical jargon, Marxists have never effectively resolved any issue with the help of dialectical laws.

C. Law 3: Negation of the negation

Finally, we can consider the negation of the negation. Let us ask first for a definition of terms. Does negation mean *destruction* of one element by the other, or does negation refer to *cyclical transformations* in which destruction is not necessary?

When Marx writes about the negation of the capitalist

system, he definitely means *destruction* and not reform or transformation. However, when Engels supports him with his numerous examples of the "dialectic" operating in nature, he is giving examples of *non-destructive cyclical transformations.*[13] The same word is used in two different senses without making clear distinctions.

A process taking place "everywhere and everyday" is, according to Engels, so simple "that any child can understand." A grain of barley:

> ... germinates; the grain as such ceases to exist, it is negated, and in its place there appears the plant which has arisen from it.[14]

Although Engels may have believed his example to be simple enough for a child, a great many thinkers, including Marxist theoreticians, have apparently been unable to understand it. Karl Kautsky, for example, pointed out that to describe germination as the negation of the grain was tantamount to saying that a child was being negated by growing up to be an adult, although he remained the same person.

If one looks hard enough, aided by terminological inexactitude, one can be persuaded that history is full of examples of negation of the negation. Because of ambiguity in the dialectical formula, almost any event can be called a negation of something prior to it.

Law 3 | **Negation of the negation**

What is negation? → **Destruction**

What is negation? → **Cyclical transformations without destruction**

Ambiguity and sophistry

The term negation is used to encourage people to think in terms of violence, contradiction and revolution. It is definitely true that cyclical transformations take place in nature, but to call these processes "negations" can be misleading. When the plant produces the seed or the chicken lays an egg, the plant or chicken is not destroyed. In fact, the plant or chicken may remain for many years producing fruit and seeds or eggs every year.

D. Conclusion: the use of Marxist "laws"

Compared to genuine empirical laws such as "energy can be neither created nor destroyed," or "gravitational force decreases inversely with distance," etc., the Marxist laws of the dialectic lack clarity and validity. Even rules or generalizations which do not apply without exceptions can have great practical significance when they are explicitly clear: "a glut of commodities leads to lower prices," "the human heart is on the left side of the chest cavity." These "laws" are not valid without exception, but they do tell us what is likely to happen or to be encountered in given circumstances, and they enable those concerned to make predictions and act accordingly. What use, however, is a "law" which tells us that, for example, an initiative in the political arena will be countered by opposition of an unspecified kind, and through the struggle between the two, a new initiative, also unspecified. will be enacted?[15]

Marxist laws are not clear, and if they are clarified, they certainly cease to be universal.

Marxist dialectics is tautological, unintelligible, and vague. It has no value in the search for knowledge and truth. Yet, it plays an important role in the hands of today's communists. It serves to confuse issues and sidetrack arguments. It helps to justify repressive and undemocratic measures taken by Marxist regimes, as well as their expansionist foreign policies. It also furnishes explanations for the persistent refusal of history to conform to the Marxist scheme of things.

IV. Historical materialism

Marx expanded his materialist analysis to all of history to try to show how history developed from earliest times, and how it would continue to develop in the future. This is known as the materialist view of history, or historical materialism.

Eduardo del Rio in *Marx for Beginners* tells us that, "the purpose of Marx's theory of historical materialism is to show us that history is made by man, not by 'destiny' or the so-called 'hand of God.'"[16]

Marxist Framework

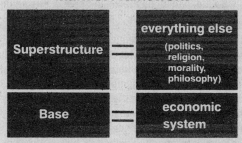

Base and superstructure

Historical materialism is based on the belief that society consists of a superstructure and a base. Marx wrote, in the frequently quoted preface to *A Contribution to the Critique of Political Economy*,

> In the social production which men carry on they enter into definite relations that are indispensable and independent of their will; these relations of production correspond to a definite stage of development of their material powers of production. The sum total of these relations of production constitutes the economic structure of society—the real foundation, on which rise legal and political superstructures and to which correspond definite forms of social consciousness.

The mode of production in material life determines the general character of the social, political and spiritual processes of life.[17]

The base is composed of the economic structure, and the superstructure consists of everything else — ideologies and institutions. This includes politics, religion, morality and philosophy. Progress begins in the base, and the forward movement of the base "pulls" the superstructure along. Thus, there are specific political and religious forms of organization which correspond to stages in the progress of the substructure. (Marx writes that the substructure "conditions" the superstructure. He is then able to apply a strong or weak usage to the word "conditions," as the circumstances require.)

This materialist perspective of human life and history colors the entire outlook of Marxists. For example, Marxists always refer to the conflict between the free world and the communist world as the struggle between two economic systems, capitalism (or imperialism) and socialism. They never regard it as a struggle between a God-affirming and a God-denying outlook. They never cast it as totalitarianism versus participatory government. They never make reference to the fundamentally different understandings of morality and ethics of the two "worlds." For the Marxist historian, these are secondary. The primary concern in the Marxist framework is economic structure.

Western conservatives who regard the Western world as first and foremost the "capitalist" world, have already stepped into the Marxist framework, and are adopting the Marxist method of analysis to a greater or lesser extent. The CAUSA Worldview will not accept the viewpoint that the economic structure is fundamental. The CAUSA Worldview regards moral values as fundamental, and the economic system as secondary.

Historical materialism, then, outlines a progression of economic structures. These changing economic structures give rise to the march of history.

A. Stages of history

1. Primitive communal society (primitive communism)

The primitive communal society is a postulated idyllic state where everyone shares everything and no one owns any private property.[18] Nevertheless, exploitation of man by man is present in embryonic form in the *family* relationship itself. Marx and Engels write:

> ... hence property: the nucleus, the first form of which lies in the family, where wife and children are the slaves of the husband. This latent slavery in the family, though still very crude, is the first property, but even at this early stage it corresponds perfectly to the definition of modern economists who call it the power of disposing of the labour-power of others.[19]

2. Slave society

According to historical materialism, as the development of productive forces continued, labor became more specialized and people began to privately own their tools. They also accumulated surpluses, which they owned. In time, they began to own each other as well. The first type of class society was thus born, the slave society. The slave society is patterned after the family, where, Marx said, the husband and father is the slavemaster over his wife and children.

In addition, according to Marx, the birth of the state occurs along with the birth of the first class society. The state in Marxism is an instrument that the ruling class uses to oppress the ruled class.

Religion, which according to Marx is the result of primitive man trying to understand natural phenomena, can also now be used by the ruling class to oppress the ruled class. Through religion, the poor are taught to be submissive to authority. Philosophies can be developed and manipulated in the same way. These are said to be nothing more than a way of justifying the socio-economic status quo. All of these new elements of the "superstructure" correspond to the appearance of the slave society.

3. Feudal society

The slave masters would like to preserve this society forever, but they cannot because the dialectic is in operation. The number of slaves and their misery grows until the slaves carry out a revolution and the feudal society is established.

In feudalism there are a number of classes: feudal lords, merchants, guild artisans and serfs. The feudal lords utilize the state, religion and philosophy to control the other classes, but the dialectic is inexorably operating. The merchants and guild artisans form a new class, the bourgeoisie, and eventually a revolution, such as the French Revolution, takes place. This bourgeois revolution ushers in the age of capitalist society. Marx and Engels write in the *Communist Manifesto*:

> We see then: the means of production and of exchange, on whose foundation the bourgeoisie built itself up, were generated in feudal society. At a certain stage in (their) development ... the feudal relations of property became no longer compatible with the already developed productive forces; they became so many fetters. They had to be burst asunder; they were burst asunder.[20]

4. Capitalist society

In the capitalist society there are two major classes, the capitalists (who own everything) and the workers (who own nothing). Possessing nothing but their own bodies, the workers are forced to sell their labor power to the capitalists, who use it as a source of profit. The capitalists do everything in their power to perpetuate this society, but again the dialectic is operating. The working class grows in numbers and in misery. Eventually there will be a revolution, and a socialist society will be established.

5. Socialist society

According to Marx, socialist society represents the first point at which the majority class owns the means of production. It is therefore a transition stage toward the abolition of classes altogether. In socialism, the norm of economic distribution is "From each according to his abilities, to each according to his *work*." Socialism will be such an efficient system, however, that soon distribution will be based only on need, and the norm will become, as Marx predicted, "From each according to his abilities, to each according to his *need*."

Although it is nothing more than a transition phase leading to the communist society, the socialist society is very important. In a socialist state, large armed forces must be maintained for defense against capitalist neighbors. In this way, for example, the Sandinista rulers of Nicaragua have justified an increase in military strength from 12,000 to 250,000 persons-in-arms.[21]

In addition, strong police forces are required to dismantle all religions, philosophies, and reactionary activities. Lenin proclaimed that "terror" would be used by the state to defend itself from class enemies and reactionaries, and began a system of prison and labor camps. Lenin wrote:

> The courts must not ban terror—to promise that would be deception or self-deception—but must formulate the motives underlying it, legalize it as a principle, plainly, without any make-believe or embellishment.[22]

6. Communist society

Eventually the state itself will wither away. In a communist society there is no more need for a state—no state, no religion, no philosophy. The communist society is the communal society re-established on a more advanced plane.

The progression from primitive classless society to

advanced classless society is held to be an example of an
affirmation-negation-affirmation phenomenon. The primitive
classless communal society is negated to give a series of
class structures, and finally these are negated once again to
return to the natural state of the human species, the communal society.[23]

B. Marxism as a pseudo-religion

We note here the characteristics of a pseudo-religion.
The components of a religious doctrine are all present; only
God is missing. The Garden of Eden is present in the form of
the primitive communal society. The fall of man is the point
where people accumulate surpluses to own property. We have
a history of sin and tribulation in the form of a succession of
class societies, and finally we even have salvation—salvation
from tribulation into paradise.

If there is going to be salvation, there must be a savior,
and in Marxism the savior is

> . . . a class of civil society which . . . cannot emancipate
> itself without emancipating all other spheres of soci-
> ety, which, in a word, is the complete loss of man and
> hence can win itself only through the complete re-
> winning of man. This dissolution of society as a par-
> ticular estate is the proletariat.[24]

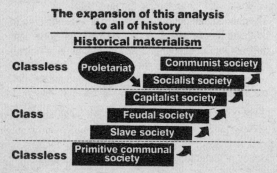

**The expansion of this analysis
to all of history**

Historical materialism

Classless — Proletariat — Communist society / Socialist society

Capitalist society

Class — Feudal society / Slave society

Classless — Primitive communal society

We see here two usages of the word proletariat. Proletariat in the role of savior is not simply the working class. The proletariat is the group of workers who have been molded by tribulation and oppression into a class which is not a class and which has nothing to lose. They have become a revolutionary weapon. They are the enlightened workers. Only the proletariat can transform this world of tribulation into the ideal world. The proletariat has no concept of nationalism or racism. They feel only class solidarity. There is no selfishness within the proletariat, because being stripped of everything has rid them of selfishness itself. It is the perfect unified, selfless class, and until the proletariat appears, there is no way to escape from the succession of class societies.

> The proletariat alone is a really revolutionary class...
> The proletarian is without property; his relation to his wife and children has no longer anything in common with the bourgeois family relations; modern industrial labour, modern subjection to capital, the same in England as in France, in America as in Germany, has stripped him of every trace of national character. Law, morality, religion, are to him so many bourgeois prejudices, behind which lurk in ambush just as many bourgeois interests.

> All the preceding classes that got the upper hand, sought to fortify their already acquired status by subjecting society at large to their conditions of appropriation. The proletarians cannot become masters of the productive forces of society, except by abolishing their own previous mode of appropriation, and thereby also every other previous mode of appropriation. They have nothing of their own to secure and fortify; their mission is to destroy all previous securities for, and insurances of, individual property.[25]

V. Critique of historical materialism

It is reasonable to say that if men and women were completely rational beings, they would reject historical materialism. It may be observed, however, that historical materialism is expanding its influence throughout the world. This is possible because of the appeal which Marxism makes to the emotional aspect of people, as well as the religious nature of men and women.

Problems with historical materialism

1. **No primitive communal society**
2. **European history only**
3. **No "capitalism"**
4. **No proletariat**

People are embracing the materialist view of history without reflecting on whether it corresponds to the historical record.

A. Historical materialism does not correspond to the historical record

1. Religious principles are timeless

In general, the Marxist view holds that the economic system is the base, and the superstructure is erected upon that. Changes occur first in the base, and changes in the superstructure result from and follow these. According to this concept, as the economic relations are progressing through stages, the religious ideas should change. A new religion should develop for each age. What we find, however, is that the fundamental religious principles are timeless.

The principles laid down in the Old Testament age, for example, are not denied in the New Testament age. They are not altered with the passage of time. Religious principles have a timeless appeal to human beings.

In general, we can say that Marx suffered from a gross misunderstanding of the origin and purpose of religion. Certainly Marx had a right to critique the ecclesiastical abuses of his day. There have been a great number of abuses carried out in the name of religion. It is our contention, however, that these are in fact violations of the true purpose of religion. It is this genuine function of religion which is of interest to us.

Marxism holds that religion is a reflection of the external world into the minds of human beings. The external phenomena become fantasies in the human mind. This is religion. Marx and Engels clearly had a tremendous contempt for religion.

An exchange of letters between Marx and Engels in 1853 examined the origin of "the Jewish so-called Holy Scripture" and the fact that the history of the East "appears as a history of religions." Marx and Engels concur that the Bible "is nothing more than a record of the old Arabian religious and tribal tradition," and the seeming religious nature of the East is due to the fact that there is "no private property in land." Engels concludes, "The absence of property in land is

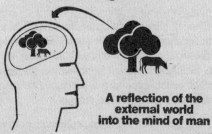

Marxist view of the origin of religion

A reflection of the external world into the mind of man

indeed the key to the whole of the East. Herein lies its political and religious history."[26]

Marx certainly felt that atheism was inseparable from communism. He and Engels wrote in *The Holy Family*:

> Just as Cartesian materialism passes into natural science proper, the other trend of French materialism leads directly to socialism and communism.

> There is no need for any great penetration to see...
> how necessarily materialism is connected with communism and socialism... Like Owen, the more scientific French communists, Dezamy, Gay and others, developed the teaching of materialism as the teaching of real humanism and the logical basis of communism.[27]

Similarly, in *Critique of the Gotha Program* we find:

> ... bourgeois "freedom of conscience" is nothing but the toleration of all possible kinds of religious freedom of conscience, and that for its part it (the worker's party) endeavors rather to liberate the conscience from the witchery of religion.[28]

In fact, it is clear that Marx thought that Christianity had already been buried by materialism, "When Christian ideas succumbed in the 18th century to rationalist ideas..."[29]

The persistance of religion is a source of concern to communists today, particularly within the Soviet Union. Books such as the handbook of *Marxist Philosophy* by Afanasayev, call upon party members to "combat all forms of spiritual oppression, including religion." Lenin wrote, "Religion is not a private affair in the eyes of the party.... We demand the complete disestablishment of the church."[30]

Within the Soviet Union today, communists have had to reconcile themselves to the fact that religion is not disappearing. Official Soviet ideologues have now softened their positions and foresee that religion may persist indefinitely even under communism. They have therefore adopted a strategy which allows certain religions to function, but requires them to keep their religious ideas and practices *strictly within the four walls of the church*. It is indeed alarming to see this same strategy being adopted in the United States.[31]

The whole notion that religion is nothing more than superstition taken advantage of by the ruling class is for us extremely unsatisfactory. Such a view does not begin to explain the fundamental drive experienced by each human being to reconcile him or herself with the Creator. This is a totally inadequate explanation for the universal emergence and continuation of religion.

The true spirit of religion which Marx failed to comprehend is twofold. *One*, God seeks after human beings, His lost children. The New Testament tells of the prodigal son who leaves his loving father. The father is not indifferent; he feels tremendous anguish. In the same way, the Creator yearns after His children. He created everything for them. *Two*, human beings seek after God. There is the religious quest of man for God.

In any case, religion is not an opium nor a drug. Religion does not exist to make people feel good. Serious religionists

The role of religion

God seeking man

Man seeking God

The most difficult human path

have often been driven to great suffering. Religion is more properly described as "the most difficult path."

From the point of view of Godism, the purpose of religion can be summarized as:

1. Resolve the alienation of man.
2. Comfort and give joy to God.
3. Elevate the human perspective towards an absolute perspective of value.

Clearly Marx had regrettable personal experiences with religion, and therefore he rejected God and failed to understand the most powerful stream in human cultural history, interpreting it in the most superficial language of economic analysis.

2. No primitive communal society

Furthermore, there is no evidence that it is against the original nature of man to own property, including the means of production. There is a great deal of evidence that it is a very essential part of human nature to want to possess property. In the view of the world's great religions, what is contradictory to man's original nature is to be small-minded and selfish with one's property. Certainly there is no archeological evidence that there was ever a primitive communal society devoid of private possessions. Quite the contrary, it appears that even animals are able to delineate certain properties as their own, and from all evidence, individuals have always owned property.

3. No resemblance to non-European history

While the general pattern of progression asserted by Marx can be seen in the history of Western Europe, the stages of historical materialism do not resemble non-European histories. Africa, Asia and pre-Columbian America have unique histories not described or explained by historical materialism.

4. No pure examples of any stage

In fact, there are no pure examples of any of the stages which Marx mentioned.[32] Marx characterized Rome as an absolute slave society, but many people consider that the Roman empire could be better characterized by calling it democratic. Rome was certainly not toppled by slave revolts. The last major slave revolt occurred centuries earlier, and slavery was not a particularly important institution when Rome collapsed from internal corruption and external invasion.

The feudal society of Europe was composed of many economic and social strata.

Marxists admit that Marx shed very little light on the nature of pre-capitalist societies other than feudal society. William Shaw notes, "Even though Marx describes the preconditions of capitalist production and some of the factors responsible for introducing and consolidating capitalism, he does not provide a theory of the transition from feudalism to capitalism—at least, not in the sense in which he tendered a theory underwriting the arrival of socialism."[33]

In bald Marxist propaganda, the absence of discussion on pre-feudalist societies is glossed over. In *Marx for Beginners*, for example, Eduardo del Rio writes, "Primitive community and the slave state are known and clear to everyone...," without making any further explanation.[34]

5. No "capitalism"

Similarly, there is no "capitalism" as Marx described it. The word "capitalism" is extremely misleading. The word comes from Marx, and it describes a system which cannot be found anywhere.

In Marx's idea of capitalism, the capitalist owns everything and contributes nothing to the process of production. The worker has nothing and does all the work. If we look at a modern free economy, it does not fit that description. The ownership of the means of production is distributed among

millions of people, most of whom are participating in the
process of production. The prosperity of the owners of
businesses can only occur *with* the prosperity of the consumers in general. If the "working class" is condemned to poverty,
no class of producers or merchants can prosper.

6. No proletariat

Finally, the most devastating critique of the whole scheme
of historical materialism is that the anticipated "savior" has
never come. The proletariat has never appeared. There is no
unified body of workers who possess only class consciousness,
who are unselfish, and who have no nationalism.[35]

A proletarian revolution has never occurred as Marx
predicted. Marxian proletarian revolutions should occur in
the most advanced capitalist countries, but such a revolution
has never taken place.

Vladimir Lenin was faced with this awkward fact when
he wanted to make the Russian revolution in 1917. There
were those, like Karl Kautsky, who said that it was necessary
to wait until the proletariat emerged. Lenin held that it was
vital to make the revolution and let the proletariat appear
later.[36] Lenin and the Bolsheviks prevailed. Lenin carried out
a revolution with an alliance of intellectuals and disgruntled
peasants and soldiers. Lenin believed that the proletariat would
emerge immediately after the revolution, but it never did. In
fact, almost seven decades have now passed and the proletariat is nowhere in sight.

B. Marxism makes false assumptions

In order to point out the fundamental misconceptions of
the Marxist method of historical analysis, it is necessary to
unmask the hidden assumptions of Marx's positivistic
approach.

1. Economic relationships are not the base of society

Marx writes that it is plainly evident that the *authentic*

Marxism makes false assumptions

1. **Economic relationships not the base**

2. **Struggle not always between classes**

3. **Violence not always necessary for change**

4. **Communism not the goal of history**

and *unique* human activity is production. Other so-called human activities may indeed be attributed to human beings, but they are just secondary results of the primary activity which is production.

> Men can be distinguished from animals by consciousness, by religion, or anything else you like. They themselves begin to distinguish themselves from animals as soon as they begin to produce their means of subsistence... [37]

In one sense, this is just one man's opinion, yet we see that Marx and Engels would certainly like to sell the idea that they deal with obvious truths, while other thinkers deal in "dogmatic" and "arbitrary" premises.

> The premises from which we begin are not arbitrary ones, not dogmas, but real premises... They are the real individuals, their activity and the material conditions under which they live. [38]

The Marxist "truth," as we have said, is that productive activity determines all other sorts of activity. In other words, productive activity represents the foundation or basis of human life, and other activities, known as institutions and ideologies, are the superstructure which rises above and upon this basis.

Why would Marx, or anyone for that matter, adopt such an extreme view? It appears that Marx adopted this view in reaction to the absolute idealism of Hegel and others. For Hegel, consciousness determines being, and in a reactionary way, for Marx, being determines consciousness. That is, production relations determine ideologies and institutions. From the perspective of the CAUSA Worldview, both "idealism" and "materialism" seem to be inadequate views.

In the CAUSA view, all beings exhibit the dual characteristics of internal character (mind) and external form (body). (Aristotle's *eidos* and *hyle* correspond approximately to these dual characteristics.) No entity can exist without both aspects.

Thus, a human being has mind and body, as do animals and even plants. Molecules, atoms, particles and sub-particles are formed from energy (external form) according to certain laws (internal character). Similarly, human relations involve internal and external components. Production relations, in other words, are relations which have a material and a spiritual component. For example, the exchange of goods is carried out based on certain moral and ethical principles. At the same time, these moral and ethical principles have no meaning until they are practiced, and material exchange is required for that practice.

A largely irrational reaction to absolute idealism is pervasive in Marxism and conditions Marx's view of man and history, but to view man first and foremost as "producer" is simply not adequate.

In the CAUSA Worldview we have a broad view of man under the general concept of "child of God." In addition, man is potentially "lord of creation." This is increasingly evident as technology progresses. Man is the only being which can experience the entire universe and the only one capable of extending God's love to all creatures.

As British philosopher Bertrand Russell observed, "Economic causes operate through men's desire for possessions, and would be supreme if this desire were supreme."[39]

2. Violence is not always necessary to bring about change

Perhaps in the course of creation, survival of the fittest was a necessary mechanism, but the concept is inappropriate in human social relations. The Creator may intend that in his role of steward to the universe, man should help to alleviate animal suffering, or perhaps what we view as suffering only appears to be suffering. We cannot think that destruction of our enemies is justified simply because it seems to be the mechanism of evolution. Yet, in Marxism, it is thought that the class struggle has brought progress to mankind.

3. Struggle is not always between classes

Indeed, it must be remarked that the most significant and determinant struggles in history have not necessarily been class struggles nor even inter-capitalist rivalry motivated by greed. Struggles have often been waged for ideals. Wars in this century have been fought to preserve freedom.

To cite Russell again, "He (Marx) regards conflicts as always conflicts between classes, whereas the majority of them have been between races or nations."[40]

4. The Marxist belief that communism is the goal of history, that it will be permanent, and that it will not be destroyed dialectically is not rational.

Where is this history, this succession of struggles headed toward? This raises a most intriguing question. Is it going nowhere? Or is it going toward a goal determined by man's "species-essence"? If the latter is true, then the origin of that species-essence is highly significant.

For the Marxist, the species-essence, wherever it comes from, dictates that history will move toward the goal of communism. This will be achieved by the functioning of the dialectic. However, if the dialectic is the law of history, why does the dialectic stop functioning when communism has been attained?

In the CAUSA view, God had a purpose when He initi-

ated the creation. Since God is an unchanging and perfect
being, His original purpose of creation must be unchanging
and perfect. Thus, He is guiding human history toward the
fulfillment of that original goal. As we have already said, the
fulfillment of that goal depends on God's work *and* man's
response, and it is the failure of man to make the proper
response to God which has produced tremendous suffering in
history.

Although this is not an exhaustive list of the errors of
Marx, it does permit us to reach the conclusion that historical
materialism is not a valid analysis or description of history. It
cannot be, because it is based on the tenets of dialectical
materialism which is not a valid metaphysical outlook and does
not explain the nature of relationship and the nature of development.

VI. Critique of the "two great camps"

Engels held that one must be either an idealist or a
materialist. By discrediting idealism, he felt that he had shown
materialism to be correct. In the CAUSA Worldview, however,
we find it unnecessary to claim that matter comes from spirit
or that spirit comes from matter.

The CAUSA Worldview, Godism, views spirit and mat-

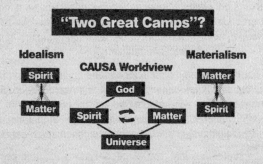

ter as existing in a subject-object relationship. Both come from the creator, and both have a purpose. The purposeful, loving creator is God.

The "two great camps" framework is designed to reinforce the belief in materialism. Both materialism and idealism are inadequate. The view of Godism has implications in social practice. Both spiritual and material values must be highly regarded, but the spiritual aspect must always be regarded as subject.

The human spirit

One area where this view can be applied is in regard to the human spirit. In the Marxist view, spirit exists. It is, however, the operation of the human brain. It is human consciousness, a function or product of the human brain.

Certain Marxist propagandists have argued that the fact that physically damaging the brain by injury or drugs causes a change in human consciousness is evidence that spirit is object to the brain. We can dispense with this weak argumentation with a simple analogy. An image appears on the screen of the television set. Destroying the screen will cause the image to disappear, yet the screen is not the source of the image. The image comes from a transmitting station, and is broadcast by means of electromagnetic waves to the television receiver.

In the same way, the physical body need not be the source of mind or spirit. God is ultimately the source of both body and spirit, and the human individual formed through the dynamic relationship of body and spirit is the creation of God. A more detailed explanation of the important relationship between spirit and body will be made in Chapter Seven of this text.

CHAPTER THREE NOTES

1. Melvin Rader, *Marx's Interpretation of History*, New York, Oxford University Press, 1979, p.179.
2. Engels, *Ludwig Feuerbach*, from *Reader in Marxist Philosophy*, New York, International Publishers, 1963, pp.47-48.
3. Ibid., p.51.
4. Frederick Copleston, S.J., *A History of Philosophy*, Garden City, New York, Image Books, Vol.7, Part I, pp.65-67.
5. V. G. Afanasyev, *Marxist Philosophy*, Moscow, Progress Publishers, 1980, p.82.
6. Afanasyev, p.98.
7. Afanasyev, p.100.
8. F. Engels, *Dialectics of Nature*, New York, International Publishers, 1940, p.26.
9. Afanasyev, p.109.
10. Lenny Wolff, *The Science of Revolution*, Revolutionary Communist Party, USA, 1983, p.29.
11. L. Kolakowski, *Main Currents of Marxism*, Oxford, Oxford University Press, 1978, Vol. I, p.290.
12. Afanasyev, p.100.
13. F. Engels, *Anti-Duhring*, Peking, Foreign Languages Press, 1976, p.180.
14. Engels, *Anti-Duhring*, pp.172-3.
15. S.F. Kissen, *Farewell To Revolution*, New York, St. Martin's Press, 1978, p.109.
16. Eduardo del Rio, *Marx for Beginners*, New York, Pantheon Books, 1976, p.142.
17. *Marx and Engels, Basic Writings on Politics and Philosophy*, Lewis Feuer, ed., Garden City, New York, Doubleday Anchor, 1959, p.43.
18. Marx and Engels wrote about several specific variations of the primitive communal society. William Shaw holds that Marx describes three basic types of primitive communism in the *Grundrisse*. These are (1) Asiatic, (2) ancient classical, and (3) Germanic. According to Melvin Rader, the stages of history in Marxism are (1) primitive communism, (2) Asiatic society, (3) ancient or classical society, (4) feudal society, (5) modern capitalist society, and (6) communism. Rader notes that in *The Critique of the Gotha Program*, Marx distinguished between the first phase of communism, known as socialism, and the latter, communism. While we do not dispute these interpretations, we have chosen to abbreviate and simplify our treatment of the progression of social structures as described by Marx as (1) primitive communal society, (2) slave society, (3) feudal society, (4) capitalist society, (5) socialist society, and (6) communist society.
19. Marx and Engels, *The German Ideology*, New York, International Publishers, 1947, p.52-53.
20. Marx and Engels, *The Communist Manifesto*, as quoted in William H. Shaw, *Marx's Theory of History*, Stanford, Stanford University Press, 1978, p.139.

21. J. Antonio Montes, "Military Buildup in Nicaragua," *West Watch*, Vol. 6, No. 6, July 1981.

22. Lenin, *Collected Works*, Vol. 33, p. 358.

23. According to Engels, it is the destiny of matter to form a communist society. The entire process of historical materialism including each of the stages culminating in communism is a manifestation of the potential and necessity contained within matter. The qualities of matter themselves dictate that at some point a communist society has to be established.

24. Marx, *Contribution to a Critique of Hegel's Philosophy of Law, Introduction, Collected Works*, Vol. 3, p. 186.

25. Marx and Engels, *Manifesto of the Communist Party, Collected Works*, New York, International Publishers, 1976, Vol. 6, pp. 494-5.

26. *On Religion*, USSR, Progress Publishers, 1975, pp. 104-109.

27. Ibid., p. 61.

28. Ibid., p. 125.

29. Marx and Engels, *Manifesto of the Communist Party, Collected Works*, New York, International Publishers, 1976, Vol. 6, p. 503.

30. Lenin, *Collected Works*, Vol. 10, pp. 85-86.

31. For a review of the threat to religious freedom in the United States see *Assault on Religious Freedom*, Washington, D.C., Coalition for Religious Freedom, 1984, 120p.

32. S. H. Lee, *Communism, A Critique and Counterproposal*, Washington, DC, The Freedom Leadership Foundation, 1973, p. 224.

33. Shaw, p. 138.

34. del Rio, p. 128.

35. B-H Levy, *Barbarism With a Human Face*, New York: Harper & Row, 1977.

36. V. Lenin, *What Is To Be Done?*, Moscow: Progress Publishers, 1969.

37. Marx and Engels, *The German Ideology*, International Publishers, p. 42.

38. Ibid.

39. *The Basic Writings of Bertrand Russell 1903-1959*, Edited by Robert E. Egner and Lester E. Denonn, Simon and Schuster, New York, 1961, p. 528.

40. Ibid.

MARXIST ECONOMIC THEORIES

As we have previously made clear, Karl Marx determined early in his life that violent revolutionary destruction of the present state of affairs was the prerequisite of significant human progress. In the elaboration of Marxism, then, we find the construction of a philosophical weapon capable of rousing anger and intensifying grievances to the point of volatility. This is the motivation for the Marxist economic theories— the labor theory of value and its extension into the theory of surplus value. These theories are the basis for all Leninist wars of "national liberation," and are being intensively taught in places such as Nicaragua where communist governments are trying to consolidate their power.

According to these theories, "capitalism" is a system which cannot be reformed, but must be violently destroyed. In *Das Kapital*, Marx elaborates his labor theory of value and theory of surplus value. Through the labor theory of value, Marx wanted to show that workers alone produce value. Through the theory of surplus value, Marx wanted to show that capitalism requires exploitation, and cannot exist without it.

Marxists consider the economic theories expressed in *Das Kapital* to be merely an objective inquiry into the functioning of the free market economy, but they are not. They were developed in order to *destroy* the capitalist system, not in order to understand it. According to Marx, efforts of reform short of the destruction of private ownership of the means of production and the forcible seizure of political power by the proletariat would never free the workers from "capitalist wage-slavery."

As the well-known Polish scholar Leszek Kolakowski

observes, Marx's labor theory of value and the theory of
surplus value do not deal in a useful way with questions
regarding "the quantity of goods produced, their manner of
sale and distribution, or even the question of exploitation."
They serve merely to "arouse indignation at the fact that the
'only real producer' gets so small a share of the result of his
work, while the capitalist, who contributes nothing to value,
rakes in profits on the strength of being a property-owner."
Apart from this moral interpretation, Kolakowski continues,
"it is not clear how the theory is supposed to throw light on
the mechanism of the capitalist economy..."[1]

Marxist economics is built around a condemnation of a
system. As Mark Blaug of the University of London points
out, "To say that an economist is a Marxian economist is in
effect to say that he shares the value judgment that it is
socially undesirable for some people in the community to
derive their income merely from the ownership of property."[2]

To be successful, however, an economic system must
function in accord with the nature of human beings. It is in
this sense more than any other that the system prescribed by
the economic theories of Karl Marx has been a total failure.
In order to condemn the capitalists, Karl Marx has put himself in opposition not only to the bourgeoisie, but more signi-
ficantly to human nature itself. The ironic result is a theory
which exacerbates the tragic conditions which Marx decried.

When Marxist principles are applied, and individual enterprise, profit production and the free exchange of goods are
considered to be criminal activities, an economic disaster is
produced. To sustain an economy under these conditions requires the continuous application of force and terror to the
population. In spite of these measures, the best which can be
achieved is stagnation in comparison with the economies of
free nations of the world.

Although Marx's economic theories have had, as Blaug
says, "virtually no effect on modern economic thought," they
are nevertheless very useful as propaganda, particularly in

the developing world. For that reason, we examine them here.

When we speak of Marxist economic theories, we are referring to the *labor theory of value* developed by the classical economists and adopted by Marx, as well as the *theory of surplus value*, which both Engels and Lenin described as one of Marx's most valuable insights.

These theories find their greatest development in Marx's *Das Kapital*, subtitled, "Critique of Political Economy." Political economy refers to the activity of classical economists such as Adam Smith or David Ricardo, who accepted the free market system as a natural and necessary system and attempted to understand it. Marx, by contrast, began with the belief that the free market system was an aberration and had to be destroyed by revolution.

As we pointed out in Chapter 2, Marx worked to advance revolution by developing an ideology, which he referred to as a "spiritual weapon." He sought also to conceal his unyielding beliefs behind a facade of "science." This process reaches its peak in his analysis of "capitalism."

"Capitalism" as Marx viewed it is quite different from what we commonly refer to as capitalism today. For Marx, capitalism was one stage in the progression of the history of class struggles. Under capitalism, the two major classes which were struggling against one another were the workers and the capitalists. The workers are those who contribute their labor toward production, yet have no property, that is, no share in the ownership of the means of production. The capitalists, on the other hand, own all the property and contribute no labor toward production. Obviously, both are necessary to generate the products.

The worker, then, contributes his labor, while the capitalist contributes his capital. Marx would argue, however, that capital contributes nothing to the value of the products. Value comes exclusively from labor. The worker, then, is the sole contributor to commodity value. Yet the worker receives only the skimpiest of wages, enough to survive, while the capitalist takes the lion's share in the form of profit.

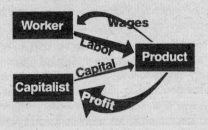

"Capitalism"

Marx set about to reveal to everyone the "true" nature of this process. He begins to do this with the labor theory of value.

I. The labor theory of value

A. Commodity value

According to Marx, the commodity is the basic unit of the capitalist economic structure. The commodity in capitalism is produced for the purpose of exchange rather than consumption. That is, the capitalist who produces it is interested in selling it rather than using it. For Marx, this is the beginning of the peculiar world of capitalism.

Marx next sets about to assign value to the commodity, and concludes that there are two types of value possible. This in turn leads him to consider two types of labor which generate these two types of value. The first type of value is determined by the particular use which is made of the commodity. This is "use value" generated by "useful labor." The use of a pen is to write; this gives it a certain use value. The use of a glass is to hold liquid. This gives it a certain use value.

The other type of value identified by Marx is "exchange value." Exchange value refers to the value of the commodity as it is circulated. That is, the exchange value is the *price* of the commodity. According to the labor theory of value, exchange value is the result of a different type of labor, "abstract labor." Abstract labor is generic labor. It is basic human effort, regardless of the specifics of the laboring activity.

In Marxist economics, when reference is made to commodity value, the value referred to is exchange value. Use value is of no interest to the economist, because it "does not embody a social relation." That is, since the commodity in capitalism is produced for exchange, the important aspect of commodity value is exchange value.

Finally, the quantity of abstract labor, and thus the exchange value of a commodity, can be measured in the form of hours of labor expended to make the commodity. This measurement must include all hours of labor expended from the point at which raw materials are taken from nature to the point at which the product can be exchanged. Labor expended to make tools and machinery must also be included.

For example, if the pen requires a cumulative total of one hour of labor to make, then the value of the pen will be one labor hour. If the glass requires altogether two hours of labor, then the value of the glass will be two labor hours. In such a case, two pens will have the equivalent value of one glass.

To summarize what has been said, for Marx, commodity value refers to exchange value, which is equal to price. And this is equal to the number of hours of labor required to produce the commodity. The number of hours refers to the average time necessary for a worker in society to produce the particular commodity.

Value = Price = Labor hours

Average labor hours

This may be regarded as the fundamental definition of terms for Marx's discussion of economics. It must be noted, however, that Marx will occasionally retract and restate his definitions in order to achieve correspondence between theory and reality. That is, faced with the fact that price has little to do with hours of labor, Marx later modified his concept of exchange value so that it is not directly related to price. If price is not equal to exchange value, or even clearly related to exchange value, then the term exchange value ceases to have empirical meaning. It comes instead to mean something akin to the medieval "just price" and it has only a moral meaning. Since that is not the way Marx developed his theories, we will retain the definition of price as being equal to exchange value.

The essential point to be noted here is that according to

Marx, value is determined in the production process, not in the market.

B. The conversion of labor hours

We immediately find that this theory contradicts what we might observe in the market place. We might find, for example, that in the market are a watch and a pile of gravel. The watch sells for $50 and the gravel for $5, yet it appears that it took five hours to produce each of them.[3]

In an attempt to salvage the labor theory of value, Marx introduces the concept of the conversion of labor hours. According to this concept, the hours of labor involved in digging gravel are simple and unskilled, while the hours spent manufacturing the watch are complex and skilled. A conversion factor must be calculated to show how much expenditure of human effort went into the different types of hours of labor. That is, both amounts of labor time must be expressed in terms of their common denominator, abstract labor hours. In this example, one complex, skilled labor hour would have the value of 10 abstract hours, while one simple, unskilled labor hour would have the value of one abstract hour. The watch is thus worth 50 abstract hours and the gravel worth five. The watch sells for $50 and the gravel for $5. The problem of the variation in the price of watch and gravel is apparently solved.

C. Critique of the labor theory of value

What is the meaning of abstract labor hours? In a Marxist economy they are supposed to serve as the basis for the setting of prices. In reality, however, they can never be determined by empirical measurement. They can only be back-calculated after prices have been set in the marketplace.

This is in fact how labor hours are calculated in the Soviet Union today. To calculate the amount of labor time required to produce even an extremely simple commodity is impossible. Such a calculation would require an almost infinite regression of calculations to determine the labor expended in

Critique of the labor theory of value

Abstract labor hours cannot be determined prior to exchange

In the Soviet Union labor hours are calculated from prices

Prices are determined in the market

each step of manufacture plus the labor expended on tools, tools used to make tools, etc. For this reason, prices in the Soviet Union are set in relation to world free market prices. Marshall Goldman describes this anomaly:

> The best analogy is the way the Council of Mutual Economic Assistance (CMEA) countries decide how to price the goods they sell to one another. Because their currencies are not convertible, and because their internal pricing systems are so irrational and arbitrary, they find it simpler just to use analogous foreign-trade prices charged for similar goods by private corporations to each other in the capitalist markets. When a Soviet planner was asked how CMEA would decide prices when, as promised, the whole world became communist, he answered with a knowing wink, "We will keep one country capitalist just for this purpose." Whether he realized that world market-prices could only be meaningful when there are numerous parties involved was unclear. [4]

The market, then, is the place where meaningful prices can be determined. Let us consider the operation of the market.

The market

In the market, producer and consumer meet. The center of their relationship is the commodity. In particular, they are interested in the use value of the commodity. The ways in which these two parties view the use value of the commodity are different, however. Let us take the example of a watch. The consumer is concerned about the usefulness of the watch. That is, he wants this watch to tell time, and perhaps perform the other functions of a modern watch. He therefore assesses the usefulness which a particular watch being offered on the market has for him.

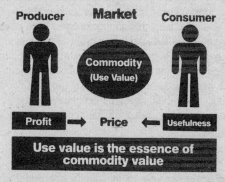

The producer sees things from a different perspective. The use value of the watch is interesting to him because of its potential to return a profit to him. Based on his assessment of its profit-returning potential (profitability) he will assign an asking price for the watch.

Let us say that the consumer comes to the market with $100 in his pocket and a certain idea of the watch he wants. The producer comes with his watch, in which he has invested $70. He asks $85 for the watch. The price is agreeable to the consumer, and the transaction is made.

We see clearly that use value is the essence of commodity value. The price-setting process does not directly entail a calculation of labor hours necessary to produce the commodity.

Why the labor theory of value?

The labor theory of value is presently considered to be a curiosity of the 19th century by most economists of the free world. It only plays an important role in economic thought in Marxist countries or communist parties where prior allegiance to Marxist thought has been given. One may ask, why did Marx saddle himself with a theory developed by the classical economists whom he detested, and rejected since that time by almost all economists?

The answer is that the labor theory of value plays an important role in the overall structure of Marxist economic theories. Marx clearly hoped to win the workers to communism by showing them that all value comes from labor. Some persons have said that Marxist revolutionaries promise the workers ownership of everything if they will join the revolution. It may be more accurately said that Marxism seeks to convince the workers that they are already the rightful owners of everything, and when capitalist economic relationships are destroyed, their ownership will be recognized and acknowledged.

II. The theory of surplus value

Engels, in his speech at Marx's graveside, cited the theory of surplus value as Marx's greatest achievement. Lenin called it the "cornerstone of Marxist economics" and based his theory of imperialism on it. Today in Nicaragua, children are indoctrinated in surplus value theory in primary school texts. Let us examine this important component of Marxist ideology.

The manufacturing process

According to the analysis made by Marx, there are three components which enter into the manufacturing process to yield the product. These are the raw materials, the machinery, and the labor power of the laborers. Let us illustrate these three with the example of the shirtmaking industry cited frequently by Marx in *Das Kapital*.

Manufacturing process

Raw Materials	+	Machinery	+	Labor Power	→	Product
Cloth		Sewing Machine		Sewing		Shirt

Sum of Values

$1	$1	$2	$7

Which capital is "variable" capital?

No	No	Yes

In the shirtmaking process, the raw material would be the cloth, the machinery would be the sewing machine and the labor power would be sewing. The product, of course, is the shirt itself. The role of the Marxist economist is to sum up the values contributed by each of these elements. Let us say in our example that the manufacturer pays $1 for the cloth needed for each shirt. He also sets aside $1 in a depreciation account for every shirt that is made. He can use this money to buy a new sewing machine when the present one is worn out. He also pays his laborers $2 for every shirt they make. Finally, he charges $7 per shirt in the market at the time of the sale. The $7 represents the real value of the shirt as determined by the labor theory of value.

> ...commodities are sold at their real values, and profits are derived from selling them at their values.[5]

Obviously, the sum of the values expended by the capitalist is $4, and yet the amount he recovers from the sale is $7. There is a difference of $3 which the capitalist calls "profit" and keeps for himself. The question posed by Marx is, does that profit belong to the capitalist? If not, to whom does it belong? To answer that question, Marx seeks to determine which of the amounts of capital expended in the manufacturing of the shirt is "variable" capital. That is, which amount of capital is increased in the process of manufacturing the shirt.

According to Marx, the capital spent on raw materials is not variable. It is "constant capital." The value of the raw materials does not undergo any change during the process of manufacturing. Marx also determines that the capital spent on machinery is constant, and not variable. Marx claims that the machine contributes its own exchange value into the products which it makes. To find out how much exchange value went into each product, take the price of the machine and divide it by the number of products manufactured before it wore out. The machine is transferring that much exchange value into each product. Marx also believed that the capitalist is aware of this amount and is setting it aside out of his revenue so that he will be able to buy a new machine when the old one is worn out.

> If we now consider the case of any instrument of labour during the whole period of its service, from the day of its entry into the workshop, till the day of its banishment into the lumber room, we find that during this period its use value has been completely consumed, and therefore its exchange-value has been completely transferred to the product. [6]

If neither the capital invested in raw materials nor that used to depreciate machinery is variable capital, then what is left? The answer is obvious. Marx maintains that the capital used to purchase the worker's labor power is variable capital. It is this capital which gives rise to the profit. The profit comes exclusively from the labor power of the laborer.

In elaborating his theory of surplus value, Marx argued that there are two time periods within each working day. The first few hours of the day are the necessary labor hours. The labor performed by the laborer during this time is sufficient to generate enough exchange value to feed and clothe him and allow him to reproduce, and this is exactly what he will be paid. The remaining hours of the day are the surplus labor hours. The worker, as he works through these hours, is generating surplus value which the capitalist takes from him. In our example, the worker on the sewing machine will generate $2 of exchange value during the necessary labor hours, and that will be his pay. Then, as he finishes the day for which he has sold his labor power, he will generate another $3 of surplus value for the capitalist.

Working day

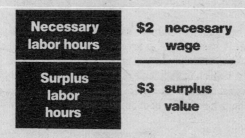

Necessary labor hours	$2 necessary wage
Surplus labor hours	$3 surplus value

Marx claimed that with this insight he had unlocked the secret of capitalist production and could now foresee the demise of capitalism. Marx said that with the $2, the capitalist in our example could buy a day of labor power for its exchange value. Remember that the exchange value is equal to the amount of labor necessary to produce the commodity. In the case of labor power, said Marx, that would be equal to the necessities of life needed to keep the worker alive.

Having purchased the labor power for $2, however, the capitalist is now in a position to see the value of his purchase expand. In our example, the value expands to $5. This $5 is the value of the labor expended by the worker during one day. This value is transferred to the capitalist in the form of the commodities which he claims to be his property. He sells the commodities, and pockets the surplus value.

This is possible, says Marx, because labor power is a unique commodity which expands in value as it is used. The capitalist buys the objectified labor power of the worker, but it is released as living labor of greater exchange value.

The conclusion of this analysis is that profit belongs to the laborer, but is unjustly seized by the capitalist. The laborer is locked into the position of being continually exploited, and the capitalist himself is driven to exploit. If he ceases to exploit his workers, he will be mercilessly destroyed by the other capitalists.

The only way out of the dilemma—the only solution to the contradiction of capitalism—is revolution. When capitalism is destroyed, exploitation will end.

The theory of surplus value has served well as propaganda. It has fueled the fires of revolution, particularly as the basis of Lenin's theory of imperialism. Tragically for those countries which have fallen to communism, however, Marxist economics and the theory of surplus value are a horrible failure as a functioning economic system.

III. The impact of Marxist economic theories in communist countries

In the Soviet Union and other communist countries, attempts have been made to make Marx's economic theories into law. In brief, the application of those theories has been disastrous for the Soviet economy.

The official Soviet economy does not allow price setting

and free exchange of goods in the market. Production is centrally planned. Factories depend on central planners to supply them with goods, and they in turn must fulfill quotas given by the central planners. The production process is thus insulated from signals from consumers which show their desires and needs. The result is inefficiency and failure to meet the needs of consumers. If plans call for the production of shoes, shoes are produced even if people need coats.

Lawrence Minard and James W. Michaels describe the ills of central planning in an article in *Forbes*.

> At Alma-Ata we visit a carpet factory. It is run by a brisk and efficient woman, Klara Nijasbayeva. By American standards it is quite small, producing about 1.2 million square yards per year with 1100 workers. Carpets are in great demand in the Soviet Union, and these seem of good quality. Nijasbayeva says she could easily sell many times the current output if she had the capital and resources. She is having trouble keeping workers, too. Why not raise the price of carpets to what the market will bear, we ask? That way the factory derives extra money for expansion and for bidding raw material and workers away from other factories. The director shakes her head. "Nyet, nyet. That would be unfair to workers in other factories. One worker would be exploiting another." In theory no one gets exploited, but few people get carpets. Those who do manage to get carpets probably bribed a shop employee. Meanwhile, wool and labor that might have gone to make much wanted carpets go instead to make shoddy jackets, which hang unsold in Moscow's GUM department store. [7]

Empirical arguments against a centrally planned labor-value economy

It is interesting to note that within the Soviet Union, almost all agricultural lands are controlled by the state. However, most of the Soviet farmers also have access to small, private plots which comprise less than 4 percent of the country's arable land. It is estimated that these plots produce 25 per cent of the Soviet Union's total crop output, an enormous proportion in comparison to collective and state sectors.[8] Clearly, the Soviet system fails to give the people the necessary incentive to work for the state.

Another example is China. In the late 1970s, Zhao Ziyang, the first secretary of the Communist Party in Si Chuan province, began an experiment whereby he permitted six factories to keep a portion of their profit. They could use that profit for reinvestment and new capital equipment or for the purpose of distributing bonuses to the workers. They also could market directly any surplus product, or diversify into new products and seek out export markets. Likewise, they had the right to reward productive workers and punish those who were not productive. Today that program has expanded from six factories to 6,600 factories which comprise more then 45 percent of the national industrial production! In December 1984, communist Chinese spokesmen went so far as to warn against rigid adherence to Marxist doctrines.[9]

The Soviet economy today

From 1951-1955, the Soviet GNP showed an annual growth rate of 6.0 percent. This rate has been steadily decreasing since that time. From 1976-1980, the rate of growth of the Soviet economy was less than 3 percent.[10]

Today Eastern Europe is $80 billion in debt to the Western world. Many people say that if the West were to cut off its support, it would be only a matter of time before these economies crumble.

Why is the Soviet bloc in deep economic trouble? Essentially, it stems from the Soviet Union's dogmatic adherence to Marxist economic principles. To cover up for the inoperability of the Marxist economic system, its adherents have opted for corruption and graft.

In *USSR: The Corrupt Society*, Konstantin Simis points

out that there is no room within the Soviet society for those who do not accept corruption. The same is mentioned by Ilja Zemtsov in *Corruption in the Soviet Union*. Simis emphasizes that within the Soviet Union anybody who is really honest about why he cannot fulfill production quotas is seen as being an enemy of the state.

Simis cites the example of an appliance factory which was expected by the government to exceed its production quota for the year. When it came down to the last few days, it was apparent the goal could not be fulfilled. In order to cover for this, the management collected the appliances of the people in the village where the factory was located, repainted them, and presented them as part of the yearly production. A few days later the appliances were returned to their owners.

As a result of this achievement, the manager of the factory received a higher post within the government. In addition to a huge bonus, his second man became the manager of the factory. The technicians also received a very handsome bonus. The workers received some praise and an evening where they had an opportunity to get drunk.

In *Analysis of a Spector*, French Sovietologist Alain Besancon concludes that the Soviet economy is, in fact, a disaster. Besancon notes, for example, that the Soviets proclaim that they are the largest steel producer in the world, but it is not at all clear where the yearly production of 145 million tons of steel is going. This quantity is equivalent to the joint output of Japan and Germany which together manufacture 12 million cars. But the Soviet Union produces less automobiles per year than Spain, it has only a slightly larger railway system than India, it has fewer paved and developed highways than France and even in terms of weaponry, its tank production cannot consume more than a few million tons of the steel that it supposedly produces.

Besancon concludes that these 145 million tons represent, first of all, the production of actual steel; secondly, the production of inferior steel; thirdly, the production of reject steel; fourthly, the production of steel for rust; fifthly, the production of pseudo-steel; and finally, the pseudo production of steel.

The notion that the Soviet Union is the second economic power in the world is also a myth. Besancon points out that the Soviet Union has fewer telephones than Spain and fewer automobiles than Brazil. Luxuries such as computers or even photocopiers are virtually unknown.

Besancon mocks the idea that the USSR has "a standard of living a little higher than that of Spain." Although the Spanish worker may need almost the same amount of time on the job as his Russian counterpart in order to buy a television, a pair of shoes, or a vacuum cleaner, Besancon notes that there are obvious differences.

In the case of the USSR, we are talking about the kind of television "one would buy in the flea market." When we are speaking of shoes, we are "talking about the kind of shoes a Moroccan migrant worker would refuse to wear." When speaking of a vacuum cleaner, we would be talking of one that only "works when you kick it."

Besancon suggests that, instead of Spain, it might be more appropriate to say the USSR has "a standard of living a little higher than that of Bangladesh."

IV. Critique of the theory of surplus value

We can group our criticism of Marx's theory of surplus value under three headings.

1. Oversimplified

Marx conceived of the manufacturing process as consisting largely of three components: raw materials, machinery and labor. This, however, is too simple a view. Marx shows very little comprehension of the role of the investor. For Marx, the investor is a capitalist. As such, he is an exploiter, and if he exploits ruthlessly enough, he will be able to pocket huge sums of money.

In reality, the role of the investor is much more demanding, more creative, more risky, and many other things. The investor must determine where and when to invest capital. He has no guarantees of success, and greater ruthlessness is not necessarily an assurance of greater effectiveness.

There are other key roles as well. These include management and secretarial, as well as inventors, engineers, researchers and purchasers. All of these must function well together if there is to be success in manufacturing.

The Product Goes to the Market

Yet this is only the first step. The product must now be taken to the market. As we have already seen, the Marxist conception of the market place is extremely inadequate. For Marx, the price was pre-fixed by the number of labor hours even before the product is taken to be sold. The profit of the capitalist is thus automatic. Reality is rudely different. Price is determined in the market, and nothing is automatic.

Prices depend on a number of factors in the market place, but chief among these are supply and demand. When there is an oversupply, the price falls. When there is a scarcity, the price rises.

In his text, *Free to Choose*, Milton Friedman mentions three important functions performed by prices in organizing economic activity:

First, they transmit information; second, they provide an incentive to adopt those methods of production that are least costly and thereby use available resources for the most highly valued purposes; third, they determine who gets how much of the product—the distribution of income.[11]

Perhaps even more fundamental in the price-setting process is product quality. If a product is of poor quality, there will be no sale no matter how many labor hours have been invested in production. (Where there is an extreme scarcity of consumer goods, such as the Soviet Union and other places, consumers may buy regardless of quality and regardless of their own personal needs. In the former case, they have no choice. In the latter, they buy when there is an opportunity and barter later with other purchasers.)

Even if we were to grant to Marx that there are only three components in manufacturing, we still find that he makes a serious oversimplification. Marx claims that labor power is the only source of profit, and that capital invested in raw materials and machinery is constant capital. We observe, however, that capital invested in machinery is not constant capital, but is in fact capable of multiplying itself, even without labor power.

Manufacturing process

Raw Materials + **Machinery** + **Labor Power** → **Product**

also can produce profit   **only source of profit**

Fully automated machines, such as a tape recorder assembly machine in the Matsushita Electric Company, are highly productive. This particular machine does the work previously done by six employees. The employees were given other less tedious jobs in the same company.

Another example is provided by robot welding machines in the Honda Motor Company. These machines are able to perform 130 welds in 45 seconds, a job which formerly required 30 people 32 minutes. Furthermore, this particular assembly line job was regarded by auto workers as one of the most uncomfortable and dangerous.

Marx viewed machinery under capitalism as an instrument of exploitation, and failed to understand the tremendous potential which machines have for liberating the worker from tedium at the same time that they generate revenues for the manufacturer. A machine is not constant capital, but is able to generate profit by amplifying the creative power of a human being.

2. Unrealistic

Marx condemned "capitalism," exalted "socialism," and predicted the coming of "communism." Yet the simple fact remains that development requires capital. This is true in capitalist countries, socialist countries, and countries such as the Soviet Union which exhibit a type of state-monopoly capitalism.

The manufacturing process can be said to require the elements of capital, management and labor. These three must act together to give the product, which in turn is taken to the market. In the market, there is no guarantee of commercial success. This depends largely on whether the manufacturer has been able to satisfy some need of the consumer. If the sale is realized, the manufacturer recieves a profit.

In the Marxist perspective, profit is evil and a crime. In the CAUSA view, however, profit is not evil. Profit is a reward which society returns to those who increase social wealth by applying their human creativity. Profit is good, but profit must be shared in a fair way with all those who join in contributing their creativity to serve society. Too often, this is not done. Herein lies the "crime of the capitalist." This crime is not in making profit, but in the frequent failure to give a fair share of profit to all those who deserve it.

This crime has resulted in a tremendous amount of resentment being generated toward businessmen and corporations. Such resentment is fertile ground for communism.

It should be remembered, however, that profit is not guaranteed. Those who demand a fair share of any profits generated must also be willing to accept a fair share of losses.

3. Incomplete

Marx said very little about the organization of communism, his ideal economic system. In the *Critique of the Gotha Program*, however, he wrote the slogan which has become popularized as the simple description of life under communism. "From each according to his ability, to each according to his needs."

This slogan has appeared to many to be a beautiful description of an ideal society, and it must be admitted that there is something poetic about it. We need to inquire further, however, to understand how such a slogan could be reality.

From each according to his ability, to each according to his needs.

Goes against human nature:

1. Desire to receive: self-improvement
2. Desire to contribute: creativity

Who determines—Abilities?
—Needs?

1. God   2. Self   3. Third party
The State

How can abilities be determined? More specifically, who can determine what a person's abilities are? Furthermore, who can determine a person's needs? We may intuitively feel that some things are necessities, and others are luxuries, but who can definitively state such things? Someone may feel that the only transportation they need is a pair of shoes, while someone else feels they need a bicycle. When they have a bicycle, they may feel they need a car. When they have a car, they may feel that their time is so valuable that they need a helicopter. Who can say?

Perhaps if there was a way for God to make known to each individual what was expected of him and what he would be allowed, we could each accept that. Since God has not made such things widely known, we may feel most comfortable making such decisions for ourselves. At least then we have no one else to blame. In the communist world, however, these decisions are made by a third party, the State. The State undertakes to determine the abilities and needs of the people through an elaborate system of quotas and allotments.

This would be fine if man were a machine. It is easy to measure the needs and abilities of a machine. When applied to human beings, however, it does not work. It goes against the most fundamental aspects of human nature. We have spoken of the nature of everyone to give and to receive. The desire to receive in a general sense may be equated to the natural desire for self-improvement. The material aspects of self-improvement are denied by the communist system.

Human nature also exhibits the desire to contribute, the aspect of human creativity. Creativity and total personal development are stifled under communism.

V. Conclusion

There can be no question that God, as the creator of human beings and the Father of humankind, wishes to provide for His children in every way. It must therefore be God's Will that an economic system be established which offers each person the opportunity to be well-cared for and satisfied in an economic sense. In the past, it has appeared to many thinkers that centralized planning would do away with economic ills and be more efficient than a free-market based economy. The dismal failures of the socialist economic experiments of this century have now shown this to be false. Highly centralized and planned economies do not work. They thwart human nature and are wasteful of resources rather than efficient.

Socialist systems abrogate the rights of private property, exert state controls and deny individual free choice. In doing so, they directly oppose three basic aspects of human nature: (1) the desire to better oneself, (2) creativity, and (3) the drive to achieve. Because they oppose these basic human traits, they are sure to fail.

God has given us a model illustrating the proper balance between central coordination and individual freedom in the form of the human body itself. We interpret the functioning of the body in human social and economic terms, holding fast to three basic principles: the sacred dignity of the person, the social nature of human life, and the obligation to assign social decisions to the level of authority best suited to take them.

The human body: model of an ideal economic system

The human body exhibits a beautiful and harmonious balance between individual freedom and central coordination. Within the body, each cell, although it forms part of some body organ or tissue, is required to maintain itself autonomously. That is, the cell is responsible for its own metabolism, and determines how much nutrients and oxygen it will draw from the bloodstream. The body, then, operates in accord with principles like those found in a free market system.

There is, however, a central coordinating of the body as a whole. The body exists in order to support the overall purpose of the individual person. The individual exists in order to love God and his fellow human beings. The brain and central nervous system coordinate the body's activities in pursuit of this purpose. In this way, the parts of the body are called upon to function in harmony. Although centrally coordinated, the organic functions of the body are largely self-regulating. The stomach resists attempts to over-stuff it. The liver responds to shortages in the blood, by releasing stored-up nutrients. The heart and lungs adjust their rates according to the body demands. The more we examine in detail the functioning

of the body, the more we see a remarkable balance between central coordination and individual autonomy and
decision-making. It is the position of CAUSA that the
body is a God-given model of a proper economic system.

The free market system

The free market system is the best system which
has been devised to try to accommodate the basic human
desires mentioned above. The desire to better oneself is
served by the opportunity which free markets give to
material incentives. The desire to be creative is served
by the freedom of the market. And the desire to achieve
is served by the opportunities created for fair competition.

The free market system, or the system of free enterprise, is the system which most closely resembles the
functioning of the human body. The free market system
allows individuals to draw from the market as they see
fit, but allows for intervention if there is a serious disorder. The system maintains medical forces to come to
the aid of stricken individuals, and security forces to
enforce laws made for the good of the whole. These forces
are only called into action as needed, however, and the
system generally functions without them.

In the free market system, the state is strictly limited. One of the clearest limitations on the state is the
principle of private property. The right to private property is a natural right, one which is further justified in
the light of the common good, for private property en-
courages the right ordering of the use of goods, providing
incentives for good stewardship and imposing upon all
responsibilities to respect the rights and property of others. Its existence is reflected in the ancient commandment, "Thou shalt not steal."

The right of private property is not absolute, however. Those who own property have responsibilities to

God, to their communities, and to their fellow human
beings. Thomas Aquinas once wrote that a human being
"ought to possess external things not as his own but...so
that...he is ready to communicate them to others in their
need. Hence, the Apostle says (1 Tim 6:17-18): 'Charge
the rich of this world...to give easily, to communicate to
others.'" Owners are temporary stewards of a portion of
the earth, and each one of us will one day give to the
Creator an account of our stewardship.

Only a free market system allows economic agents
regular, reliable, ordinary liberties. Only a market system respects the free creativity of every human person,
and for this reason respects private property, incentives
(rather than coercion), freedom of choice, and the other
institutions of a free economy. A market system obliges
its participants to be "other-regarding," that is, to observe
the freely expressed needs and desires of others, in order
to serve them. A market system is not morally validated
because it is productive, for any economy can achieve a
certain productivity through coercion. A market system
is moral because it is the only system built upon the
liberty of its participants.

The market is not an "Invisible Hand" which makes
everything right. A market is only an arena which provides us an opportunity. It allows us liberty of conscience.
What we make of it determines our character and prepares us to meet our Judge and live out our eternal lives.

Critique of Western economies

Western societies may be considered to be composed
of three integrated systems: an active political system,
a dynamic economic system, and a vital moral and cultural system. It was Karl Marx who first named the
economic system of "bourgeois democracy" (which he regarded as a fraud) "capitalism." He did so in order to

condemn it. In this chapter, we have rejected Marx's critique of free economies. At the same time, we must look at our Western society to see what is the real source of its ills.

It is the view of CAUSA that the cause of the ills of the economic system lies in the degeneration of the underlying moral and cultural system. Marx held that morality was part of a "superstructure" rising above the economic "base," but in the view of CAUSA, *the moral system is the base*. Because of basic flaws in human nature, there exist exploitation and abuse in the economic sphere. These flaws are part of man's "fallen nature." They are a result of the human fall from God and the multiplication of human sin. They are the nature of alienated man, and it is part of the task of religion to instruct people in the ways to overcome their selfish fallen nature.

The CAUSA solution

Complacency, non-belief and particularism have handicapped our society today in its function of guiding people to be unselfish and Godly. CAUSA maintains that a spiritual solution is necessary. By spiritual solution, we mean a solution involving the human heart and spirit. We need to experience God, and this will bring about an internal revolution of man.

We in the West may take instruction from the remarkable economic miracles which have occurred in recent years in Asia. The emergence of Japan from the ashes of destruction, and the multiplication of many "Japans," such as South Korea, Taiwan, Singapore and Hong Kong, are a testimony to the importance of moral, cultural and spiritual factors. In particular, these societies adhere to a strong "family ethic." The society as a whole is regarded as an extended family. A business enterprise, for example, is regarded as a family. Workers are not laid off in times of crisis, but rather the entire family suffers through while providing for its own. In return, the enterprise demands loyalty from its employees. In this way, much job-hopping is avoided, and this may benefit the enterprise greatly.

Amazingly, these are societies which are based upon Confucianism rather than Christian ethics. Because Christianity views God as the Father or Parent and humanity as the children of God, one would expect that such family ethics would be a part of our Western societies. This would be the case were it not for the predominance of materialist thinking in the West. It is this viewpoint which must be transformed and replaced by a Godly viewpoint. Although in name we are Christian, in practice, we have often been materialists.

The family itself is the building block of a free society. One can understand neither democracy nor a market economy apart from the sound structure of family life. It is no accident that totalitarians always seek to infiltrate, weaken and destroy the integrity of the family, sowing mistrust and suspicion in this sanctuary of human trust and love. Both in person life and in the reliable functioning of a society, the family is a crucial institution. It is a bridge between personal morality and social morality, the school of both personal virtues and social virtues, and without it, neither personal life nor economic life can survive and prosper.

CAUSA calls for freedom in family life and freedom in the market place. Above all, CAUSA calls upon us to become the unselfish and virtuous persons who can bring God's love and justice into the society, nation and world. The best economic system for the present time is a free market system run by God-centered men and women.

CHAPTER FOUR NOTES

1. Leszek Kolakowski, *Main Currents of Marxism*, Vol. I, Oxford University Press, 1978, p.330.
2. Mark Blaug, "Economics," in *The New Encyclopaedia Britannica*, 1983, V.6, p. 265.
3. Let us assume for this example that it is possible to calculate labor hours, although we will later show that this cannot be done.
4. Marshall I. Goldman, *USSR in Crisis*, New York, Norton, 1983, p. 50.
5. Karl Marx, *Wage-Labour and Capital, Value Price and Profit*, New York, International Publishers, 1983, p.37
6. Marx, *Capital*, New York, International Publishers, 1967, Vol. I, p.203.
7. Lawrence Minard and James W. Michaels, "Why workers won't work in the Soviet Union," *Forbes*, December 6, 1982, p.144.
8. Goldman, p. 83.
9. *The New York Times*, December 8, 1984.
10. Goldman, p.47.
11. Milton and Rose Friedman, *Free to Choose*, Avon Books, New York, 1980, p.6.

IMPERIALISM AND THE THIRD INTERNATIONAL

"No nation can be free if it oppresses other nations."
V. I. Lenin[1]

Without Vladimir Ulyanov Lenin, the social theories of Marx might have fared the same as those of Saint-Simon, Fourier or Owen. Marx would probably be seen today as just another social thinker whose writings could be found in a remote corner of the municipal library. Because of Lenin's crucial contribution to communist theory, most radical thinkers see his work as a necessary prolongation or addendum to Marxist thought. In this section, we will focus on Lenin and his view of imperialism.

I. Marxism in search of a mentor

With the death of Karl Marx in 1883 and the death of Frederick Engels in 1895, Europe's communist movement needed a mentor who could serve as an interpreter of Marx's writings.

A. Bernstein

After the death of Engels, a large portion of the Social Democratic (communist) movement gravitated toward Eduard Bernstein (1850-1932). Bernstein was a German thinker who had followed Marxism since having been influenced by Engels' *Anti-Duhring*. For several years, he had worked directly with Engels and was recognized as an expert in Marxist theory.

Bernstein, nevertheless, maintained that there were certain shortcomings in Marx's thought. He pointed to the three laws of economic movement which Marx had observed in capitalist society:

(1) The centralization of capital. Marx had predicted that as time went by, capital would become more and more concentrated in the hands of a few capitalists. This would occur because of wealthy capitalists resorting to unscrupulous practices such as bribery and selling at artificially reduced prices in order to destroy their competition. Likewise only the most prosperous capitalists could purchase the latest machinery. Ultimately, all capital would be controlled by a tiny minority.

(2) Decrease of profits. In accord with the theory of surplus value, Marx maintained that the worker constitutes the only source of profit in the production process. Marx recognized that companies were purchasing more and more modern machinery and replacing workers. By reducing the number of workers, Marx maintained that the capitalists eliminated the only real source of profit. Therefore, the rise in machinery and the decline in workers would cause a decrease of profits.

(3) Increase of poverty. Marx maintained that the concentration of capital would force owners of small companies to abandon their businesses and return to the labor force. The increased use of machinery would multiply unemployment and poverty. Marx predicted that the misery of their living conditions would lead both new and old members of the working force to revolt against the capitalist system.

Marx's Laws of Economic Movement

1. **Centralization of Capital**
2. **Decrease of Profits**
3. **Increase of Poverty**

Bernstein's perception

By the end of the 19th century, Bernstein concluded that Marx's predictions were not coming to pass. In fact, profits increased and the situation of the workers improved by the end of the 19th century. Bernstein, therefore, maintained that Marx's economic analysis was incorrect and unscientific. He likewise challenged Marx's view of history and even concluded that Marxism was great not because of the dialectic, but "in spite of" it. Bernstein thus denied the scientific necessity for a violent revolution and instead advocated, as expressed by the title of his book, not the need for revolutionary but *Evolutionary Socialism* (1889).[2]

Bernstein's Perception

End of 19th Century

1. **No Decrease of Profits**
2. **No Increase of Poverty**

Bernstein's theories achieved a broad level of popularity. Initially his positions were refuted by orthodox Marxists such as the German Karl Kautsky. In 1899 Kautsky attacked Bernstein in *Bernstein and the Social-Democratic Program, an Anti-Critic.* By 1910, however, Kautsky had changed his views and came to support Bernstein's revision of Marxism. Followers of Kautsky and Bernstein spoke of a "return to Kant." They concluded that society would not be transformed spontaneously through revolution. Individuals needed to undergo a moral change.

This perspective was naturally interpreted as being

"idealistic" or "utopian" by Marxist purists as well as by
Lenin, who claimed that societal transformation was contingent upon violent revolution.

As time went by, Karl Kautsky became the foremost
political figure in favor of this revision of Marx. Lenin,
therefore, referred to those who adopted this position as
"Kautskyans."

B. The Communist Internationals

By the beginning of the 20th century, the socialist movement had already proceeded through various stages which
will be briefly examined here.

First International
(1869-1876)

Second International
(1889-1914)

Third International
(1919)

1. The First International (1869-1876)

The First International was headed by Karl Marx himself.
It was not at all limited to supporters of Marx's theory; it
involved various groups committed to workers' rights.
However, because of Marx's control, the First International's
basic direction tended to reflect only Marx's opinions in its
policy-making. Marx himself was a conflictive, impulsive, and
scattered personality. Marx's sarcasm and his stubborn nature
provoked the First International's demise.

2. The Second International (1889-1914)

The second attempt to organize the socialist movement

was far less structured. It recognized that socialism had to be related to the character of each nation. There was not a single path to socialism.

The Second International split, first, because of disputes about membership and again later due to different socialists' attitudes toward World War I. Kautsky's supporters wanted a very broad definition of membership. Kautsky felt that essentially anyone who supported the basic worker movement could be viewed as a social democrat or communist. Vladimir Lenin, on the other hand, had a far more restricted view of membership. He wanted membership restricted to a highly disciplined revolutionary core who could educate and raise cadres in that same tradition. Basically the debate was quantity vs. quality.

Individuals such as Lenin also advocated international socialist solidarity in opposing World War I because of its "imperialist" nature, whereas Karl Kautsky and most other principal leaders of the Second International opted to support their respective nations during that conflict.

3. The Third International (1919)— An Affirmation of Lenin's Views

The Third International served basically as an affirmation of Lenin's principles and his particular interpretation and

What is a member of the Communist Party?

Lenin's View— Disciplined, totally dedicated individual

Kautsky's View— Any sympathizers

application of Marxism. Almost all the participants at the
Third International were Russians. Lenin sardonically
denounced the Second International, referring to it as the
"Yellow" International.[3]

C. Lenin

Born in 1870, Vladimir Ulyanov (Lenin) had acquainted
himself with the basic writings of Marx by the age of 18. By
his early 20s, Lenin acted as the coordinating point for most
communist activity within Russia. A survey of several of his
key revolutionary writings reveals the particular character of
Lenin's interpretation of Marx (as affirmed by the Third
International). Here we will just briefly touch on a few of the
major themes:

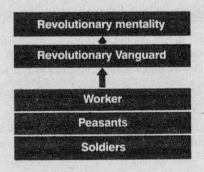

(1) *What is to be Done?* (1902) In this text, Lenin concludes that workers by themselves cannot achieve a proletarian consciousness. They need a professional revolutionary
vanguard to educate and prepare them for revolution. The
vanguard should have a restricted membership and operate
on the basis of absolute secrecy. In his text Lenin also advocates jumping from feudalism to socialism. For Lenin there
was no need to pass through the stage of capitalism prior to
advancing to socialism.

(2) *State and Revolution* (1917) This text was written

just prior to the October Revolution during Lenin's exile in Finland. Here Lenin speaks of the process by which society moves from a bourgeois state to communism. Lenin maintains that the state which has served as a special repressive force benefitting the bourgeoisie must now be replaced by a state with a special repressive force committed to benefitting the proletariat. This constitutes what Marx and Lenin defined as the "dictatorship of the proletariat."

This dictatorship, Lenin insisted, will remain during the socialist stages and gradually the state, in accord with Marxist principles, would wither away. During this process, the communist party would serve as the vanguard leading the whole people to socialism.

(3) *"Left Wing" Communism, an Infantile Disorder* (1920) Here Lenin clarifies the nature of Marxist morality. Lenin called for iron discipline in the party and for an attempt to win the proletariat of all nations. Lenin emphasized that communists must work on two levels, one being legal or parliamentary, the other illegal and employing subversive or underground methods aimed at advancing the cause. He advocated compromise with the bourgeoisie if it permits communism to advance. Statesmen should measure and prepare the appropriate moment for the proletariat to seize power. Lenin maintains that the right time was a moment when the ruling class is in a state of governmental crisis. Likewise at the same moment the "exploited" would find themselves in a state of crisis.

II. Lenin's view of imperialism

"National liberation," "self-determination," and "imperialism" are terms frequently encountered within socialist and revolutionary circles. This terminology and these concepts are found in Lenin's view of imperialism, particularly as developed in the text *Imperialism, the Highest Stage of Capitalism.* Lenin wrote this book in 1916 with a very controlled style. In that way, he succeeded in having it accepted by the Czarist censors. We should not, therefore, feel that

Visible political activity

**Subversive political
and
terrorist activity**

Imperialism, the Highest Stage of Capitalism is an exhaustive presentation of Lenin's views.

Lenin's writings between 1913 and 1917 constitute the basis for a new theory of world revolution. Lenin frequently wrote on imperialism, and his views can be seen developing in such diverse writings as *Backward Europe and Advanced Asia* (1913), *Theses on War* (1914), *On the Slogan for a United States of Europe* (1915), and *The Socialist Revolution and the Right of Nations to Self-Determination* (1916).

Lenin's views contradicted Marxist orthodoxy and maintained that revolution would not first occur in the developed industrial nations but in backward countries such as Russia.

Lenin's writings on imperialism were influenced by German Marxist Rudolf Hilferding's *Finance Capital*, written in 1910, and by J.A. Hobson's *Imperialism*, written in 1902. Interestingly, Hobson was a Christian reformer and Hilferding eventually allied himself with Kautsky.

Lenin's analysis of imperialism justifies the failure of Marx's predictions to come to pass. Lenin maintains that a delay in profits decreasing and poverty increasing is to be expected. In *Imperialism, the Highest Stage of Capitalism*, Lenin shows that there is in fact a centralization of capital, or what he refers to as a "concentration of production." He gives U.S. Steel, Rhine-Westphalen Coal Company, General Electric, and others as examples to show that step-by-step various corporations are forming monopolies.

Lenin agrees that the other two laws of economic movement mentioned above — the decrease of profits and an increase of poverty — have not been occurring as predicted by Marx. This is because, Lenin asserts, a new strategy has been developed between financiers and entrepreneurs. Through their collaboration, Lenin maintains that a new financial strategy has been formulated focusing on the "exportation of capital." Lenin notes that the great capital needs of the developing world are being met by the financiers of the developed world. They are able to charge high interest rates and also dictate what the borrowing nations can purchase with the funds they receive. Furthermore, Lenin maintains that a theft of raw material is occurring because the imperialist powers, such as the United States, Britain, and France are not giving a just remuneration for the raw materials they receive from the developing nations.[4]

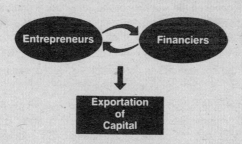

Lenin presents his observation that the world has been divided into colonized spheres of control. For instance, Britain controls a certain sector of the world and its market. Britain determines what can be imported from those colonies and what can be exported to them. France also has its sector. The world has been divided among imperialist powers. Lenin maintains that the only way the markets of the world can be changed is by means of war. For that reason, Lenin defines World War I as an imperialist war. The purpose motivating the war is that certain nations are trying to extend their colonial influence, thereby enhancing their economies.[5]

By exporting capital into these nations, exorbitant profits reach the developed world, according to Lenin. The workers of the developed world receive a small portion of those profits, as a kind of bribe. It is this bonus that is preventing these workers from awakening to their exploited condition.[6] Likewise, they remain indifferent to the condition of their fellow workers in the developing world. Leninism concludes that the only way to awaken the workers of the developed world is to end imperialist domination of the Third World.[7] As Che Guevara said:

American workers... cannot gain clear consciousness of their exploitation as long as they continue to get the crumbs which North American imperialism tosses to them from the feast.[8]

To awaken the workers of the developed world, national liberation movements must, therefore, succeed in cutting off the Third World markets of capitalist nations such as the United States.[9] Leninism maintains that it is the responsibility of the communists to defend the self-determination of all peoples.

Although colonialism has largely disappeared since World War II, communists maintain that the Third World still finds itself in a state of de facto imperialism.[10] For example, the United States controls the economy of much of Latin America. For that reason communists want to support national liberation movements throughout Latin America — their ultimate target being the United States.

Che Guevara insisted that national liberation militants need not be taught Marxism until after their nations have been "liberated."[11] In the examples of Nicaragua, Cuba, or even Vietnam, one can see that this has indeed been the case. For example, in Cuba, people such as Huber Matos and William Morgan fought for "national liberation." They did not fight for communism. Yet that is what they received due to Castro's application of Leninist strategy.

III. Critique of Lenin's view of imperialism

In many parts of the world, young men and women have dedicated their lives to revolution. Many of them have died for their cause. If we study the cases of Nicaragua, El Salvador, Vietnam or Angola, we can recognize that people were stimulated to participate in revolution, not because the workers were being deprived of "surplus value" (Karl Marx's view), but because of a commitment to "national liberation." This view largely has its origins in the writings of Lenin.

It is important, therefore, to determine whether or not Lenin was justified in his position. Let us consider the matter, point by point.

> **Critique of Lenin's Theory of Imperialism**
>
> 1. **Centralization of capital?**
> 2. **Bribery of the workers of developed world through exportation of capital and exhorbitant prices to Third World?**

A. Centralization of capital?

If we observe the phenomenon occurring in the developed world, we find that instead of a centralization of capital, a distribution of capital is occurring. Today many major United States corporations such as General Motors, IBM and U.S. Steel have literally millions of stockholders. Many of those stockholders are workers who participate in profit-sharing programs. In fact, the number of "capitalists," instead of decreasing, is multiplying. Lenin emphasized that to control a corporation, a single shareholder needed at least 40 percent of the stocks.[12] Today there are many corporations, such as the Chase Manhattan Bank or General Electric, where there is no one who controls anywhere near that amount of stock.

Marx predicted that centralization of capital would occur through various unethical business practices. In his analysis of history, he saw government as a superstructure to protect capitalist interests. However, by 1914, the United States had enacted the Clayton Anti-Trust Act in order to discourage monopolies. Similar measures were taken in Europe. Marx's and Lenin's affirmations are, therefore, denied first by the tendency towards distribution of capital, and secondly, by government measures aimed at blocking the formation of monopolies.

B. Export of capital?

Although the concept of export of capital is a key aspect of Lenin's theory of imperialism, it cannot be justified historically. Specifically, in contrast to Lenin's claims, export of capital cannot be shown to be characteristic of a late stage of capitalism.[13]

Lenin maintained that the export of capital correlated with a capitalism that had become "over-ripe." Tied in with the concentration of capital and the control of the domestic markets was the concept that the profitable areas in the domestic market become saturated. This stagnation leads to the imperialistic export of capital abroad, and a consequent struggle for territories. However, there is not any reason that export of capital cannot correlate with, and be the result of, a booming domestic market.[14] One can note that:

More than 40 percent of the capital exported from
Britain in the hundred years before 1914 was used to
finance railway investment overseas. British-financed
railways abroad was not only the result of booming
conditions at home, but also the cause of further
domestic expansion. [15]

It is notable that the greatest amount of foreign investment for Britain and other developed countries, at the height
of their colonization, went actually to developed countries,
and not their colonies or underdeveloped countries. [16]

Historically, export of capital has actually been a feature
of capitalism at all stages, even where the least tendency
toward any monopoly has been seen, [17] and several free market countries that were acquiring territories were actually
capital importers. In addition, imperialism is not limited to
capitalism. It is found in feudal societies such as the Roman
Empire and it is also practiced in socialist societies such as
the Soviet Union. [18]

C. Bribery of the workers of the developed world?

Was there in fact a bribery of the workers as Lenin
maintained? It is interesting to note the case of France and
Scandinavia. At the turn of the century, the standard of living
of the worker in France (a nation allegedly with colonies
enough to provide bribes for its workers), was inferior to that
of the Scandinavian worker (Scandinavia meaning the nation
existing prior to the division of Sweden and Norway, which
did not have colonies). This suggests inaccuracies in
Lenin's analyses.

D. World markets controlled by developed nations?

The theory that more world markets are controlled by
more developed nations is basically not true in the Free World.
For example, prior to World War II, Japan had many colonies.
Because of the war, Japan lost all of those colonies, yet today
Japan is flourishing. The overriding factors in the Free World

> **Lenin's Theory of Imperialism**
>
> ⌃
>
> **Marx's Laws of Economic Movement**
>
> ⌃
>
> **Theory of Surplus Value "Cornerstone" of Marxist Economics**

are not "control" or domination, they are factors such as quality and demand.

E. The false foundation of Marxist economics

Lenin constructed a theory, but his theory was built on Marx's theory of surplus value, a faulty foundation. The Soviets maintain that Lenin's economic theories are a logical extension of Marx's economic theory. Lenin's theory of imperialism, in fact, served to defend Marx's three laws of economic movement. As we know, Marx's three laws of economic movement are based on his theory of surplus value, a theory that Lenin maintained was "the *cornerstone* of Marxist economics."[19] However, we have seen that this theory of surplus value is false. Lenin constructed his thesis on this faulty "cornerstone." Because Marx's three laws of economic movement, based on the theory of surplus value, are false, Lenin's view of imperialism (a defense of these three laws) must also be false.

While Lenin uses imperialism in support of Marx's three laws of economic movement, it is very interesting to note the divergence of Marx and Lenin in their views of imperialism. Lenin effectively reversed the traditional Marxist view in that he considered imperialism to be an unwelcome, reactionary force. Marx and Engels, and even Lenin in his earlier days,

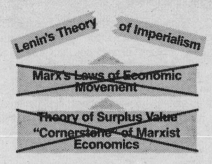

Lenin's Theory of Imperialism

Marx's Laws of Economic Movement

Theory of Surplus Value
"Cornerstone" of Marxist Economics

considered imperialistic expansion to serve a valuable, progressive role in expanding economic advancement throughout the world.[20] According to Bill Warren, himself a Marxist:

> ... the proposition that imperialism was reactionary,
> in Marxist terms, could be sustained only by clouding
> the issues in ambiguity, by distorting history and
> rejecting some fundamental precepts of Marxist
> economics.[21]

F. Imperialism and exploitation of developing nations

There is not any clear reason why imperialism and exploitation of the Third World should necessarily correlate with
capitalism. More likely, any such exploitation can be considered to coincide with selfishness of nations or the greed of
the people in power. Capitalistic nations may or may not act
imperialistically, depending upon their greed. Not only capitalistic but any kind of powerful government can act imperialistically and can exploit other countries.[22] History has been
replete with examples of strong nations subjugating weaker
ones. In fact, perhaps the most imperialistic nation exploiting
the Third World today may well be the totalitarian USSR, a
nation which ironically decries "imperialism." This will be
elaborated upon in the following section.

G. National liberation

The kind of national liberation which Lenin called for, and which present-day Marxists support, often appears directed less toward the "freeing" of countries than towards sovietizing them.

At the time of the Bolshevik revolution, Vladimir Lenin advocated an end to Russian imperialism. Lenin maintained that each nation has the right to determine its own destiny. Today we recognize that this is not the phenomenon which is occurring in our world. The classic example for this is the case of Somalia.

In 1960, Somalia gained its independence. It had been divided among Italy, Britain and Ethiopia. Britain and Italy gave independence to Somalia, but the Emperor Haile Selassie of Ethiopia decided to keep Ogaden, which was the Ethiopian-controlled part of Somalia. In 1974, Somalia became a communist country. Somalia then proceeded in a war against Ethiopia in order to regain Ogaden.

Somalia called for outside help. The Soviet Union responded by sending to Somalia nearly 5,000 Cuban soldiers. This war of "liberation" went relatively well, as did similar operations in Angola, Mozambique, and elsewhere. The Soviet Union and Cuba were truly seen as champions of the oppressed.

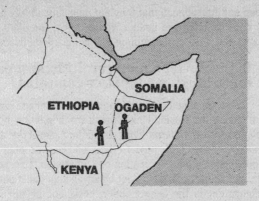

In 1975, however, a coup d'etat occurred in Ethiopia. Emperor Haile Selassie was overthrown. For the next three years there was an internal battle for control of Ethiopia. It ended when Colonel Haile Mengistu Meriam seized control in 1977. Mengistu soon afterwards proclaimed himself a Marxist-Leninist.

Even after the start of the Mengistu presidency, communist Somalia continued in its efforts to liberate Ogaden from Ethiopia. Mengistu therefore asked help from the Soviets, who were still assisting Somalia.

Considering that the Soviets are practical, and considering that Ethiopia with its 30 million inhabitants was a more important country than Somalia (with a population of four million), they simply chose to withdraw the 5,000 Cuban troops from Somalia.

A short time later, Cuban troops arrived in Ethiopia. In May 1978, those Cubans, with the help of East Germany and the Ethiopian military, attacked Somalia with napalm.[23]

Today the Communist Party of the Soviet Union maintains that, at a certain stage in the development of a nation, movements of national liberation are, in fact, "historically justified."[24] It is manifestly clear through cases such as

Ogaden and Afghanistan that they are only "historically justified" until nations have been sovietized. We therefore are speaking not of national liberation but national sovietization.

IV. Is the Soviet Union revolutionary or imperialist, socialist or capitalist?

Lenin supposedly wanted to end capitalism and imperialism. Today the Soviet Union proclaims a solution to the problems in these systems. They clamor for national liberation. But as one assesses the Soviet Union, one is confronted with the question: With its occupation of Afghanistan, Czechoslovakia, and Hungary, is the Soviet Union an imperialist power? Furthermore, is the Soviet Union socialistic or in reality capitalistic?

> **"No nation can be free if it oppresses another nation."**
> **Lenin, 1916**

> **"The Russian people do not want to become Poland's oppressor again."**
> **Lenin, 1916**

> **"All those who...back the right of nations to self-determination must stand for the right of the Ukraine to secede from Russia."**
> **Lenin, 1916**

A. The USSR as imperialist

Through both political and economic imperialism, the Soviet Union has dominated and exploited other regions of the world.

Before the Bolshevik revolution, Lenin warned about the dangerous ambitions of the Russian empire. In 1916, Lenin warned that Czarist Russia's aim was to bring Afghanistan under control of the Russian empire.[25] Ironically, what Lenin denounced, his successors accomplished in 1980.

Lenin said, "The Russian people do not want to become Poland's oppressor again."[26] He spoke about the need for Poland to be able to choose its own direction, and yet the Soviets denounced Lech Walesa and forced the Polish leadership to suppress Solidarity. Furthermore, Lenin stated that "all those who back the right of nations to self-determination, must stand for the right of the Ukraine to secede from Russia."[27] He called for and defended the right of all nations that were a part of the Russian empire to become independent. Yet, by 1919, Lenin himself had dispatched troops to win back the whole of the former Russian empire. Lenin then joked that former Russian colonies had "the right" to secede from the Soviet Union, but that they would not have "the opportunity" to do so.[28]

The Soviet Union still maintains that these colonies have the right to secede from the Soviet Union. Yet in the Soviet constitution, there is no procedural means to secede from the USSR.

Through economic imperialism, the USSR has dominated and exploited large sectors of the world. According to the magazine *Peking Review,* between 1955 and 1973 the Soviet Union siphoned off $11 billion in unjust profits from the Third World.[29] The Soviet Union pays only 38 percent of the world's price for Angolan coffee. It pays only one-half of the world's market price for Afghan natural gas. It lends money to India but specifies that it must only be used to buy Soviet products, or build factories managed by Soviet personnel. The USSR gets back a 560 percent return on its Indian loans.[30]

In his text, *Imperialism, the Highest Stage of Capitalism,* Lenin attacked the socialist Kautsky and warned against a phenomenon which could occur. Kautsky had defended the participation of Germany in World War I and supported Germany's right to have colonies. Lenin referred to Kautsky's position as "social imperialism." Lenin defined the social imperialists as those who are "socialistic in words" and "imperialistic in deeds."[31] The Soviet Union ironically corresponds to this definition.

Communist:
Cambodia
Vietnam
Laos
Guinea Bissau
Sao Tome and Principe
Angola
Mozambique
Ethiopia
Afghanistan
Nicaragua
Cape Verde

Communist:
Cambodia
Vietnam
Laos
Guinea Bissau
Sao Tome and Principe
Angola
Mozambique
Ethiopia
Afghanistan
Nicaragua
Cape Verde

Wars:
Guatemala
El Salvador
Peru
Lebanon
Chad
Colombia

Communist:
Cambodia
Vietnam
Laos
Guinea Bissau
Sao Tome and Principe
Angola
Mozambique
Ethiopia
Afghanistan
Nicaragua
Cape Verde

Wars:
Guatemala
El Salvador
Peru
Lebanon
Chad
Colombia

Radical or Uncertain:
Iran
Zimbabwe
Uganda
Sudan

B. The USSR as capitalist

According to both Marx and Lenin, capitalism, in its final days, would be transformed into state-monopoly capitalism. In other words, in the ultimate stage of capitalism, all industry, all factories, and all banks would be controlled by the state. This, of course, is the situation of the Soviet Union today.

Lenin also maintained that the state is an instrument of the ruling class. Now, if the Soviet Union, with its state monopoly capitalism, has a ruling class, then it is definitely capitalistic.

To know whether there is a ruling class, one must ask: "Who benefits from the income of the Soviet Union?" Is it the worker who benefits from this income? According to *Forbes* magazine, the Moscow worker receives 171 rubles per month, while he needs 210 rubles in order to survive. The situation outside of the capital is even more grim. In other words, the worker in the Soviet Union is clearly receiving a subsistence level salary of the type that Marx mentioned in *Capital*.

On the other hand, there is another group of people which has many privileges. In 1980, the official magazine *Moscow News* proclaimed, "Yes, one can become a millionaire here."[32] Supposedly, the Soviet Union has 13,000 millionaires. These individuals are part of the Soviet "nomenklatura." The members of the nomenklatura avail themselves of all important posts in the government. Their children attend special schools. They themselves have access to foreign exchange privileges and special shops where they can buy the most recent products from Paris and New York. The books that they write are assured of publication and of royalties, sometimes totalling hundreds of thousands of dollars.

In his text, *La Nomenklatura*, former Soviet official Michael Voslensky makes a very strong attack on the Soviet leadership, maintaining that they live on a parasitic basis. The nomenklatura protects its own interests at the expense of the workers whom they supposedly represent and defend.

Who is the economy serving?

Ruling class

Soviet economy

~~Workers~~

Because of the nomenklatura, one must conclude that today in the USSR, there is a ruling class.

Who is the Soviet state serving? Let us consider the Soviet collective farms. Alienation, according to Marx, results from the fact that an individual works on a certain product only to see that product taken away from him by a capitalist. This actually is what occurs in the Soviet collective farm system. The farmers work only to have what they produce taken away. Do the farmers themselves decide what to do with their products? Do they decide to take it to the market? Do they decide when and to whom to sell it? Do they decide how to use that food? Not at all. That is all determined by the ruling class. The nomenklatura always makes sure that it has what it needs. Trotsky warned about the danger of the emergence of a new aristocracy and yet it is apparent that this is what has occurred.

This phenomenon is not limited to agriculture. In November 1917, industry and factories were placed under the direct control of Soviet laborers. They were to determine their own hours, their own production, etc. This lasted until the summer of 1918 at which time Soviet bureaucrats took control of industry. It has remained the same since then. The situation of the Soviet laborer is as alienated as ever.

While a very small class in each communist country lives very well, the rest of the population remains in misery. In his book, *La Corruption en Union Soviétique,* former Russian functionary Ilja Zemtsov speaks of the living conditions in Azerbaijian near the Iranian border. The majority of the citizens of Azerbaijian are of Islamic origin. Thirty-two percent of them live in communal residences where each person has only three square meters of living space. The author says that even today, there are countless thousands of illiterate people along with many children who have never even been to school. To express the misery of the people, Zemtsov gives the example of one report which came across his desk:

> On the 13th of February, 1970, a resident of Kirovo-bade, Mrs. Roubaba Gouseinova, 42 years of age, with a primary school education, divorced, with three children, two boys and a girl, covered herself with oil and burned herself alive.
>
> She had lived for 13 years in a cave and had asked the city's executive committee 19 times to find her a dwelling place. This, the 20th time, she chose a different direction. She left a letter on which could be read the words, "This time they will give us one."[33]

Zemtsov maintains that not only in Azerbaijian but in many other places in the Soviet Union, many people still live in caves. They have no running water; they have no heat. Is this the grand promise of communism?

It is said that communism will liberate us, that it will bring us to a new level of technological superiority. But what kind of technological superiority is this if after 60 years, there are still millions of people living in absolute misery?

V. The nature of Soviet imperialism

As we have seen, Marx predicted that certain phenomena were to occur in the capitalist world. These included:

(1) A centralization of capital
(2) An increase of poverty
(3) A decrease of profits

These phenomena did not occur in the West. As we have seen, even a "centralization of capital" did not occur. More and more, a distribution of capital has taken place.

While these three processes did not occur in the free market system of the West, these processes *are* occurring in the totalitarian system of the USSR.

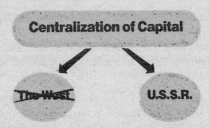

A. Centralization of capital

First of all, there is a centralization of capital. Marx predicted:

> Today, therefore, the forces of attraction, drawing together individual capitals, and the tendency to centralization are stronger than ever before... In a given society the limit would be reached only when the entire social capital was united in the hands of either a single capitalist or a single capitalized company.[34]

In the case of the Soviet Union, that single company is the state. However, the profits are not distributed on an equitable basis. Instead, the leadership class benefits the most from any economic surplus.

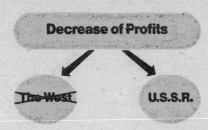

B. Decrease in profits

Marx predicted a decrease in profits. Although the West has sporadically experienced recessions and other economic setbacks, the overall tendency of development has been positive. On the other hand, as various sovietologists such as Besancon have indicated, the Soviet Union survives largely on the basis of a parasitic relationship with the West. The West continues to pump in aid and encourage certain trade policies which extend the economic life-span of the Soviet Union.

C. Increase in poverty

Increasing poverty is also a phenomenon which is occurring in the Soviet Union. As we already mentioned, in the past 20 years, the Soviet male life expectancy decreased from 67 to 62. The infant mortality rate more than doubled over the past 10 years.[35] From being an exporter of wheat, the Soviet Union has become an importer of wheat. Instead of a new prosperity and the formation of a communist state by 1980 (as Khrushchev promised) we notice that the Soviet Union remains in a condition of deprivation. In most respects, instead of improving, these conditions continue to worsen.

Lenin foresaw the occurrence of these three phenomena in the West, but in fact, a typical case of their occurrence is

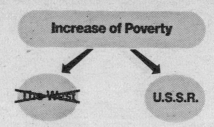

manifested in the present situation of the USSR. Lenin
asserted that the capitalists had delayed this process through
an exportation of capital and goods to the developing world.

In fact, this is the phenomenon which is occurring today
in the Soviet Union. It is the Soviet Union which attempts to
distract the Soviet citizens from seeing the true state of
affairs by constantly emphasizing the "threat from without"
as a justification for its brand of imperialism. In the case of the
Soviet Union, imperialism is advanced not only by an exportation of capital but also by an exportation of revolution. Each
day the Soviet Union provides Cuba with at least $9 million of
economic aid. In return, Castro lends Cuban soldiers and
advisers to the cause of Soviet imperialism. The results of
Soviet imperialism are always the same, yet little attention is
paid to it. While the world was appalled by the human rights
violations of certain rightist, authoritarian regimes, virtually
nothing was said when Soviet surrogates murdered 150,000
Angolans after the communist takeover of that country.
Because the Soviets lend lip service to a better society, we
fail to examine the real results of the extension of their influence in nation after nation.

VI. The solution to imperialism and exploitation

Communism, while decrying imperialism and social

injustice, has not solved these problems. In fact, communism itself has become a problem which must be solved along with the problems it sought to correct. The question still remains as to what is the solution to imperialism and social injustice.

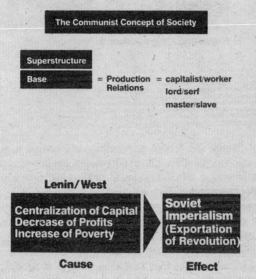

Communism has been unable to stop social injustice because of its distorted world view, founded on wrong principles. It ignores the basis of injustice — selfishness. The communist view of society is a distorted view. It stresses two dimensions — the base and the superstructure. The essence of the base for the Marxists is the production relations, or class relations. For the Marxist, all other aspects of society, such as religion, law, philosophy, politics, etc. are built upon this foundation. However, Marxist theory fails to recognize relationships which are actually more basic than economic ones: (1) the family (informal education), and (2) the school (formal education).

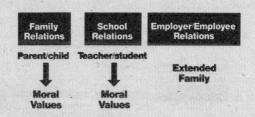

Family and school relationships are central to forming a person's character. The importance of the family, especially the parent, in the development of the child's personality is widely recognized. Likewise, the teacher, acting in the role of parent, is very important. Certainly these two aspects preceed the employer-employee relationship. Parents and teachers must have moral values and communicate these to the child. If children do not properly develop, then this will be reflected at a higher level as they take their place in society. The real bases of any society are its moral principles and their application.

Marxists have not solved the problems of imperialism and social injustice because they have not understood the source, selfishness. Any system, whether free-market, feudalist, socialist, or whatever, has the potential to act imperialistically toward other nations because of greed on a national level. It is not inherent to capitalism, as most Marxists would like us to believe. Destruction of capitalism will not lead to an end of imperialism and social injustice. Marxism, based on an illogical and empty ideology, seems to have resorted to attacking imperialism and social injustice more as a strategy for expansion than as a real attempt to solve social ills. The ultimate irony is that the USSR can decry imperialism and social injustice, and yet exhibit the worst forms of both.

That exploitation and injustice exist in free market societies we cannot deny. However, we can deny that it *must* exist (as Marx and Lenin maintained). Economic or social injustices are not a result of the economic structures of Western society; they are a result of human greed.

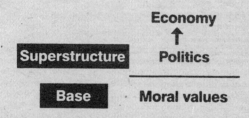

The Soviet exploitation of nations such as Angola and Afghanistan and likewise the Soviet Union's exploitation of its own people prove that while Lenin may have made cosmetic changes in the economic structure of Russia, he did not eradicate selfishness or corruption. To bring about that kind of change, Lenin needed not a political but a moral revolution. His adherence to Marxist principles made that impossible.

CHAPTER FIVE NOTES

1. V.I. Lenin, *Collected Works*, Moscow, Progress Publishers, 1980, Vol. 22, p.343.
2. Pierre et Monique Favre, *Les Marxismes Apres Marx*, Paris, Presses Universitaires de France, 1980, pp.18-25.
3. *Encyclopedia Britannica*, 1983, Vol. 16, pp.965-973.
4. Vladimir Lenin, *Imperialism, the Highest Stage of Capitalism*, New York, International Publishers, 1974, pp.65-66.
5. Pierre et Monique Favre, pp.39-42.

6. Ibid., p.107.
7. Andrei Melvil, *"La Concepción Leninista de la Política Exterior,"* in *Ciencias Sociales*, Moscow, Academia de Ciencias, 1981, pp.171-185.
8. Che Guevara in ed. George Lavan's *Che Guevara Speaks*, New York, Grove Press, 1968, p.105.
9. *Documents on Major European Governments*, ed. Randolph L. Braham, New York, Alfred Knopf, 1966, pp. 191-206.
10. Ibid.
11. Che Guevara in ed. George Lavan's *Che Guevara Speaks*, p.18.
12. Lenin, *Imperialism, the Highest Stage of Capitalism*, p.48.
13. Bill Warren, *Imperialism: Pioneer of Capitalism*, London, Verso, 1980, p.57.
14. Ibid.
15. Ibid.
16. Ibid., p.46.
17. Ibid., pp.60-64.
18. Ibid., p.67.
19. Michael Voslensky, *La Nomenklatura*, Paris, Belfond, 1980, p.182.
20. Warren, p.46.
21. Warren, Ibid., p.48.
22. Note that imperialism can be defined as "the policy, practice, or advocacy of extending the power and dominion of a nation, especially by direct territorial acquisition, or by gaining indirect control over the political or economic life of other areas." (*Webster's New Collegiate Dictionary*). This is the common, broader definition, and not the narrow Marxist definition which strives to restrict the term to capitalism. (Such as the definition given by Lenin that ". . . imperialism is the monopoly stage of capitalism," from *Imperialism, the Highest Stage of Capitalism*.)
23. See Ezzedrine Mestiri, *Les Cubains et L'Afrique*, Paris, Editions Karthala, 224p. The case of Soviet duplicity with regard to both Ogaden and Eritrea is also discussed in Richard Nixon's *The Real War*, New York, Warner Books, 1980, pp.25-27.
24. *Documents on Major European Governments*, ed. Randolph Brahan, New York, Alfred Knopf, 1966, pp.191-206.
25. V. I. Lenin, "Notebook Imperialism," in *Collected Works*, Vol. 39, p.676.
26. Lenin, "Peace without Annexations," in *Collected Works*, Vol. 22, p.139.
27. Ibid., p.140.
28. Voslensky, p.403.
29. *Peking Review*, March 29, 1975.
30. *Is the Soviet Union Socialist or Capitalist*, Oakland, The New Voice, 1980, pp.4-72.
31. Vladimir Lenin, *Imperialism, the Highest Stage of Capitalism*, New York, International Publishers, 1972, p.109.
32. Quoted by Patrick Meney of Agence France-Presse, *San Francisco Chronicle*, May 8, 1980, p.28.
33. I. Zemtsov, *La Corruption en Union Sovietique*, Paris, Hachette, 1976, p.128.
34. Marx, *Capital*, New York, International Publishers, Vol. I, pp.626-627.
35. Cullen Murphy, "Watching the Russians," *The Atlantic*, February 1983, pp. 33-52.

CONFUSION IN THE WESTERN VALUE SYSTEM

The world today has attained a level of technological development that few dared to imagine only fifty years ago. Men have stood on the moon and can mine the ocean floor. We can communicate with any part of the world in seconds. Scientists from many nations working together have been able to find solutions and cures to problems which have plagued our civilization for centuries.

Yet with all our great advances, humanity is still plagued by hunger and war. Our cities worldwide are experiencing unprecedented levels of crime. Drugs, racial strife, corporate crime, and even political assassinations, have all left their scars on contemporary society.

The fact that these problems go beyond national boundary lines, and affect every social sub-group, suggests that such problems are not simply caused by the local environment. The problems are deeply rooted; therefore we cannot respond to them superficially. The problems which confront 20th century man cause us to reflect on the philosophical and moral bases of society. The following is an examination of the present Western value system, its historical origins and its impact on current affairs.

I. The ideal world and reality

Two thousand years ago Jesus Christ offered the Lord's prayer in which we find the words, "Thy Kingdom come, Thy Will be done, on Earth as it is in Heaven." These words express Jesus' desire to see God's Will fulfilled on Earth. Physically (externally) at least, this hope has not yet been fulfilled. Humanity continues to suffer.

In history, various individuals have attempted to fulfill the words of Christ's prayer. In more recent times, the Second Vatican Council (presided over initially by Pope John XXIII) addressed the immediate need to respond to the deplorable living conditions of the world's poor. "Liberation theology," which has gained considerable popularity in the Americas, also alludes to building the Kingdom of God on Earth and eradicating social injustice. We can say that even Marxism, in terms of its ultimate goal and purpose, imitates the Kingdom of God on Earth, and attempts to construct a utopian world from which God has been excluded.

Although various methodologies aiming to build an ideal society have emerged, none have been successful. This causes us to re-examine the bases upon which a just society can appear.

The bases of a truly just and moral society

Although there are some who believe that society shapes the individual, it is generally accepted that the individuals who make up a society project their way of thinking into the institutions of that society. For that reason, in order to build a just, moral, and God-centered society, we would first need individuals of real integrity. Unless God-centered, moral individuals dwell in an ideal society, it will eventually be corrupted.

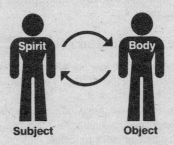

What then is the basis of a moral person? Within the human being, there is both a mind and a body. A harmonious relationship should exist between these two dimensions. Essentially the mind, or spirit, which seeks the godly, should guide the body, which relates to the material. Both of these aspects have great importance, but the relationship between them should be properly balanced.

The Apostle Paul speaks of the discordance between mind and body in the seventh chapter of his letter to the Romans. He confesses, "In my innermost self, I delight in the law of God, but in my members I see another law warring against the law of my mind..."[1] It is this contradiction between mind and body which causes a struggle within the self.

Ideally, as we have stated, a reciprocal relationship of subject and object, with the mind guiding the body, should exist. Instead, we find a relationship of subject-subject. In other words, a relationship of conflict exists between the desires of the mind and those of the body. This conflict has found expression in the historical tension between two trends in human cultural tradition — one stressing faith and the other reason and sense experience.

II. The religious and humanistic traditions

Western society traces its roots back to two great traditions. Hebraism, or the religious tradition, is based on faith. Truth is found in the transcendental and it can only be known and understood through faith.

Hellenism, or the humanistic tradition, on the other hand, links truth with reason and sense experiences. We can summarize the tension between the two as a question of faith vs. reason. These two traditions have greatly influenced the foundations of Christianity and continue to influence us today.

Over the centuries, philosophy and culture developed from the humanistic tradition as well as from the religious

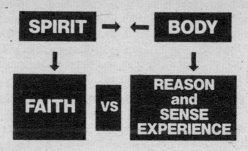

tradition. Only rarely have there emerged great thinkers, such as Augustine and Thomas Aquinas, who strived for saint-hood as well as for intellectual understanding, and who helped to bridge gaps between these two parallel roots of Western culture.

The general nature of the religious and humanistic traditions

The religious tradition is symbolized by the Israelites and their leader Moses. Moses turns to heaven for guidance and receives from God the 10 Commandments. If we examine Exodus, we notice that it teaches that all problems stem from man's failure to unite with God. When the people diso-bey God, there is suffering, and they are called to repentance and obedience once again.

In contrast, in his text *The Rebel*, French philosopher Albert Camus sees Prometheus as a prototype of the human-istic tradition. Prometheus was the immortal responsible for taking fire from Zeus and giving it to humankind. Zeus punished Prometheus for this act by chaining him to a mountain. Accord-ing to Greek mythology, Zeus sent his eagle day after day to devour Prometheus' liver. During the night, Prometheus' liver supposedly grew back again, and the process was repeated. Prometheus encountered this torment because he refused to repent before Zeus. Zeus for him was an unjust god. Camus maintains that this view of God as unjust is typical of the Hellenic tradition which, he says, glorifies the greatness and the goodness of man, and belittles the justice of the gods.[2]

Whereas Hellenism posits the injustice of God, Hebraism focuses on the justice of God and the moral weakness of men. When we study history, we can recognize that time and again, struggles have occurred between these two divergent viewpoints. The religious tradition has manifested itself in the mystic, the saint, and the religious reformer. Humanism has manifested itself in the intellectual, the scientist, and the artist. Though not necessarily contradictory in nature, these different perspectives have resulted in historical divisions and conflict.

III. Religious tradition and humanistic tradition in recent history

In this presentation we cannot study the whole development of the religious and humanistic traditions. We will limit ourselves here to considering the impact and influence of these two traditions upon modern society. When we turn to 15th and 16th century European history, we recognize that two important phenomena took place: the Renaissance and the Reformation. The Reformation constituted a re-awakening of spiritual values and is characteristic of the religious tradition.

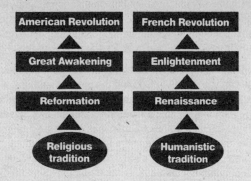

The Renaissance results from a resurgence of humanism. Both of these trends have had a great impact upon the development of today's religious, moral, and sociopolitical institutions.

A. The Reformation

The best known champions of the Reformation are the Protestant reformers, such as Martin Luther and John Calvin. However, the impact of the Reformation is not limited to Protestantism. Through the Catholic Counter-Reformation, there was also a spiritual awakening within the Catholic Church which produced such mystics as Theresa of Avila and St. John of the Cross.

The character of the Reformation and Counter-Reformation was internal. It inspired men and women to reflect upon their relationship with Christ and their understanding of the Bible. It brought about a reawakening of moral values and a sincere re-examination of the implications of faith.

B. The Renaissance

The Renaissance provoked a very different phenomenon. Most particularly, the Renaissance challenged many concepts which people had blindly accepted for centuries. For example, in *The Prince*, Machiavelli implicitly challenged the concept of

REFORMATION:

1. Internal

2. Need for a personal relationship
   with God and the Bible

the monarch as the "elect of God." He likewise challenged the Christian ethic and opted for what was "pragmatic" in the gaining of power. The prince depicted by Machiavelli must be pragmatic, and he must be ready and able to step outside the boundaries of Christian conduct if it allows him to maintain power. It is from Machiavelli that we develop the concept that the "end justifies the means," and the end for Machiavelli is political power.

We can term the Renaissance as "external" in nature. Rather than reflecting upon the moral character of humankind, it focused upon intellectual advances. Revelation and mystical experience were rejected as not being valid modes of acquiring knowledge. Descartes and Bacon raised up rationalism and empiricism as new standards for discerning the truth.

C. The Great Awakening

Approximately two centuries after the high point of the Renaissance and the Reformation, we find similar patterns of development in the religious and intellectual tradition through the Enlightenment and the Great Awakening.

The Great Awakening certainly can be said to represent a kind of second Reformation. The Great Awakening occurred primarily in the United States, however its roots are also related to France and England.

RENAISSANCE:

1. External

2. Focused on the development of
   intellectual understanding and the
   glorification of man.

During the 17th century, France replaced 16th century mystical Spain as the spearhead of a Catholic renewal. With reformers like St. François de Salle and St. Vincent de Paul, the 17th century in France was called the Century of the Saints. Popular religious practice attained levels never reached before in French history. In the intellectual field, the philosopher Blaise Pascal propagated a Christian doctrine that taught the experience of God through the heart rather than through reason.

During the same epoch, Puritanism developed as a movement of purification in the Church of England, seeking to carry the Reformation beyond the stage it had reached in the previous centuries. The religious, social, economic, political and intellectual institutions of the modern Anglo-Saxon world remain deeply influenced by the Puritan spirit.

In England in the 18th century, the Wesley brothers, John and Charles, founded the Methodist movement aimed at sparking a new spirit in the churches. According to many historians, the great popular outreach of the Wesleys' evangelical and social action helped England to avoid the violent revolution which neighboring France had to endure.

The Great Awakening, in some sense, constituted a departure from the intellectual developments of the 18th century. Instead of emphasizing intellectual understanding of God, the Great Awakening emphasized faith and a relationship with God.

The Great Awakening inspired a religious revival throughout New England. Its God-centered direction came to have a great impact upon the spiritual and cultural development of America. One of the foremost figures of the Great Awakening was Jonathan Edwards. Preachers such as Edwards emphasized the need for developing a personal relationship with God and Christ and also called Christians to study and apply the teachings of the Bible to daily life. Many historians relate the spiritual and cultural roots of the American revolution to the events which surround the Great Awakening.

Pietism and the Great Awakening

1. **Reaction to Formalism and Intellectualism**

2. **Bible Study**

3. **Need for Personal Religious Experience**

D. The Enlightenment

The Enlightenment largely had its origins in France. One of the highlights of the Enlightenment was the development of the Encyclopedia by Diderot and D'Alembert. The Encyclopedia provided a means whereby the cultured individual could have quick reference to any number of topics, including music, philosophy and art. The French philosophers of the Enlightenment challenged religion as a social institution as well as the traditional view of God as a personal being able to intervene in man's life, accomplish miracles and guide the history of Providence. (see Chapter 2)

The Ptolemaic View:

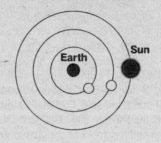

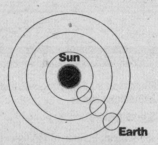

Copernican View

The Enlightenment thinkers contributed to an anti-religious attitude in 18th century France. Through such individuals as Voltaire, the Enlightenment challenged the traditional view of God. Voltaire and others adapted the discoveries of 17th century British Deism.

The Deist view of the universe as a machine stemmed from Copernicus. It was Copernicus who first challenged the Ptolemaic notion which placed the earth rather than the sun at the center of our system. Copernicus, a contemporary of Luther, was rejected by Protestantism and Catholicism alike. When, in the following century, Galileo espoused the same position, he was also exposed to ridicule and religious persecution. Through the later discoveries of Newton, it became clear that Copernicus' observations had been accurate. This caused some to question Christianity's credibility and to search for a new approach to religion. That view was Deism. Deism emphasized the role of science and the mechanistic character of the universe. To a large extent, however, there was no conflict between Christianity and British Deism.

For 18th century French Deism, God assumed the role of an indifferent machine-maker and the universe the role of a machine. God had created the universe, His machine, in accord with rational laws which were discoverable by men. After creating the universe, God had withdrawn. He would not interfere with the processes of nature and the works of man. Humankind alone bore the responsibility for effecting change in the world. Human beings should not rely upon God; His help would not be forthcoming.

The Enlightenment connected itself strongly to science. The development of science and technology, Newton's discoveries of the laws of motion, and the Industrial Revolution left people with a great sense of optimism. Many felt that universal human progress was inevitable and that through the advance of science, humankind would ultimately succeed in solving all problems within society. This optimism encouraged the Industrial Revolution, but allowed social injustice to go unchecked because social theorists felt that the injustices suffered by laborers were a necessary evil in order to open the way to a utopian future for humanity.

E. The American Revolution

In the latter part of the 18th century, these two trends in human cultural history became manifested in two revolutionary models — one based on God and the other denying the existence of God.

Although these two revolutions occurred approximately at the same time, they had two different philosophical origins. Generally, we can attribute the philosophical basis of the

Enlightenment

1. **Questioning of Doctrines and Values**
2. **Individualism**
3. **Universal Human Progress**
4. **Empirical Method**
5. **Rationalism**

French Revolution to the Renaissance and the Enlightenment. We can attribute the philosophical basis of the American Revolution more to the Great Awakening. Let us consider each of these revolutions.

An important factor in the founding spirit of the United States was the attitude of many of the pioneers who came to the shores of Massachusetts, New York and Maryland. They came to America not merely in search of economic prosperity but because they sought the right to practice the faith of their choice in freedom. The Pilgrim Fathers who crossed the Atlantic in the Mayflower risked their lives in order to practice their religious beliefs and ideals.

The importance of God in their lives is clearly reflected in the wording of the charter which they created before disembarking from the Mayflower. During their first winter in Massachusetts, 47 out of 102 settlers lost their lives due to the harsh conditions. These pioneers were prepared to make such sacrifices because, for them, nothing was more precious than to worship God as they saw fit. After harvesting their first crop, the Pilgrims gathered together in prayer and thanksgiving in commemoration of the God who had protected them. Some of the early pioneers viewed America as a New Israel and a nation of Providential design.

When we study the documents which surround the American Revolution, we find constant references to Divine Providence and to the belief that, without the guidance of the Almighty, the revolution could not have accomplished its goal. When the Constitution of the United States was written, the first article of the Bill of Rights read, "Congress shall make no law respecting the establishment of religion, or prohibiting the free exercise thereof." In his first inaugural address, George Washington dedicated one-third of his message to expressing the need for America to rely on God as she took her first steps toward nationhood. When Washington became president, he received broad, interdenominational support. Catholics, Jews, Methodists, and Episcopalians all pledged their prayers and their support to his presidency and called upon God to guide their new nation.

Even though the roots of the American Revolution are essentially religious, one should also take into account the influence of the humanistic current upon it. The pioneers of political liberalism, Locke and Hobbes, served as a major inspiration in the development of the American Revolution.

The key for the success of the American Revolution was that it was able to harmonize the Christian and humanist currents (unity of Christians and Deists). The ideas of the Enlightenment, such as Deism, were not foreign to the American people. These ideas penetrated deeply in America, but the militant incredulity and anti-clericalism of the French philosophers never found an echo in the American people. For them, the respect of religion was a guarantee of the stability of democratic institutions and the safety of individuals.

Observers of American history such as Alexis de Tocqueville, wrote that you cannot separate American democracy from underlying religious principles. In his text *Democracy in America*, he said that religious beliefs are an integral part of the American political practice. American democracy has to be understood in that way. De Tocqueville wrote that he searched for the greatness of America in the places of commerce, in the harbors, and in the places of industry.

American Revolution

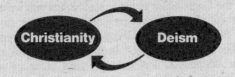

However, he did not find it there. It was not until he went into the churches and found the pulpits aflame with righteousness that he understood the greatness of America. He wrote, "America is great because America is good, and when America ceases to be good she will likewise cease to be great."

This God-centered tradition continued in America in the 19th and 20th centuries. Prayer opened each daily session of the United States Congress. All across the country, millions of students began their day with prayer. Always, even in the darkest moments in American history, a leader has come forth and upheld the God-affirming tradition. Abraham Lincoln, for example, had a profound understanding of the deep sin represented by slavery. On the wall of the Lincoln Memorial are carved the words of Lincoln's Second Inaugural Address. It reads:

> Fondly do we hope, fervently do we pray, that this mighty scourge of war may speedily pass away. Yet, if God wills that it continue until all the wealth piled by the bondsman's two hundred and fifty years of unrequited toil shall be sunk, and until every drop of blood drawn with the lash shall be paid by another drawn with the sword, as was said three thousand years ago, so still it must be said, "The judgments of the Lord are true and righteous altogether."

Lincoln had an understanding that the nation had sinned and the nation was paying for its sins. He realized that we cannot ignore a deep wrong such as the wrong of slavery. Lincoln called the country to join together in a national day of repentance marked by prayer and fasting on April 30, 1863.

F. The French Revolution

The French Revolution took a much more chaotic and bloody course than the American Revolution. Why? What was the basic difference between American history and French history?

The French *Ancien Regime* society was characterized by absolute monarchy and the absence of religious freedom. Louis XIV, known as the "Sun King," had centralized France to an extreme degree. He proclaimed: *"L'Etat, c'est moi!"* (The state is me!) He persecuted mystical groups within the Catholic Church such as the Quietists of Madame Guyon and the Jansenists. He retracted the Edict of Nantes which had granted religious freedom to the Protestants. Against them, he launched bloody massacres known as "les dragonnades."

According to many historians, Louis XIV's repressive policy explains why the Enlightenment philosophy and the French Revolution took the form of a violent reaction against the French crown and Christianity (which the crown supposedly defended).

When the French Revolution occurred, several of the foremost revolutionary figures such as Diderot and D'Holbach called for the de-Christianization of France. Christianity was viewed as an instrument through which the monarchy had justified its power. Certain proponents of the French Revolution even maintained that whereas in the past, the monarchy had justified repression through Christianity, this would be the appropriate moment to avenge this by crushing Christianity and its hierarchy.

Thus, Alexis de Tocqueville could speak of the "anti-Christian genius" of the French Revolution. "Among the passions born from that revolution," he wrote, "the first ignited and the last extinguished was the anti-religious passion. Nowhere did anti-religion ever become a general, ardent, intolerant, or aggressive passion, but in France..."[3]

This fanatical and militant incredulity is the fundamental difference between the French Revolution and the American Revolution. Both revolutions originally sprang out of the same desire for liberty and democracy, but they took a completely opposite orientation. The French historian François Furet explains it in the following way:

> The American Revolution founded institutions guaranteed by God, while the French Revolution established institutions which had no foundation but themselves. The aim of the French Revolution was to create a new man and a new society without any reference to Transcendence, serving in reality as a substitute to any kind of Transcendence.[4]

A quite significant phenomenon is that, in the French Revolution, as opposed to the American Revolution, the Deists united with the agnostics and the atheists to violently oppose the Christians. Therefore two camps — a Christian camp and an anti-Christian secular camp — pitilessly confronted each other. This was characteristic not only of the French Revolution, but also of the Russian Revolution which followed its tradition. Equally significant was the ambiguous position which the French Revolution took on religious freedom in the French Declaration of the Rights of Man and the Citizen:

> No one may be disturbed on account of his opinions, even his religious ones, as long as the manifestation of his opinions does not interfere with the established law and order.

In this formulation, there is clearly reluctance in guaranteeing respect of religious freedom. By 1791, the French Revolution would actively attempt to de-Christianize France. In the beginning of the revolution, most clergy

French Revolution

Deism
Agnosticism
Atheism

Christianity

supported efforts in favor of democracy and the abolition of
the privileges of the aristocracy, however, they soon found
themselves under growing pressure. Priests were forced to
swear on the Constitution under threat of being sent into
exile. The monastic orders were suppressed and public
processions forbidden. Revolutionary communes were given
the right to close down local church parishes. The churches
were transformed into temples of Reason where effigies of
the martyrs of the Revolution replaced effigies of the saints.
In the department of Nievre, the revolutionary leader Fouche
tore down all the religious emblems at cemetery gates and
replaced them with signs reading: "Death is an eternal sleep."

Certainly the anti-religious development of the French
Revolution was a factor which led Karl Marx to view the
French Revolution as a most significant event. More particularly, Marx maintained that this had been a revolution of class
and was, therefore, a vital step in the development toward
the ultimate revolution of class, the communist revolution.

IV. Social abuses and injustice in the 19th century

A. The emergence of Social Darwinism

As we have mentioned, Deism, which gained prominence

during the Enlightenment and the French Revolution, perceived the universe as a machine. The question arose as to how the machine had come to life. Various explanations for the origin and development of life arose. Initially, the view which gained the most popularity was that developed by French biologist Jean Lamarck. Later, Darwin's *Origin of Species* made an even greater impact.

Darwin observed that, within nature, some organisms randomly inherited traits which made them more apt to survive than others. The principle of "natural selection" would then operate to select out those who were most fit for survival and allow them to perpetuate the species.

For example, let us say that there were two varieties of a given species of deer, one with longer legs than the other. Should a predator come, the deer with the longer legs would have a greater chance to escape from it. We can say that those deer would have a greater possibility of both surviving and reproducing. Darwin would observe that the offspring of such deer would potentially inherit this same trait. By this process of natural selection, a species would advance or develop. The guiding principle would thus be what is referred to as "survival of the fittest."

It is one thing to apply this principle to nature, another to apply it to human society. Herbert Spencer, British thinker

Random mutation

Natural selection

Survival of the Fittest

and contemporary of Darwin, maintained that "survival of the fittest" applied not only to animals but to human society. For Spencer, some members of the human species were more "fit" than others. Some were inherently destined to live in prosperity, whereas others were biologically destined to live in poverty. For Spencer, certain races were also biologically destined to dominate other races.

Spencer's theories made a great impact upon the thinking of the early part of the 20th century. Social Darwinism (as Spencer's theory is usually called) served as a philosophical justification for selfishness. Likewise, it served to justify the exploitation of the weak by the strong. Certain industrialists and entrepreneurs used Social Darwinism to justify a ruthless form of "capitalist" business practice.

B. Religion's response to Social Darwinism

We would expect Christians to respond to this degeneration of the Western tradition and come to the defense of the weak, based on the belief that all people are children of God. Unfortunately, Christianity did not strongly maintain this position. There were exceptions such as John Wesley, who advocated rights and protection for laborers, Bartolomé de las Casas, who defended rights of native Americans, and Albert Schweitzer, the great humanitarian and missionary.

**Social Darwinism served
as an excuse for injustice**

Tragically, however, we see that the Christian response was stifled by the misapplication of John Calvin's theological view on predestination.

Briefly, predestination is the theological position which stressed that the spiritual destiny of each person was predetermined by God and no amount of human effort could change that destiny. Predestination was later misapplied by interpreting it in a socio-political context to justify one race dominating other races. It also served to justify Christians being insensitive to the needs of others. The financial prosperity of a Christian came to be interpreted as an affirmation of salvation. The poverty of others testified to their damnation. Some were predestined to salvation and therefore economic prosperity. Others were predestined for damnation and abjection.

This created a tragic parallel between Christianity and Social Darwinism. In other words, the "predestined" individual coincided with what Spencer and Darwin termed "the fittest." In "affirming" their own salvation, Christians ignored the situation of the poor and the suffering. Many felt theologically justified in doing so. Yet when Christianity failed to address problems such as poverty and exploitation, Marxism did so instead.

**Predestination in a Sociopolitical
Context Justified
"Survival of the Fittest"**

C. Western society today

Because of a twisted application of predestination, some of our most basic Christian principles, such as "love of neighbor," were laid aside. Revolting against the discrepancy between Christian words and deeds, young people have resorted to drugs and other tragic deviations, which allegedly serve as an alternative for what they perceive as hypocritical piety. This had led progressively to deeper levels of revolt. Many find themselves totally disillusioned.

V. Western expansionism and the three world wars

In the 20th century, we find that the entire democratic world is encountering various challenges. From the viewpoint of the loss of human life, no greater calamity exists than the ideologically-based wars, which have occurred and continue to occur in this century. Let us review some of the events and circumstances which led to these three world wars.

A. World War I

In the 19th century, Europe initiated a great movement of imperialist expansion in Asia and Africa. The two main democratic countries of the continent, Great Britain and

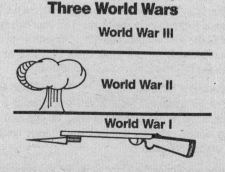

Three World Wars

World War III

World War II

World War I

France, took the lead in this movement and built powerful and prosperous empires.

Many theories were developed at that time to justify imperial expansionism. For British imperialists, it was the providential, civilizing and humanitarian mission of the British race, superior and predestined by its qualities, virtues and institutions to expand throughout the world. "If there is a God," wrote British empire-builder, Cecil Rhodes, "He works in a visible manner to make the Anglo-Saxon race the chosen instrument through which He will bring a social state founded on police, liberty and peace." In this view, educating and training the lower peoples were the "white man's burden," the moral responsibility of the British people.

Among the movements that rose to elaborate a British imperialist doctrine, the most famous was the Round Table Movement founded in 1909 by young liberals gathered around Sir Alfred Milner. These young patriots believed in the inherent superiority of British civilization and in the Englishman's duty to carry the fruits of that civilization to humanity. Their ideology was a combination of Social Darwinism and the Christian ethic. "This is the law of human progress," said Milner, "that the competition between nations, each seeking its maximum development, is the Divine Order of the world, the law of Life and Progress."

The Round Table's primary aim was the reinforcement of the political unity of the British Commonwealth as the basis of Anglo-Saxon supremacy in the world. This supremacy, which they saw as the best contribution to stability in the world, had to be established by force if needed, for the greatest benefit of all in the end.

At the end of the 19th century, the French Third Republic asserted itself as the regime which would build France's greatness through colonial expansion, as opposed to the monarchy which had lost most of the French colonies to England in the 18th century.

For the leaders of the Third Republic, colonization was a

mere prolongation of the republican ideal in the line of the French Revolution. They regarded French humanistic civilization as the most advanced, the most progressive, and the most universal. During the Revolutionary Wars, France had tried to bring the principles of equality to the rest of Europe. After the failure of the Napoleonic epic, France's mission was to reach out to the backward peoples of the world, hastening the day when all mankind would be united at the highest level of human culture. This "civilizing mission" implied rights as well as obligations. "The superior races," said Republican leader Jules Fery, main promoter of French imperialism in the 1880s, "have a right toward the inferior races... because they have the duty to civilize the inferior races."

The theories of Darwin were used to reinforce such views. Colonization presents "all the characters to which one recognizes the forces of nature." (Charles Gide) "The need for expansion... is so intimately linked to the instincts dispensed to all beings that one can see there one of the essential manifestations of life." (J. Harmand)

In the late 1880s, the United States, following the example of the European powers, abandoned the traditional isolationistic orientation of her foreign policy and launched an imperialist drive in her sphere of influence, Latin America and the Pacific. The U.S. strategy did not consist of establishing colonies, like European powers mostly did, but in building up a system of formal or financial protectorates.

New intellectual currents emerged providing historical, philosophical and religious justifications for U.S. expansionism. The arguments advanced were often a curious blend of materialistic considerations of self-interest and altruistic concepts rooted in Christian idealism. Darwin's doctrine of "the survival of the fittest" was used by many theoreticians to justify the superiority of American democratic institutions and Anglo-Saxon civilization. Historian John Fiske developed a Social Darwinist theory describing the American system as the "fittest" in the world and necessarily destined to be applied to all other nations. The Congregationalist pastor Josiah Strong used the theory of evolution to support his idea of the innate superiority of the Anglo-Saxon race. In his book *Our Country* he explained how God invested the American people with the mission to bring the great principles of civil liberty and "spiritual Christianity" to all the weaker, backward peoples of the world. Other thinkers, more purely altruistic, described the role of the United States as protector of all the freedom-fighters and democratic movements in the world rather than defender of its selfish national interests.

The mixed motivations of the colonizers and expansionists produced mixed consequences. Positive results of Western expansion for the native populations could be witnessed in the fields of technical development, public health and education. But, on the other hand, it was mostly conducted with an obvious lack of sensitivity for the local needs.

Sometimes the most sordid intentions would appear, like in the Opium War which broke out in China in 1839. At that time the British, who dominated India, where cultivation of the opium poppy was flourishing, were looking for new markets for the drug. They succeeded in developing the vice in China, where users gathered in the notorious "opium dens." Upset by the resulting destruction of its own people, the authorities of the city of Canton threw 20,000 opium chests into the sea. After demanding payment of an indemnity for the lost opium and meeting a Chinese refusal, the British launched the bloody Opium War.

At the turn of the century, another great power arose, imperial Germany, gaining supremacy on the European continent with its booming economy and powerful army. The Germans had somehow been left behind by the English and the French, however, in the race for control of new markets and new materials overseas, thus limiting the scope of German expansion. Everywhere on the world scene, Germany butted against the more successful colonial powers.

Kaiser Wilhelm II liked to be constantly told he was the

greatest sovereign on earth and the founder of German supremacy. Joseph Chamberlain's words describing the British as "the greatest people of conquerors ever seen in the world" grated strongly against him. The increasing tension between European powers finally brought about the First World War.

After the fall of the Russian Czarist Empire and the entrance of the U.S. in the war in 1917, a mostly democratic block led by France, England and the U.S. opposed a coalition of central autocratic nations led by Germany, Austria and Turkey.

The democratic nations came off victorious from that war, but the new world order they shaped in 1918 created the conditions for a second global confrontation.

B. World War II

The English and especially the French wanted to prevent Germany from recovering as a big power. They adopted a revengeful attitude, setting war damages to a level beyond the possibilities of the German economy, then in shambles. "Germany will pay!" was the central motto in French politics in the 1920s. And in 1923, Premier Raymond Poincare sent troops to the Ruhr region to force the Germans to start the payment. This humiliating move did much to create additional resentment among the Germans and allow the rise of National Socialism.

After Adolf Hitler took power in 1933, England and France adopted an attitude of weakness. Trying to systematically avoid direct confrontation with the new leaders, they yielded to each of Hitler's aggressive moves.

The United States refrained from taking international responsibility immediately after the war. She went back to her old isolationist tradition and did not even take part in the League of Nations which she had helped to create. Encouraged by this passivity, the Japanese challenged U.S. strongholds in the Pacific and emerged as a new imperialist power.

Thus, the lack of courage and commitment of the democratic nations resulted in the rapid rise of German Nazism, Italian Fascism and Japanese militarism. Convinced that the morally weak democracies would not respond, the Axis powers launched the Second World War.

The Allied democratic nations (United States, England and France) survived this new challenge and won the confrontation, but once again they created the conditions for a third global conflict by shaping a new world order which gave enormous advantage to the war's co-winner, the totalitarian Soviet Union.

C. World War III

All the post-Second World War period has been marked by a constant confrontation between the Free World and the communist world on the global level. For that reason, many observers consider that World War III has already started. The Third World especially became the field of East-West competition (Korean War, Cuban crisis, Vietnam War, Portuguese decolonization, Central American crisis, etc.)

What is the real nature of the world wars? World War I and World War II constituted threats to Christian or democratic ideals. In the case of World War I, we saw democracy challenged by the authoritarian nations of Germany, Austria-Hungary and Turkey. In the case of World War II, the challenge stemmed from Adolf Hitler who viewed himself as a "deliverer" and interpreted history on the basis of racial elitism. If the non-democratic forces had prevailed in either of these wars (particularly World War II), the situation of Western society would be tragic. Like it or not, the world already finds itself in the midst of another global conflict.

1. The romantic appeal of communism

Communism constitutes a deviant form of humanism. Basing itself in scientism, communism has demonstrated a unique ability to win the young and the idealistic. It promises a world of equality, freedom, and harmony. Its slogans and its vision have been able to attract millions.

Communists romanticize their revolution. In his text *From Good Savage to Good Revolutionary*, Venezuelan writer Carlos Rangel analyzes the mentality of the Latin American revolutionary and sees him as one in search of an identity as a "noble savage," lost due to colonialism. Rangel maintains that some believe that through the revolution, the noble savage will be restored and indigenous cultures will return to what Rangel views as a mythical state of innocence. Communism has not liberated any nation. It has, however caused tremendous suffering.[5]

2. Communism and Christianity are not compatible

Instead of opposing it, some Christians have often tried to compromise with communism. In Latin America, "liberation theology" provides Christians with a Marxist analysis of history and has led thousands to communism. It is generally acknowledged that without a support base among Christians, the Sandinista revolution could not have succeeded. For many Nicaraguan Christians, the source of that support was "liberation theology." There are various forms of this theology but the most militant ones view violent confrontation with the system as part of the Christian mandate. This analysis is so powerful that it led priests such as Colombia's Camilo Torres to dedicate their lives to revolution. For Torres, the true Christian is he who, as did Torres, goes to the mountains with a rifle to participate in the communist revolution.[6]

In Latin America, communists never approach the Christians in an aggressive manner. They try to win their trust by telling them: "Of course we have nothing against keeping your faith in God. All that we ask is that you accept our view of history." Once they have convinced a person to accept historical materialism, they can proceed to the next step, which is the teaching of dialectical materialism. This leads to the denial of God's existence.

From a logical viewpoint, however, Christianity and

Marxism are not at all compatible. Liberation theology accepts the Marxist interpretation of history. However, Marx's interpretation of history is nothing other than historical materialism, which denies the existence of God. For this reason, the two are incompatible. God or no God, it is here that Christians are called to take a stand.

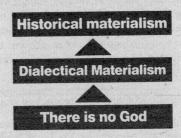

In the United States, an intermediary stage prior to communism may be secular humanism. Secular humanism is outlined in the "Humanist Manifesto," published in 1933, 85 years after the *Communist Manifesto*. It expresses, in the humanitarian style of the agnostic and atheistic ministers and professors who formed it, essential points of materialism, including belief in a universe which is self-existing and not created, and a human being who is a product of his interaction with nature. Secular humanism glorifies all that is charitable and good in human life, states that all problems are to be solved by humans alone, and although it does not deny the possibilities of "realities as yet undiscovered," believes that only that which can be proven by the scientific method exists as a reality. The 14th article of the Manifesto reads,

> The humanists are firmly convinced that existing acquisitive and profit-motivated society has shown itself to be inadequate and that a radical change in methods, controls, and motives must be instituted. A socialized and cooperative economic order must be established...[7]

Secular humanism denies the reality of spiritual experiences. It limits truth to what can be proven either rationally or empirically. This position can lead to Marxism, and at the least it has served to dull the spirituality of 20th century man.

3. Communist persecution of Christians

The Sandinista revolution in Nicaragua received much support from the Church. However, when the Sandinistas came to power they began to persecute Christians, to destroy their faith, and consequently to provoke their spiritual separation from God. Before taking power, communists always promise to respect freedom of religion. In Nicaragua, in the beginning of the revolution, the Sandinistas proclaimed unity of action with the Christians: "Let's join our forces," they said, "to destroy Somoza's dictatorship."

Once solidly installed in power, however, the Sandinistas launched a violent campaign in the official press and organized large demonstrations against the Protestant and Evangelical churches, which they depicted as "cults" ready to invade the country. They also closed down the only Jewish synagogue.

Concerning the Catholic Church, their strategy was more subtle. They attempted to break the unity of the Church by promoting a "popular Church" led by infiltrated communist agents against the hierarchy still faithful to the Pope. Pope John Paul II vigorously denounced this attempt of internal subversion in his visit to Nicaragua in 1983, and in 1984 ordered Catholic priests to leave positions in the Sandinista government.

Former Sandinista collaborator Humberto Belli describes the serious situation in Nicaragua:

> The present report intends to show that Christians' hopefulness regarding the Sandinista revolution has been mistaken. The difficulties which Christians are now facing from the Sandinista government—as well as the government's curtailment of basic freedoms, cooperation with Cuba and the Soviets, and so on —

are the result of the fact that the Sandinistas are fundamentally Marxist-Leninists. These policies are due to the Sandinista leader's explicit and firm commitment to Marxist-Leninist ideology. Given this commitment, it would be inconceivable that they would pursue any other set of policies, besides those which they have.

The implications of this situation are very serious for Christians in Nicaragua. They face a government which has expressed its dedication to building a communist state in Nicaragua which has no place for churches that are in any way independent of the government — no place for churches that want to preserve the integrity of Christian teaching and outreach. The government has already indicated its willingness to use every means to manipulate, divide, vilify, intimidate, and otherwise persecute Christians who do not give their wholehearted support to the Sandinistas' policies.

It is imperative that Christians outside Nicaragua should open their eyes and properly understand the circumstances that their fellow Christians in Nicaragua confront today. Failure to understand what those circumstances are has led many Christians to abstain from supporting their fellow Christians in Nicaragua and, even worse, it has led sometimes to their supporting those who are persecuting them. This has been a repetition of a pattern that developed after the communist revolution in Cuba.

Armando Valladares, a Cuban Christian and poet released last year from 22 years' imprisonment in Cuba, wrote that the most painful experience of Christians in Cuba has resulted from Christians abroad giving their support to the Marxist government rather than Christians persecuted by the government. These are his words:

"During those years, with the purpose of forcing
us to abandon our religious beliefs and to demoralize
us, the Cuban communist indoctrinators repeatedly
used the statements of support for Castro's revolution
made by some representatives of American Christian
churches. Every time that a pamphlet was published
in the U.S., every time a clergyman would write an
article in support of Fidel Castro's dictatorship, a
translation would reach us, and that was worse for
the Christian political prisoners than the beatings or
the hunger. While we waited for the embrace of
solidarity from our brothers in Christ, incomprehen-
sibly to us those who were embraced were our
tormentors."[8]

The physical effects of communism have been the same
everywhere: violence, hunger, elitism, and death. The West,
however, has failed to stop the growth of communism. We
have lost our idealism and our vision, and for that reason, we
have failed to offer a viable response to Marxism.

4. The lack of Western awareness of the communist threat

Although Lenin declared from the outset that the
communist revolution would not end until the world was
communized, we in the West have been unable to grasp the
extreme seriousness of the Soviet threat. In Western cities
such as Boston and New York, thousands of young people
participate in protests against cruelty to laboratory animals,
but fail to protest communist cruelty to their fellow human
beings.

At the same time, citizens of the West show great
concern regarding the build-up of Western armaments, but
fail to show similar concern regarding the massive Soviet
build-up. Nevertheless, Soviet leaders have declared their
objectives and have been consistently moving to achieve
effective world domination.

Conclusion

To conclude, let us summarize the development of the religious and humanistic tradition over the past five centuries. The Reformation and the Catholic Counter-Reformation culminated in the 16th century. This was followed two centuries later by the Great Awakening in America and the Pietist movement in Europe. These religious renewals served as a basis for the American Revolution as well as a basis for Western democracy.

Although, in the West, we still pay lip service to religious ideals, our societies are becoming increasingly materialistic. Today all humankind is in need of a world view, which has the ability to revive idealism and altruism in the Free World, which can offer solutions for social and personal problems, and which can promote cooperation and peace among the many developed and underdeveloped nations.

On the humanistic side, the Renaissance was followed two centuries later by the Enlightenment. This humanistic view contributed not only to the French Revolution but it also established the philosophical foundation for the communist revolution. French philosopher Maurice Clavel observed that through the Renaissance, man denied sin, through the Enlightenment, he denied revelation and through communism, he denied God.

After a toll of millions of lives, communism has produced

no utopian society, nor is it approaching that goal. Today Eastern Europe is rampant with crime. Every five minutes, there is a violent murder (provoked by hold-ups, robberies, etc.) committed in the Soviet Union. [9] Today in cities such as Budapest, young people resort to drugs. [10] Furthermore, because its society is composed of a rich and powerful elite (the nomenklatura), we can say that its fruits are materialism and selfishness.

We can conclude that neither communism because of its atheistic foundation nor contemporary Western society because of its present confusion of values have effectively responded to human problems. For that reason, we need a new response—one which can unite these two developments. We refer to this as Godism.

Introducing Godism

In the past, scientific theory has often contradicted religious thought. Society and even some scientists were asked to choose between their traditional religious beliefs and recent scientific findings. Since the Enlightenment, people have often opted for science.

This has changed in the present century. Materialism denied the existence of a spiritual element at work in the physical world, and it sought to rationalize all phenomena on

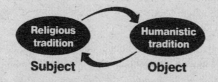

the basis of scientific observation. In *The New Class Divided*, Alfred Parry points out that today, more and more, Eastern bloc scientists find a contradiction between recent scientific discoveries and communist materialism. Among Soviet scientists, communist theory is perceived as unscientific and outmoded. In light of continued scientific discovery in fields such as nuclear physics and cybernetics, the days of communist absolutism seem to be numbered.[11]

Regardless of the process by which humans developed, materialism cannot deny the unique role of the human being in the overall universal order. Only the human being can relate to and appreciate every dimension of the creation — the sea, the stars, plants, fish, reptiles, or mammals. Today scientists argue that there is increasing evidence that the world was made for man.

God

Humanity

Creation

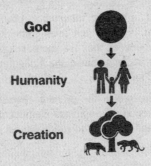

God chose humanity as an instrument to express His love to the whole creation. For that reason, we can appreciate the whole of nature.

The true value of the human being is infinite. Every man is a son of God. Every women is a daughter of God.

Mother Theresa of Calcutta once said that the first time that she saw a man dying in the streets, she was repulsed. But something called her to that person and led her to pick him up and bring him back to her home. As she looked in the

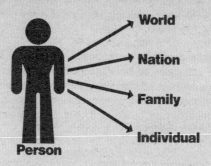

eyes of that man, she saw Christ. She discovered the true value of her fellow man. The implications of the Judeo-Christian tradition are boundless. Every man and every woman has unique and divine value. Every man and every woman, for that reason, merits our respect, our love, our care and our concern.

People are often blind to others because of selfishness. As we have seen in the 19th century, selfishness was philosophically justified by materialist world views. Yet the reality of the latter part of the 20th century challenges such materialist perceptions.

Ultimately each of us has to reflect about our own selves. Who is my life for? Myself? My family? The nation? The world? God? The great individuals of history were those who were able to live for the sake of their nation and beyond. Such a lifestyle requires one to go beyond selfishness. We cannot go beyond selfishness without God and an appreciation of the value of each person as a child of God. We are one family under God. Because we are one family under God, we can go beyond race and creed, and realize a brotherhood of man. Harmony between the religious tradition and humanism, and among cultures and nations is the goal of the CAUSA Worldview and the task of modern man.

The late U.S. President John F. Kennedy spoke eloquently to the hearts and imaginations of many people when he said:

> To those people in the huts and villages across the globe struggling to break the bonds of misery, we pledge our best efforts to help them help themselves, for whatever period is required—not because the communists may be doing it, not because we seek their votes, but because it is right.[12]

CHAPTER SIX NOTES

1. Romans 7:22-23.
2. Albert Camus, *The Rebel*, New York, Vintage Books, 1956, pp.26-27.
3. Alexis de Tocqueville, *The Ancien Regime and the Revolution*.
4. François Furet, Interview, *New York Tribune*, July 4, 1983, p.1B.
5. Carlos Rangel, *Du Bon Sauvage au Bon Revolutionaire*, Paris, Robert Laffont, 1976, p.318.
6. Camilo Torres, *Revolutionary Priest*, edited by John Gerassi, New York, Random House, 1971, pp.324-326 and p.426.
7. *The New Humanist*, Vol.VI, May-June 1933, No.3, p.3.
8. Humberto Belli, *Nicaragua: Christians Under Fire*, Garden City, Michigan, Puebla Institute, pp.7-8.
9. *A l'Est*, edited by Alain Brossa and Juan Yves Potel, Paris, Seuil, 2 Mai, 1983, p.57.
10. Ibid., p.219-224.
11. Alfred Parry, *The New Class Divided*, New York, MacMillan Company, 1966.
12. John F. Kennedy, Inaugural Address, January 20, 1961.

INTRODUCTION TO
THE CAUSA WORLDVIEW

CAUSA Worldview I
General Overview of Godism

Preface

The CAUSA movement is an ideological movement, not a religious movement. We consider communism to be an ideology. Communism can only be defeated by a superior ideology or world view. We offer here a world view based on philosophical and scientific reasoning.

The CAUSA Worldview is centered on God. Therefore, readers will find certain religious expressions and reference to some general religious principles. As a "rule of thumb," if any statement in the CAUSA Worldview conflicts with the readers' own religious beliefs or theological principles, we ask that they keep their own views. CAUSA's purpose is not to change anyone's religion.

What is the purpose of presenting the CAUSA Worldview?

1) Our purpose is to promote and strengthen understanding of God and man's relationship with Him. Why? Because that is the fundamental weapon that we need to defeat communism, because communism is an ideology which is based on the denial of the existence of God. God alone can overcome godlessness.

2) Furthermore, CAUSA wishes to present certain universal principles which God-believing people can use as a rallying point. We seek a common ground upon which all religious people and people of conscience can unite. We invite you to examine this section looking for what unites us, instead of what divides us.

3) Another purpose of the CAUSA Worldview is to inspire men and women to a higher spiritual awareness. Materialism is prevailing in more than just the communist world. The West has likewise adapted itself to various materialistic world views such as secular humanism and Social Darwinism.

An awakening into higher spiritual values is vital to bring change in our society. Confusion in the value system of the West has brought about the chaos of today's Western world. We have had the experience at our seminars of CAUSA presentations "striking a chord" and awakening the dormant spirituality of men and women. Many participants claim that they have gained a higher understanding of spiritual values through the CAUSA presentation.

We need a spiritual and moral awakening in order to ignite the true revolution of men, which alone can bring the needed change in our society. We believe the CAUSA Worldview will make us better Christians, better religionists, better scholars, better soldiers, better statesmen, better journalists, and better men and women. The only thing we cannot guarantee is that we will make anyone a better communist.

4) The CAUSA Worldview is based on universal principles that are in conflict with no religion. The CAUSA Worldview is respected in Buddhist countries as well as in Christian nations. It can also be taught very effectively in the Islamic and Hindu cultures. In countries such as Japan and Korea, which are primarily Buddhist, the CAUSA Worldview is flourishing.

Because American readers are aware of the Judeo-Christian tradition, we use some biblical quotations. We do so simply to facilitate understanding.

5) We speak frequently of God, but there are certainly readers who may not believe in God. What does a God-centered world view have to do with them? We are not excluding anyone from associating with CAUSA as long as they are

men and women of conscience believing in moral and ethical principles.

We in CAUSA believe that the conscience of man is the agent of God. There are men and women in our world today who live godly lives without professing any particular belief in God. We believe that when you are obeying your conscience, you are actually obeying the voice of God. Therefore, men and women of conscience can be great defenders of freedom, and can work with us.

These are the basic five points CAUSA wants to make clear before beginning this section. This will hopefully avert misunderstandings in this area.

Introduction

The ancient Chinese war tactician, Sun Tzu, once observed that if a person knows neither himself nor his enemy, then in 100 battles, he will suffer 100 defeats. Likewise, Sun Tzu observed that if one knows either one's enemy or oneself, it would be possible to win 50 out of 100 battles. He asserted that the only way to win all 100 battles was in knowing both one's enemy and oneself.

Until now, we have devoted a lot of attention to our enemy, international communism, which is also the enemy of God. We have systematically refuted each of the major pillars of communist ideology. Beginning with this section, we want to understand something more about ourselves, our potential and our responsibility.

One hundred and fifty years ago, the famous French historian, Alexis de Tocqueville, wrote:

> There are now two great nations in the world which, starting from different points, seem to be advancing toward the same goal: the Russians and the Anglo-Americans.
>
> Their point of departure is different and their paths diverse; nevertheless, each seems called by

some secret design of Providence one day to hold in
its hands the destinies of half the world.

Amazingly, what de Tocqueville foresaw 150 years ago
has become a reality today. But the one thing which de
Tocqueville failed to predict was the role of ideology. In 1917,
Russia became a central part of the Soviet Union. Since that
time, the Soviet Union has advanced and emerged as one of
the two great powers in the world. Today, concern grows
about the Soviet Union and communism. People ask how to
stop this force.

In his article, "Why I am against communism," Dr. Fred
Schwartz, a distinguished anti-communist for decades, notes,

I am against communism because I am against war,
dictatorship, monopoly, slavery, fascism, fratricide,
cannabilism, imperialism, atheism, materialism, spiritual infanticide, and idolatry. Communism advocates
and practices all of these.

Dr. Schwartz is correct; these are all problems. They
are all symptoms of applied Marxism. But like any disease,
there must be a cause, or an original virus which has produced these symptoms. For that reason, we need to ask,
What is the virus or core evil of communism? Unless we
discover this, we cannot prescribe a cure. That means we
can never stop communism.

Many explanations have certainly been advanced. Some
people have argued that communism's core evil stems from
its deprivation of freedom. Ironically, when we study Marx,
we realize that he claimed to have designed a philosophy
which would allow for true human freedom. This being its
supposed goal, can we say that the deprivation of freedom is
communism's core evil?

In the United States, some people seem to feel that the
core evil of communism stems from its stated goal of abolishing
private property. However communists often deny their intention to abolish private property. Lenin promised the Russian
peasants that after the revolution he would bring them "bread,

What is the core ✪ evil of Communism?

land, and peace." In El Salvador today, the communist FMLN also promises land, and in communist China and the USSR, peasants do have tiny plots of land. Likewise, the Soviet leaders have villas and new Mercedes Benzes, so can abolition of private property be the essence of the evil within communism? Refugees from Eastern Europe often testify that communism's greatest evil is its violation of human rights. Yet no one group presents itself as a more vocal proponent of human rights than the Marxists.

Writers such as Erich Fromm feel Marxism can restore human dignity, and communist propaganda persistently accuses many non-communist governments of corruption and short-comings. Communists speak of their intention to build a world where no one will live in fear, or be without enough to eat. They portray themselves as the world's true humanitarians, therefore it is difficult to establish that the violation of human rights is communism's core evil.

Political writers, such as Hannah Arendt, might argue that communism's core evil is found in its totalitarian nature. However, the communists counter that repressive rule will not continue forever. It is only a stage. Once the world has been freed from the threat of counter-revolution, there will be no need for repression; there will not even be any need for government. Men and women will be completely liberated.

This cannot be the core evil either because theoretically totalitarian rule is thus only a stage in a process.

The Nightmare of Man

Workers' living hell
1. Workers' utopia
New class — cruel masters
2. Classless society
Total enslavement
3. Total freedom and democracy
Economic disaster
4. Abundance of goods

Communism: promises versus reality

Marx's slogan from his text *On the Gotha Program* sounds poetic: "From each according to his ability, to each according to his needs." Communists predict a glorious future for humanity. Soviet Premier Khrushchev predicted that a communist "paradise" would appear on earth by 1980. Khrushchev commissioned many Soviet scholars to do studies on this supposed "new society." They anticipated a classless society. Communism was to provide total freedom and true democracy. All human needs were to be abundantly satisfied. Today those studies are an embarrassment for the Soviet Union and communism stands as a failure.

Rather than fulfilling man's dreams, communism has come to be a nightmare for all of its victims. Rather than a workers' utopia, we find a workers' inferno with poor living conditions which have provoked widespread worker revolts. The unrest in Poland may very well be only the tip of the iceberg visible to the Western press.

Instead of a classless society, we have found in every communist nation a new and powerful elite known as the *nomenklatura*. They are cruel masters who live in luxury at the expense of the common people. Instead of total freedom and democracy, communist society has encouraged abuse and slavery. Furthermore, instead of an abundance of goods, the communist economies are in the midst of inordinate economic crises.

What has provoked all of this? What is behind all of this suffering? CAUSA feels that communism's core evil does not lie in its attacks on private property, its violation of human rights, its deprivation of freedom, or its totalitarian rule. These are only symptomatic of a more profound problem.

Then, once again, what is the core evil of communism? It is communism's militant denial of the existence of God. We find this militant posture beginning with Marx's earliest writings. Furthermore, communism militantly denies the eternal life of human beings. If there is no God, and no eternal life, then there is no basis for absolute values. At the bottom of any atheistic ideology is the belief that man is responsible to no one greater than himself.

When an ideology is constructed which denies God and the eternal human spirit, and this ideology is adopted as official state policy, what is the result? All of the unrestrained power of the state is brought to bear on any dissenters and state atrocity and barbarism come to rule. The core evil of communism emerges when the denial of God and the denial of the eternal life of man become state policy.

This we have seen in Stalin's Russia, Mao's China, Pol Pot's Cambodia, Ortega's Nicaragua, and in every other nation where communism has been implanted. Such patterns led French new philosopher Bernard Henri Levi to refer to communism as "barbarism with a human face." Behind a facade of hope and promise there is a philosophical basis for abusing human rights. When God is denied by the official ideology, the state can lie, kill and extort without any remorse. The state becomes a beast. In fact, the communist state is worse than a beast. It violates human dignity, and does so with all of the ingenuity of the human mind, something no animal could ever do. Communism philosophically justifies barbarism and genocide.

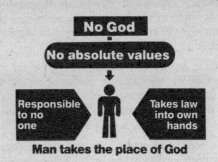

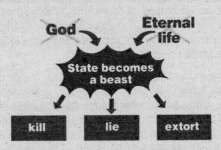

As French philosopher Albert Camus observed,

We are living in the age of the perfect crime. Our criminals are no longer children who can use passion as their excuse. They are adults and they have the perfect alibi, philosophy which can be used even to transform murderers into judges.

Communism is the perfection of the Machiavellian concept that "the end justifies the means." The human cost of communism has been 150,000,000 lives, and this amount is increasing at the rate of one victim every fifteen seconds. Communism thus constitutes the worst enemy of God and the worst crime against humanity.

If a killer were to come into the room and start systematically killing people, what would you do? You might be engaged in some important activity, but you would drop everything and try to stop the killer, no matter what the price. This is just the situation which we are facing today. The room is our world, and the killer is communism. In such a situation, it is the first responsibility of everyone to respond to the extraordinary emergency, stop the international lawlessness of communism, and safeguard the planet earth.

How does one respond to the threat of communism? For CAUSA, traditional anti-communist approaches are good but not enough. In order to awaken the young and the idealistic, we cannot only attack the deeds of the communists. We in the West also are guilty of shortcomings, and we must admit to them. Furthermore, to win intellectual people to our cause, we must point out the ideological fallacies of Marxism and show that even when social problems are real, communism brings no solution to them. Then, we must offer a real solution to the moral and social ills which have created fertile ground for communism.

We need a positive solution. We have been defensive too long. In order to win, we have to take the offensive. Since this war is a war of ideas, we must initiate an ideological offensive.

Marxism thrives by exploiting humanity's religious sentiments. It engenders passion and supplants the religious experience with a political one. We need to recognize communism as a godless form of religion. A godless religion can only be subjugated by God Himself. Therefore, an ideological offensive against communism must be launched from the point of belief in God. Just as light dispels darkness, the knowledge of God overcomes atheism.

To achieve this, we need a God-centered world view. CAUSA calls this world view "Godism." We use the term "Godism" in order to emphasize that we are not attempting to preach the viewpoint of a particular religion or denomination — instead, we are speaking of a philosophical perspective broad enough for all religionists and for all people of conscience.

As this section proceeds, it should become clear that Godism constitutes a solution to communism and a foundation for a lasting peace. It can also provide the foundation for a just and moral society. In other words, the solution to the problem of communism is only an intermediate goal. Our ultimate goal must be the fulfillment of the age-old human dream — the dream of a just and moral world.

One reason for the success of communism up to this point has been its appeal to the natural aspiration of people for an ideal world. In history, both good and evil men have addressed this aspect of human nature. On the positive side, Martin Luther King, Jr. inspired millions of people when he spoke of his dream of a society free from racism. On the negative side, Hitler rallied millions to the task of building a "Third Reich." Such appeals have been successful because for good or for bad, they touch the innate human desire to see God's ideal established on the earth.

In the same way, communism speaks of the realization of utopia, and asks people to sacrifice for the "workers' paradise," but after 70 years, this utopian dream has turned out to be a nightmare. There can be no good and moral world where God is excluded. The ideal world must be established with God at the center. In religious terminology, this is known as the Kingdom of God on Earth. This is our dream.

CAUSA Worldview

GODISM

**Solution to Communism
Foundation for Lasting Peace**

**Realization of Age-Old
Human Dream**

Godism

CAUSA proposes Godism as the means to achieve our ultimate dream. Belief in God is the basis of all religion. It is true that there are certain religious traditions which do not explicitly profess the existence of "God." When we examine these traditions, however, we find that they are seeking the fulfillment of ultimate justice, truth and love. In essence, then, they recognize the existence of absolute values based upon an Absolute Being.

Men and women of conscience

If we are to unite all religious people upon some common ground, that common ground must be the belief in God. There is nothing more fundamental than this. Godism is a world view based on the belief in God. By using Godism as a common ground upon which to unite, the God-affirming forces of the world will be able to effectively oppose the God-denying forces of communism.

In the future, historians will record that a showdown occurred between Godism and communism. Godism must prevail, for it is based on the truth of God's existence.

Godism also provides ground for the unity of those men and women who do not recognize the existence of God, but who are nonetheless directed toward absolute values by their consciences. As we said in the preface, the conscience of man is the agent of God. Man's conscience is created by God to seek after His eternal moral and ethical standard. When one is obeying his conscience, he is actually following the voice of God based on His moral principle. Thus, no one seeking after absolute goodness would be excluded from the common ground of Godism.

It frequently happens that conscientious people poignantly realize the existence of God when they come to study Godism. This is because hearing truth brings an awakening of the spirituality of man.

A. Overview of Godism

In this section, we want to provide a bird's eye view of Godism. We will introduce four areas:

1) The characteristics of God
2) God's ideal of creation
3) The world of reality: a world of evil
4) God's will of restoration

1. The characteristics of God

Godism begins with an affirmation of the existence of God. God is the creator of all things, and human beings are

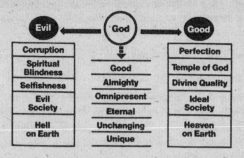

His highest creation. This assertion is the starting point of Godism.

Let us consider the nature or characteristics of God. What kind of God is He? To answer this question, we can look at God as He is described in the Bible. The biblical God is good, almighty, omnipresent, eternal, unchanging and unique.

This might be called the common sense view of God. God is good because as the Creator, he defines goodness. He must also be omnipotent, since he is the ruler of creation and the lord of history. Then He must be omnipresent. Why? Because God cannot be limited in space. He is infinite. He is transcendent of time — eternal. The God of Abraham is the same God today. The same God which created the first human ancestors is watching over our destinies. That God must be unchanging. He is governing the world with timeless law. His standard of value does not change. His moral principle remains forever. Finally, He must be unique. He must be the only God. There could not be another God like Him.

We consider these to be the general characteristics of God. If there is God, He must be all of this and more. If He does not exist, then it is an entirely different story. Either there is a God as we have described Him or there is not. There can be no in-between.

Now, this God is the Creator of the world and man. What kind of world and man would He create?

That world must be good, and man must be good. Would a good God, if He is truly almighty, create anything other than a good world and good men and women?

2. God's ideal of creation

The perfection of man: perfect union with God

Man is created with the potential for perfection. Today, however, people are not serious about perfection in the creation or in themselves. Since we constantly experience human imperfection, we are seldom aware of the original blueprint of God for the perfection of man. Nevertheless, could God create anything that was not perfect? If God is omnipotent and perfect Himself, He can only design and create perfectable beings. Jesus said, "You therefore must be perfect as your Heavenly Father is perfect." (Matt. 5:48) These words can only mean that God has created each man with the potential for perfection. That is, the potential to be like God.

It is important here that we define clearly what perfection means. It does not mean that perfected man does not make mistakes, or that he could not injure himself in an accident. Perfection does not imply having superhuman powers. We are speaking about the perfection of man's *character*. Perfected man would live totally in accord with the will of God, experiencing complete union with God. A man of perfection would never desire to separate himself from God, nor would he be capable of being corrupted. To use a biblical expression, perfected man is intended to be the temple and dwelling place of God. As Paul wrote, "Do you not know that you are God's temple and that God's spirit dwells in you?" (I Cor. 3:16) When man becomes a house and God is the master of that house, then how could that man do anything other than God's will?

Perfection, therefore, means man's maturity and his perfect union with God. This is the kind of union which Jesus described in the Bible when he said, "I am in the Father and the Father in me." (John 14:10) The Father and the Son are one.

Man is originally endowed with divine character

When a man reaches this perfection and becomes a temple of God, then that man will possess a God-like or divine character. The God-like character of perfected man means that he not only exercises his five physical senses to perceive the reality of the world of creation, but also uses his full spiritual capacity. For this divine man, the spiritual reality is no longer a matter of "belief," but it becomes a matter of "fact." He "knows," instead of "believes," that God exists and the spiritual dimension exists. He then experiences the totality of God's creation. When man becomes spiritually mature, he becomes a divine, totally unselfish person who can exercise perfect love. His every action is motivated by his love for God. This is the meaning of man's perfection, as it is taught by and manifested in the life of Jesus Christ.

Ideal society — the Kingdom of God on Earth

As the Judeo-Christian tradition maintains, God intended the first human ancestors to reach perfection and multiply this perfection by having children. The human family should have started with one couple achieving perfection, and that perfection would have been passed down through the human lineage to those who are alive today. Clearly, had this occurred, we would all be living in a perfect society. It is quite reasonable to think that this is the way in which God intended to create the ideal society, or in religious terms, the Kingdom of Heaven on Earth. God intended that ideal society on earth first. When God created this world, he had every intention to create His ideal on earth. Thus, Jesus asked us to pray, "Thy Kingdom come, thy will be done on earth as it is in heaven."

Problem: religious people tend to neglect life on earth

At this point we recognize one important problem with our religious world. Religion in general has tended towards "other worldliness." Too often, those who have been suffering from exploitation and poverty are told that they must bear such injustice until they reach a better life after death. Some Christians, in particular, have turned away from the world's problems because they are waiting to be lifted up into the air with Christ in a supernatural way. Of course, we must prepare for our eternal life. Yet, it is because our eternal life is so important that we must work for justice upon the earth, because the earth is where we prepare for eternity.

As long as we ignore earthly realities, we can never win over communism. If we look exclusively toward the next life, the communists will take this world and make it impossible to pursue spiritual values here. Communism is single-minded in its goal of world domination. After all, for the communists there is no other world. If religious people surrender this world to communism, the future will be tragic.

In the CAUSA view, the earth is the first place where we must realize God's ideal. We must build God's kingdom on earth before we even look to our reward in heaven. God did not create this earth in order to give it to communism. God created the earth for the realization of His ideal. The importance of establishing God's ideal on earth was clearly stated by Jesus when he said, "Whatever you bind on earth shall be bound in heaven, and whatever you loose on earth shall be loosed in heaven." (Matt 16:19)

This is also found clearly in the Lord's prayer, "Thy kingdom come, thy will be done, on earth as it is in heaven." (Matt 6:10)

Therefore our "manifesto" to the communists could be this: "Communism has no business on the earth. This is God's world. We as His children claim ownership. We shall build His kingdom here on earth; we shall realize His ideal. His children have a right to live and flourish here on earth. A God-denying force has no place here. Communism get out!"

3. The world of reality — a world of evil

When we look around ourselves today, we see that we are not living in a perfect world. We are living in a society which is corrupt and far from perfection. What happened to God's original ideal? It is apparent that it has not been realized as God intended.

Man's separation from God brought about fallen society

We recognize that a deviation from God's original plan must have taken place. In other words, man has departed from God and entered the realm outside of the principles of God. The process of man's separation from God is known as the fall of man. This is the real alienation of man — it is a spiritual alienation, not an economic alienation as Marxists see it.

Due to the fall of man, the unprincipled or evil world came into being. God never planned to have this kind of world, yet it came about. Some might ask, How is this kind of deviation possible? We can answer by saying that God allowed man freedom, and gave him the right to decide his own destiny. Man has misused his freedom and ignored his God-given responsibility. In this way, he has departed from God. Because of man's separation from God, man has become corrupted instead of perfected. We must underscore, however, that God has to allow man such freedom, even though it may be abused. (The reason will be explained later in CAUSA Worldview IV.)

According to Judeo-Christian teachings, the human fall was preceded by deception. In the symbology of the Bible, the serpent lied to the first woman, telling her that God was deliberately hiding the most desirous gift from man. The woman ignored the truth from God, and listened to this lie. In this way, man's tragic separation from God occurred.

Spiritual blindness

This is the beginning of man's corruption or alienation, which has resulted in man's spiritual "blindness." Man has lost his understanding of the deepest aspect of himself, the spiritual aspect. Since the fall, man has lived with a strong awareness of the physical aspect of life, but his awareness of spiritual reality has been weak and in many cases has been extinguished. Man's corrupted human nature is manifested in selfishness, greed, jealousy and immorality.

The reality of evil

This corrupted nature began with the first man and woman, and has been multiplied from that point. Coming from these same original ancestors, all human beings have suffered the same destiny. Instead of multiplying perfection and goodness, imperfection and corruption have been multiplied, and spiritual darkness has plagued the human race. The sinful society which we find today can accurately be called "hell." It has become a reality here on the earth.

The ideal society can be characterized as a society in which honesty, trust, cooperation, mutual love and happiness prevail. The fallen world, on the other hand, is characterized by frustration, hatred, struggle, exploitation, immorality, crime and war. Though we live in a world of tremendous technological capability, the simple fact is that no amount of material wealth will lift off spiritual darkness, and we are still in the world of "hell."

We clearly recognize that communism is not the beginning of human evil. The fall of man, the separation of man from God, occurred at the beginning of human history, while communism is a product of the 19th century. However, communism has brought the perfection of evil. We cannot imagine any more dangerous ideology than one which harnesses and perverts man's natural aspiration to build an ideal world, and puts it to work constructing a human hell. Communism has created the ultimate hell.

Perfect Model

Human Body

Microcosm of the Universe

Microcosm of Ideal Society

Ideal society — what is it like?

No one has seen the original world that God intended, because it was never realized, so it is difficult to picture it correctly. Yet we find a model of this society in the functioning of the human body. The human body consists of over 400 billion cells composing many body organs and parts. Each of these cells is working harmoniously for the common purpose of the body.

There is no conflict between the cells or the body parts. A person's right arm does not quarrel with his left arm; his two legs cooperate and move the entire body wherever he wants to go. Although it is the mouth which enjoys the good taste of food, the hand carries the food into the mouth without any complaint. How is it that all the different parts of the body work so harmoniously? There are two important factors.

First, the entire body has one whole purpose which is commonly shared by all the parts. Every part is working for the well-being of the entire body, while at the same time all parts are partaking of the benefit of the whole. When you eat, for example, the stomach works for the entire body, and the whole body, including the stomach, receives the benefit.

Second, there is one coordination center for the entire body: the brain. The brain is also working for the well-being of the entire body. It will give proper communication and coordination so that the whole body can function harmoniously. Seen from this point of view, the human body provides a vivid example of how an ideal society could function.

In an ideal society, the whole society functions like the human body. First of all, there is one common purpose shared by all mankind. That purpose is the very purpose of God's creation — the joy of God and peace and happiness of all men. Each works for this common purpose and each is benefitted by it.

This is possible because there is one common center for all humankind, God. If we compare the universe to the human body, then God is in the position of the brain. God works for the overall purpose and coordinates all things for the fulfillment of that purpose. This is how "heavenly society" should function. Such a society is where the full potential of individual man can be realized. This is the God-centered society. The Bible says, "For just as the body is one and has many members, all of the members of the body, though many, are one body, so it is with Christ." (1 Cor 12:12)

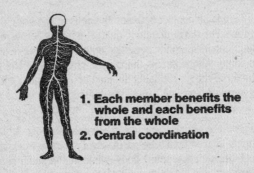

1. **Each member benefits the whole and each benefits from the whole**
2. **Central coordination**

Ideal human relations

How can people really relate to each other as brothers and sisters? There is only one way. All people — John, Susan, Jim and Mary — must recognize that they have the same parent, God. We are all brothers and sisters only when we recognize one common parent above us.

In the original ideal of God, every person experiences the love of God. John, for example, is the loving son of God. In that sense, he is governed by God's will. He is a temple of God. The same God is dwelling in Tom, Susan, Jim and Mary. Then the same will of God is governing them also. How could there be hate and conflict between them? It is impossible. They must be in harmony and unity because they are responding to the same will of God, the parent of all. The vertical union with God brings about the horizontal union among men.

When men and women are separated from God, they are also isolated from one another. They have no feeling for the goals and desires of the other person. The purpose of the whole is lost. When man lost God, he lost his fellow man as well.

Human alienation came into being when man became disconnected from his original source — God. From that point everything has been disoriented and disorganized. This is the far-reaching significance of the human fall.

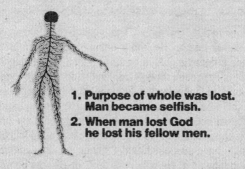

1. Purpose of whole was lost. Man became selfish.
2. When man lost God he lost his fellow men.

Fallen society

What is fallen society? It is like a sick or injured body.

Our society is like a person whose central nervous system is broken down. Because of this breakdown, each person's connection to God has been lost. Since the vertical connection to God has been damaged, it is difficult to establish good horizontal connections between men. Since the "nervous system" is paralyzed, we can kill, steal and hurt one another, and still we do not feel any pain from it.

If the cells of the body begin to destroy one another, as in cancer, the body will surely die. Throughout human history, we find a continuous succession of countless wars, struggles, atrocities and killings. This is not the fulfillment of God's purpose of creation. We are living in a world of deviation, a perverted kingdom, a kingdom of living hell.

4. God's will of restoration

We have now described two contrasting worlds: one is the ideal society which God originally intended, and the other is the society which we find today, outside of the realm of God's ideal. Furthermore, until now, human society has been creating a fallen history. Given this situation, the most important question is — what is God doing about this world? If God has no power or plan to do anything, then humanity has no hope. We would have to live with this sinful reality forever with no way to restore ourselves to wholesomeness.

Fortunately, this is not the case. God is almighty and omnipotent. Just as He had a definite purpose in creation, God has a definite goal in human history, and that goal and purpose is the restoration of mankind. God is going to restore this world of imperfection into the world of goodness and perfection which He originally planned. His determination has been clearly recorded in the Bible. In Isaiah 46:11 the prophet records the promise of God, "I have spoken, and I will bring it to pass. I have purposed, and I will do it." It is not written that God may do it, He will try to do it, or He may be thinking about it. In no uncertain terms, the scripture states, He will do it.

God has spoken of an ideal world. Therefore, by all

means He will bring that world to pass by restoring man to goodness. He has purposed a world of joy and satisfaction, and that is what He will do at any cost. No matter what, He will accomplish. This is the absolute goal and will of God.

Restoration is re-creation

God's goal and will is truly the hope of mankind, and restoration is truly man's hope of salvation. We know that God had the wisdom and power to create this world in the first place, and we know that the same God, with the same wisdom and power, will re-create mankind into the originally intended perfection and goodness. Therefore, restoration is re-creation. Yet God does not have to re-create too much. The only part of God's creation that has deviated is man. Everything else is perfect. Even the physical or biological aspect of man is perfect. It is only the internal aspect of man that needs re-creation. Of course, this is the most important part. The spirituality of humanity must be re-created.

Every person will eventually be able to restore his original character and essential value. All men and women shall become "perfect as their Heavenly Father is perfect." We shall create a society in which trust and love prevail and harmony and cooperation shall be the natural order of daily life.

CAUSA Worldview
On History

1. **History has a goal**
   Moves toward the fulfillment of God's original ideal of creation
2. **History of restoration**
3. **The role of men and women in history**
   Partners with God in restoration
4. **History of struggle**
   Between good and evil

B. The CAUSA view of human history

Communists look at human history as the history of class struggle. They apply the law of the dialectic to human history and arrive at an apocalyptic conclusion. They believe that the time has arrived when the capitalists must be eliminated, and through the process of socialism the ultimate communist utopia will dawn. Of course, this theory is based upon materialism with the assumption that there is no God. This is a false assumption, and the predicted utopia has never been realized.

By contrast, the CAUSA Worldview offers a God-centered view of human history.

1. History has a goal.

Human history is not merely a random collection of events. History is being guided by God, and the course of history is closely related to His will. God is the Creator, and His work of creation was carried out to fulfill a distinct purpose. This original purpose of God has never changed. History is the record of God's efforts working with mankind to fulfill His original purpose.

When we recognize God and His will in history, there must be a definite goal to reach. Ever since creation this goal has not changed. The goal which God originally intended to accomplish by His creation is the very same goal God is working to accomplish now.

2. Human history is the history of restoration

We have already emphasized that a good and almighty God can only design a good world. God began with an original ideal. This is the world in which men and women become true temples of God, and their God-given nature fully blossoms. In this world, each person would possess a God-like character. This is the world where the perfect union of each person with God prevails, and this is the world where people are incapable of corruption. Such an ideal society has not been realized because of the fall of man.

Human beings, separated from God, brought forth here on earth the totally opposite result. This is evil — a world of decay and corruption, a history of war and crime.

We believe that God is almighty and that He has a plan for this fallen world. That plan must be the restoration of the original world. This restoration of the original world is the will and goal of history. History is the history of restoration. God is going to restore all things and men and women to His original ideal. When that is consummated, and restoration is completed, God's new history of goodness will begin.

3. The role of men and women in history

People have a vital role in history. They are the partners of God in restoration. God's will or goal cannot be achieved unless people fulfill certain portions of responsibility. Even though God has a certain schedule, whenever someone fails to respond to the schedule, God's program is prolonged. This is happening over and over again due to the failure of key individuals. Let us take one example from the Bible. God ordered the Israelites to make the exodus from Egypt to Canaan under the leadership of Moses. If they had responded to God's will 100%, that distance could have been covered in 40 days. Due to the chosen people's constant faithlessness and rebellion, it was prolonged to 40 years. Furthermore, Moses as God's chosen leader could not even enter into Canaan and was succeeded by Joshua and Caleb. Only the second generation born in the wilderness entered the promised land. It was not God's desire for this to happen, but human failure in responding to God brought this misery. This type of failure has caused an incalculable prolongation of human history.

Even today God needs men and women who are dedicated to the consummation of His ideal. History cannot be fulfilled without people doing their role. This is God's greatest source of anguish, yet God endures and has great hope that we will respond to Him and fulfill our responsibilities. In this respect the old maxim must be reversed to yield: "God proposes and man disposes." Now is the time when we must stand up and must respond to God's urgent call. In the fight against communism, people must be the champions of God. So far, too few men and women have responded. Too few Christians have responded. CAUSA is bringing the call of God all over the world so that all righteous men and women can respond. When people respond to God, human history will dramatically change.

4. Human history has been the history of struggle between good and evil

If the fall had not occurred and man had reached perfection, this world would not have seen the history of struggle. God did not plan to have human beings struggle, because progress and prosperity can be brought about through the laws of cooperation. However, the day evil was introduced into the world, the history of struggle began.

The history of struggle has not been the history of class struggle as communism proclaims. It has been the history of the struggle between good and evil. God is always working to spread goodness among humankind. Over and over again, however, evil men have attacked the side of goodness, but goodness will always endure and finally prevail. It is God's will that all people one day abandon evil and come to the side of goodness.

Good and evil defined

What is evil? Anything that goes against the will of God and anything that blocks the fulfillment of God's ideal is evil. Anything in accord with the will of God is good. In this respect communism today is the worst evil human history has ever seen. This ideology has not only denied the existence of God, but itself tries to take the position of God. The struggle between good and evil has never before achieved the global dimensions of the struggle between communism and the Free

World. This is truly God's emergency of all time. It is a time when all good and righteous people of the world must rally together, not only to stop the spread of communism, but also to liberate the communist world with a God-centered world view. This is the time men and women must respond to God's will and take action.

The internal struggle of good and evil

When this task is carried out on a worldwide level, there still remains the internal mission of solving the problems of good and evil within ourselves. The root of evil must be removed so that man can enter the realm of perfection in total communion with God.

When communism fades away, it obviously does not mean that all the world will instantly become heaven. The ultimate consummation of history will come when every individual passes through a purification process and restores himself, thus eliminating the tendency toward evil residing within his own character.

Ever since the fall, every individual has been destined to go through this internal struggle to overcome the fallen nature within himself. Truth will give him the power to do this. Only with the help of a clear world view can the human tendency toward evil be overcome and each person be enabled to advance toward perfection.

America's mission in history

God has given America an important mission to fulfill. The United States is chosen to lead the fight against the God-denying ideology of communism. America must first awaken to the will of God, and must demonstrate faith and obedience. In this way, America can serve to unite the forces of goodness in the world.

God has chosen America as a guardian of freedom and a defender of belief in God. America must bear the burden of global responsibility. America must be faithful to God and altruistic towards the world. This nation will only flourish when it fulfills the mission which God has given. Otherwise, America will go the way of decadence which previous great powers, such as the Roman empire, have gone. America's awakening is therefore the most crucial factor that will decide the outcome of the global struggle against God-denying communism. This is why CAUSA is making the greatest efforts in America.

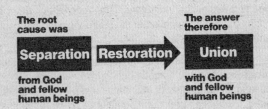

The root cause was **Separation** **Restoration** → **Union** **The answer therefore**

from God and fellow human beings

with God and fellow human beings

Conclusion

To conclude this section, and to make more clear the meaning of human responsibility, we recall the story of a man in a small town which was threatened by a flood. An emergency was declared, and the town was evacuated. This man, however, refused to flee from the floodwaters.

"Don't worry about me," he told his friends. "God has promised to save me."

Soon, however, the streets were flooded with water, and the National Guard came by with a boat to pick him up.

"Go away! Go away!" he shouted. "God will take care of me."

Within a few hours, the waters had risen up around the sides of his house, and he had to retreat up to the roof. A rescue team in a helicopter flew over the house and lowered a basket, while the crew shouted to him to climb in.

"Take it away!" he shouted back. "God will save me."

However, while they watched helplessly from the helicopter, the man was swept away by the flood and drowned.

Now it so happened that he went up to heaven and demanded to see God. When he came before the throne of God, he was boiling mad. "Mr. God," he burst out, "you were supposed to save me. We had an agreement. You broke your promise."

God looked at him with great love and some frustration. "My son," He said, "I did everything I could for you. I sent you a boat. I even sent you a helicopter. What else could I do?"

In the same way, many people in America today feel that if God wants to destroy communism, He can easily do so. They are content to engage in mundane pursuits and have a great deal of apathy toward God's will. They never consider that they may themselves be the people whom God has chosen to solve the problem. This is the most acute and serious problem in America.

God always works through His champions on the earth. God needs our arms, legs, mouths and hands to carry out the physical dimension of His work. God looks to inspired men and women on the earth who are determined to do His will. At this time, God is looking to America to truly be "one nation under God."

CAUSA Worldview II
God vs. Communism

A. Four fundamentals of communism

As we already established, communism is an ideology based upon a certain metaphysical, economic and historical viewpoint. Essentially, we have recognized that communism is based on four fundamental principles.

1. Absolute materialism
2. Law of dialectics
3. Historical materialism
4. Man as a product of his economic environment

These are like four pillars supporting communist theories. Let us review them briefly one by one.

1. Absolute materialism

The first of these is absolute materialism. Marx thought that he had been successful in perfecting all of the materialisms of the past. He had gone beyond the materialism of mechanists such as Voltaire, and likewise he had gone beyond the humanistic materialism of Feuerbach. Like them, Marx believed that there is no God. However his atheism differed from that of others in its degree of militant opposition to theism. For Marx, religion had served as a tool used by the ruling class to oppress the weak.

According to Marx, the essence of the universe is matter in motion. Somehow matter has within it the potential to evolve toward certain natural, biological and even political ends.

2. The law of dialectics

As a second fundamental, Marx universalized the laws of

the dialectic. Citing various examples from nature, Engels maintained that certain laws and principles were inherent to motion. What was it that caused motion to occur? It was the dialectic. Because of the conflicting, or dialectical relationship between the thesis and antithesis, ultimately one will destroy the other. This confrontation will contribute to a new development, or synthesis, which will combine the best qualities of the thesis and antithesis.

Marxists interpreted the dialectic developed by Engels as the guiding principle within nature. They then applied it to human society and history.

3. Historical materialism

Marx maintained that history had developed on the basis of the dialectic. He emphasized that man has passed through various stages. The foundation for each stage of history was determined by the economic relationships of that stage, and these in turn were subject to the laws of the dialectic. Marx pointed to six different historical stages: (1) primitive communal society, (2) slave society, (3) feudalistic society, (4) capitalistic, (5) socialistic, and ultimately (6) communistic society.

Marx maintained that the advancement of history was predestined to culminate in a communist society. As we have seen, Engels' *Dialectics of Nature* affirms that even if the universe is destroyed, the dynamic of matter is such that an evolutionary process will begin again, ultimately culminating in the formation of a communist society. In other words, matter itself will always evolve towards this same social end. Thus, communism is inevitable. This is the mandate which the dialectic gives to history.

4. Man is a product of his economic environment

Marx maintained that man is a product of his economic environment. He believed that the essence of evil was economic alienation. He discarded any religious concept of alienation, and emphasized that religion and God have served as tools to maintain economic domination by one class or another. Marx furthermore maintained that the only way to change man was to change the economic system. Marx also asserted that the elimination of private property, particularly the private ownership of the means of production, would bring about an ideal, or utopian, society.

Four Fundamentals of Communism

1. **Absolute Materialism**   No
2. **Law of Dialectics**   No
3. **Historical Materialism**   No
4. **Man as Product of His Environment**   No

B. Counterproposal: based on truth and absolute values

We have seen through our critique of Marxism that these points are not true. They are lies and deception masquerading as scientific reasoning. We have now removed the disguise and exposed the lies. Beyond exposing the lies, however, we must formulate a counterproposal.

Any counterproposal to Marxism must be founded on truth. Light alone overcomes darkness. Truth alone overcomes lies. For CAUSA, truth can only result through a God-affirming world view, which we call Godism.

The most fundamental truth is the existence of God. Communism is based on the assumption that there is no God. When the existence of God is clarified, absolute materialism is exposed as false.

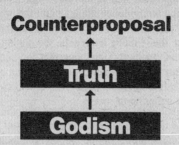

Questioning God's existence

For CAUSA, the most important question in life is, therefore, "Does God exist?" If God does exist, then there are absolute values. If there are absolute values, this will be the foundation for a moral and ethical standard. That moral and ethical standard must be permanent and unchanging, just as God is unchanging. We can say, "The buck stops here." All human behavior is accountable to and will be measured against the absolute standard of God.

For many people the question of God's existence remains unanswered. Certainly in the 20th century, the question arises,

1.

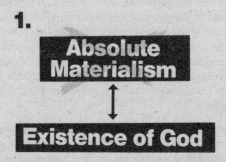

"If God exists, then why is there so much evil?" This question has had a tremendous impact upon the whole mentality of 20th century man. In many respects, the mentality which emerged in the United States in the 1960s stems from atheistic existentialism. One thing that led both Camus and Sartre to deny God was their own observation of the injustice in the world. If God was a good God, how could He possibly permit such suffering of man?

If there is no God, there cannot be absolute values. In that case, communism would be correct in its belief that values are relative to circumstances. At least communism offers, based on relativism, a convincing explanation of human life and history. For that reason, the question of God's existence is a fundamental question. It is *the* fundamental question.

Does God exist?

Does God exist? This is not a new question; it is ancient. But upon this question hinges our entire view of life and the world. In seeking answers, two contrasting views have emerged. One view holds that men come from a Creator, God, and the entire world is God's creation. Based on this belief, religions have come about, and the values, ethics and spiritual heritage of our world have developed.

A fundamentally different view maintains that there is no God, and that this world was not created. This is the atheistic communist or Marxist position. In this view, matter alone has always existed and is the essence of the universe. Human life is seen as nothing more than a phenomenon associated with matter, and human beings must thus create their own meaning and purpose, as well as their own solutions to life's problems. In this view, "God" is a concept found only in the human mind.

The problem we face today is that of determining which view is the truth. If God exists, then communism must be wrong; if God does not exist, then communism may be correct. God or no God: two contradictory beliefs cannot

both be true. There must be a showdown in which the truth
will prevail.

GOD

?

GOD

↓

Absolute value

This showdown is now occurring. There are basically
two worlds around us: one that is based on the belief that
God exists, and the other based on the belief that He does
not. The former is represented by the Free World, and the
latter is represented by the communist world. This showdown is occurring in our individual lives as well. In every
person's life, the decisive moment comes when he must face
the awesome question squarely: Is there a God? The question — God or no God — is still the most fundamental

question for modern man. The answer to this question affects our behavior from simple daily life to global events.

Knowing God: a common sense approach to religious epistemology

The problem of knowing God is complicated because the very nature of God means that He is invisible and not material. That is why no one has yet confined God to a "test tube." Any "God" which we could touch and see and photograph would not be the God we are seeking. Then how can we understand God? Although we will not try to define God, the Judeo-Christian tradition provides us with a description of Him. The God which we are speaking of must be good, infinite, omnipotent and omnipresent, eternal, unchanging and unique. He is, as St. Anselm observed in the 11th century, "the Being than which no greater can be thought of." Thus, God must be bigger than yourself, bigger than the world, bigger even than the whole cosmos. God certainly cannot be fully grasped by any single individual's perception. Such a God would not be God.

Our inability to directly perceive God seems to present a dilemma. A child knows and recognizes his father. Children do not have to make any effort to believe in their parents. They know them as a matter of fact. In the same way, we

How can we know God?

1. Science
2. Philosophy
3. Personal experience

would expect that there must be some way that the children of God can recognize Him as their Creator and Father. This avenue to knowing and recognizing God must be open to all of His children, not just to those who may be trained in theology or science. God would not make man without giving him the capability of knowing his Creator. There must be a way to recognize God.

CAUSA proposes a common sense approach to knowing God, as opposed to complex theological or philosophical methods. We believe that it must be possible for everyone to become convinced of God's existence. To achieve this, we have outlined a common sense approach to learning about God.

There are basically three ways to recognize the existence of God. These are by science, by philosophy and by experience.

Science

How do we learn about things? One way is through science. Science begins with empirical observation. That is, science begins by seeing, hearing, smelling, tasting and touching things. Then, through the application of logic and reasoning, science extends the powers of human perception. This is done by means of scientific experiments. For example, air is invisible; we cannot see it directly. We can, however, blow on a piece of paper, and we can interpret what we see happening. We then understand that air is moving against the paper.

Philosophy

There is a second general way in which we can extend our knowledge, and it is closely related to science. That is through philosophy. Philosophy also uses observations, logic and reasoning. Philosophy calls upon us to carefully examine our ideas and ways of thinking to make them better.

Philosophy demands that we consider various problems. By means of philosophy, for example, we can explore the question of the existence of our minds, which are totally invisible and untouchable. We conclude that every human being has a mind.

Personal experience

Thirdly, however, beyond science and philosophy, we can know things through personal experiences. We experience our mother's love, for example. This experience goes beyond science and philosophy. Once we have had such an experience, no power under the sun could bring us to doubt that the love of our mother is real.

In perceiving God, then, and in affirming the existence of God, we can use the same methods: (1) science (2) philosophy and (3) personal experience. Personal experiences with God are called personal religious experiences. People either believe in or know the existence of God by one or all of these three methods.

1. Science and the existence of God

It should first be made clear that it is not the role of science to *prove* God's existence. Since God is not a material being, His existence is beyond scientific proof.

However, while science has not proven God's existence, the advance of science has taught us a great deal about the universe in which we live. Some of the insights of science have amazing philosophical and religious implications. For this reason, we can say that science has brought human understanding to the threshold of God. Science leads us to the conclusion that the universe can only be completely described by a view which encompasses the First Cause.

Dr. Paul Davies, for example, in his book, *God and the New Physics,* notes that "right or wrong, the fact that science has actually advanced to the point where formerly what were once religious questions can be seriously tackled, itself indicates the far-reaching consequences of the new physics."

Davies continues, "In my opinion, science offers a surer path to God than religion."

Communist faith in science

There was a time, mainly in the 18th and 19th centuries, when the proponents of materialist world views, like communism and its precursors, anticipated that science would develop to a point where it would destroy every notion of God. Marx and Engels clearly felt that science was their ally. They called religion, "the opium of the masses."

This attitude has prevailed into the present century in the Soviet Union. In the early days of the Soviet space program, Moscow's propagandists joked that the exploration of space by cosmonauts would prove that there was no God in heaven, and that notions of God and Christ would soon be relegated to mythology. Quite contrary to this expectation, a survey of the remarkable advances of 20th century science and technology shows that quite the opposite is occurring. The present trend of science suggests that it is communism, rather than Christianity, which will be relegated to mythology.

Science and the nature of life

The origin of life has always been an intriguing question for biologists. The theory of biogenesis, that life comes only from life, was put forth in 1858 by Rudolf Virchow in Germany. A few years later, the work of Louis Pasteur in France offered convincing proof of the biogenesis theory.

Recently, however, great efforts have been made to show that spontaneous generation of life is possible. Until now, these efforts have not been successful. It has been shown that when a mixture of ammonia, methane, water and hydrogen is subjected to electrical discharges, amino acids, the building blocks of proteins, are formed. However, no protein chains can be formed without additional efforts to synthesize them. Until now the principle remains that life comes only from life. Only a living being can create and generate other living beings.

What would be the cause of all living beings? The logical conclusion would be that the cause of all living beings must be another living being. That first cause must be alive. In other words, God, the Creator, must be a living being.

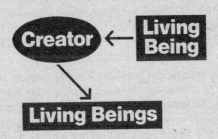

Matter and energy

We can also approach the question of God's existence by considering the nature of matter and energy as viewed by physics and chemistry. As time has gone by scientists have refined drastically their notions of matter and energy. The nature of energy and its relation to matter has been obscure through most of history. Greek philosophers had certain insights regarding matter and energy, but their efforts are crude by today's standards. Democritus held that matter consists of "atoms" which are solid, rigid, indivisible, internally homogeneous and spatially extended. At the same time, heat (a form of energy) was thought to be a fluid permeating a substance.

The development of mechanics helped to define more clearly the concepts of force and energy. Later, it was shown that various types of energy — such as mechanical, radiant and chemical — were interconvertible.

A major revolution in our understanding of energy came with the development of nuclear physics. Just prior to the outbreak of World War I, the English physicist Ernest Rutherford discovered that the atom consists of a tiny core, called the nucleus, surrounded by a tenuous cloud of electrons. In 1934, the Italian Enrico Fermi split the uranium nucleus into several fragments, releasing a sizable amount of nuclear energy, but he did not realize what had happened. Within a few years, however, scientists began to understand more about the process, and in 1940 the first controlled chain reaction was carried out in a secret laboratory under the abandoned football stands of the University of Chicago's Stagg Field.

In splitting atomic nuclei, we find that a certain amount of matter becomes completely converted into energy. We could say then that the most recent advance in understanding matter and energy is the realization that they are the same thing.

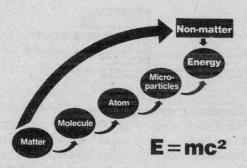

Marxist materialism consigned to the dustbin of history

Marxism was based upon a certain perspective of matter being solid, being real, being tangible and being reducible to indivisible particles. In the 20th century, particularly because of the discovery of nuclear energy, it becomes clear that this view of matter is primitive. In fact, the conversion of matter to energy was predicted by Einstein's theory of relativity.

According to this theory, energy and matter are interconvertible and interchangeable. At this point, the communist belief that the universe is matter having motion as its "attribute" is clearly seen to be antiquated, and must be thrown into the dustbin of history.

Energy and matter, considered together, appear to be "conserved." That is, they can be neither created nor destroyed. The question then becomes, how does energy become matter? How does it develop to a higher and higher level of sophistication? Certainly it is not by accident or random selection.

Question?

How does energy become...

Matter?
The Universe?
Man?

The universe exhibits precise discipline and orderliness. How did it come about? Materialism offers no explanation. From the Christian, Jewish and Moslem points of view, God is the cause of both energy and lawfulness, and the creation has come about as God has expressed His character into material form through the medium of energy. This is how a disciplined, orderly universe came into being. The basic assumption of science itself is that nothing occurs without cause. Thus, science supports the existence of an orderly First Cause.[1]

The third law of thermodynamics states that unless energy is added to a closed system, it will tend to move to a state of greater disorder (greater entropy). What we find, even according to evolution, is that there has been an upward

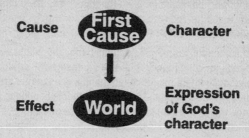

development toward man. Things are advancing to a more sophisticated level. At this point, we must recognize a "creative will" behind the developmental process.

The reality of a First Cause is becoming more and more apparent. Einstein's studies in science led him to one conclusion: there must be a God. Einstein himself concluded: "I want to know how God created this world. I want to know His thoughts, the rest are just details."

Regarding Einstein's views, scientist and author Robert Jastrow writes:

For Einstein, the existence of God was proven by the laws of nature; that is, the fact that there was order in the Universe and man could discover it. When Einstein came to New York in 1921 a rabbi sent him a telegram asking, "Do you believe in God?" and Einstein replied, "I believe in Spinoza's God, who reveals himself in the orderly harmony of what exists."[2]

To the total disappointment of the followers of Marx and Engels, science has turned out to be God's disciple instead of an ally of communism.

So far science has done a remarkable job of helping us affirm the existence of God, bringing us to the threshold of knowing the existence of God. We cannot ask anything further of science. At this point, we turn to philosophy to tell us more about God's existence.

2. A common sense proof of God

Have centuries of philosophical thought produced any convincing proofs of God? The fact is, they have produced a bewildering array of proofs of God, and a bewildering array of critiques of these proofs. The German theologian Hans Küng recently wrote a best-selling book 800 pages long entitled, *Does God Exist?* In it, he examines scores of arguments and counter-arguments. However, we do not want to plunge head-long into the treacherous waters of theological debate. Furthermore, we want to avoid the technicalities of these sophisticated discussions. Let us, therefore, take a common sense look at proofs of God.

We can consider the question in an analogical way. We recognize many man-made objects in an auditorium, such as lights, podium and microphones. Did these things come about by chance? No, absolutely not. First, someone made these things. Even prior to making them, there must have been a necessity and a distinct purpose. Second, that purpose was not conceived by the object which was created. The purpose was first conceived in the mind of the creator. All of these objects existed first in an invisible form in someone's mind, then were projected into reality, not randomly or by whim, but by will.

The same principle may also be applied to the creation of the universe. Nature and man could not come into being without the action of an organizing, willful Creator. Likewise, there must also have been a distinct purpose which preceded the creation of the universe. The whole creation was initiated with purpose, existed first as an idea in the mind of the Creator, and became manifested in reality. That is the process of creation. By scientific analysis and analogical reasoning, we are led to the understanding that there must be Someone existing prior to the universe who conceived the purpose of the universe, designed it and willed it into reality. That Someone must possess the Cosmic or Universal Mind.

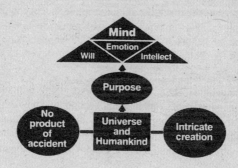

We can call that Someone by many names — God, Jehovah, Allah, etc. However you name Him, it does not change the truth. The truth is that there is a Creator, God. To fulfill His distinct purpose all things were created.

God: a being of heart and emotion

All the objects we see around us serve a definite purpose. Purpose always precedes creation. The Maker or Creator conceived the purpose before beginning to create. That is, the act of creation is carried out to fulfill a definite purpose, that is, to satisfy the desires felt by the Creator.

How did the plan of creation become a reality? Through what process did God create?

To understand the process of creation, let us use the analogy of a sound amplification system. Before any product can be manufactured, there must be a purpose in the manufacturer's mind which it would serve. The purpose in this case is to amplify sound so everyone in an auditorium can hear a lecture. The necessity, or the purpose, exists before the substantial amplification system. How then is the purpose fulfilled?

To substantially fulfill the purpose, the various parts of the human mind come into play. The mind of a person consists of three components: emotion, intellect and will. Emotion is the center of the three. First, someone feels that the purpose must be fulfilled (emotion). Knowledge (know-how) is then needed to generate a design, but knowledge alone is not enough. A design is still not a reality. For design to become reality, will (drive) comes into play.

In general, then, this is how everything is made. Purpose gives rise first to feeling, second to knowledge, and third to will. These correspond to the three components of the human mind. In order to create and fulfill the purpose, these three components of the mind must work together.

The creative work of God is centered on purpose: (1) Within the heart of God, the seat of emotion, purpose is felt. (2) Within the intellect of God, purpose is understood, and the design and plan of creation is generated. (3) Within the will of God, the determination and drive develops to fulfill the purpose and carry out the creative act.

What is the most important part of God's mind? Like the human mind, made in His image, the core of God's mind is emotion or heart. Emotion is as central for God as it is for man. Human emotion is the ultimate source of desire. Just as human beings have the ability to feel emotions, God also has the ability to feel — feel every sadness, joy, loneliness and pain. Even more than human beings, God experiences a vast spectrum of emotions.

We sometimes forget that God is a God of emotion. We totally misunderstand and think that God is like a super-computer having infinite knowledge, infinite will and infinite power. Our concept of God may resemble that of a giant robot with no heart and feeling. This would be a serious error in our understanding of God. God is first of all a God of emotion, therefore He has a capability to understand love and feel it. He is an infinite personality with a truly sensitive heart, watching every human affair and participating in every human drama. He watches His children and experiences their joys and sufferings, sharing their emotions with the deepest heart of a devoted parent.

3. The purpose of God's creation of man

Finally, we must know why God has created all things and mankind. What was His purpose in creating? Along with the question of the existence of God, this is among the most fundamental and crucial questions of life. No religion or philosophy has yet completely answered this question, but without this essential understanding, human life cannot help but be beset by confusion and chaos.

Creation should fulfill the purpose of the Creator. God intended that all men would know the purpose of God's crea-tion and live for that purpose. Only in this way can we feel fulfillment and happiness. When we try to live for another purpose, confusion and unhappiness follow. To achieve happiness, then, we must understand the purpose of creation.

Why did God create man? We can approach this question by asking another question: Why does anyone do what they do in life? Every living person has a certain ambition. Some want to succeed in business, make a lot of money and become millionaires. Others study hard to become accomplished and recognized scholars. There are some who are working day and night to become virtuosos in music or highly accomplished in other forms of art. Others still give their utmost effort to become champion athletes.

Have you ever asked yourself, "Why am I doing this?" Most of us, upon reflection, have come to feel that knowledge, honor, wealth or fame cannot be the ultimate goals of life. Suppose you attain wealth and honor, accomplishment and fame — what will all these things do for you? How are they good for you? What then is the ultimate purpose — the innermost purpose — in life? The answer to this question may be simpler than we think. Is not the most important purpose for each of us to be happy? We want most of all to feel joy and satisfaction.

We may seek after knowledge, wealth, honor, accomplishment and fame, but only because we know that these provide us with happiness. Happiness or emotional satisfaction is the bottom line.

God, being a God of emotion, must have the same emotional goals. This explains why God created man. God wants to experience happiness. Unlike man, God does not need money, knowledge or power. These things would not give God any joy and satisfaction. God would seem to have everything and have no need of such things. God is already the King of knowledge, He has the power to create, and He has no need for wealth. All creation is His. What else is there that would give joy to God? Love. Love is the only thing that gives God joy. Love is the one thing which God cannot experience all by Himself. Love by its nature demands a reciprocal relationship. There must be a complete circuit for the exchange of love. God needs someone to love and someone to love Him in return.

In the position of that someone, God created man. Man is God's object, able to receive God's love and return love back to God. In this exchange of love, God can experience joy.

God created men and women to receive His love and respond to His love. Human beings are the children of God. Without men and women, God cannot derive His joy and satisfaction. When men and women receive the love of God and return their love to Him, God experiences great joy. Man is created to constantly stimulate God with love. This, and this alone, will satisfy God. Man is God's masterpiece and supreme creation, because man is able to return God's love and be the source of His greatest joy.

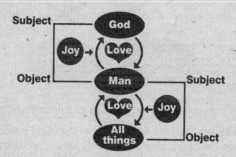

The universe is for man to love

The magnitude of God's love for man is truly awe-inspiring. The Bible records God's initial blessings to mankind, "Be fruitful and multiply, and fill the earth and subdue it; and have dominion over the fish of the sea and over the birds of the air and over every living thing that moves upon the earth." (Gen. 1:28) By this we understand that in order to give His children the actual experience of lordship, God created the entire universe as the home of man.

The universe is not simply cold and inert energy. The personality of God is projected into the universe as well as mankind. Because the beings of the universe are partial reflections of God's character, the universe may be called the symbol of God, while men and women are the image of God. All beings in the created world respond to the love of man, just as man responds to the love of God. The natural world is ours to make beautiful or to abuse. We are the gardeners, and the great garden of the universe depends on us to transmit God's love to it.

4. God's purpose of creation has not been fulfilled

The problem we have today is that God's purpose of creation has never been fulfilled. Man is like a distorted mirror which fails to properly reflect God's image. We are separated from God and have perverted our original nature, thereby losing our original value. Therefore we are not good objects of God's love. Men and women have failed to fulfill their original potential to respond to the love of God. This is the cause of human alienation. It is alienation from the love of God.

In the parable of the prodigal son, Christ compared God to a human parent with children. If a child chooses to leave the parent and rejects the inheritance which the parent wishes to give him, the parent cannot stop him by force. He must allow him to leave. However, how would this parent feel? He would certainly be heartbroken.

The situation of mankind today is even more serious and tragic, because many people today do not even know that God exists. How can children respond to the love of their father and return that love to him when they do not even know that he exists? In our world today, there is very little exchange of love taking place between God and man, and this is the worst tragedy for both God and man.

God is a God of deep feelings, and God is heartbroken over the loss of His children. God cannot receive joy or satisfaction from children who are spiritually deaf, dumb and blind. The history of God has been the history of weeping for the sake of humanity, and thus far humanity never knew that God was suffering in this way. Still, God has never given up hope. His constant goal and determination is for man to be restored to his original nature and value, and someday become a wholesome object to God, responding to God's love and returning joy, love and glory to Him. On that day, God's joy and satisfaction will have no end. For the first time, the purpose of creation shall be fulfilled.

Until God experiences happiness from the freely loving response of human beings, the attempts of men and women to achieve their own happiness will always be in vain. When we as children of God relieve completely the pain of God first, we solve the greatest problem of man as well — the search for love and happiness. The two problems are not separate, but are interlocked. When God is living in joy, man can also live in joy. People are frantically trying to be happy, but we can never achieve it if we neglect God.

5. The characteristics of God

Causality

Science is based on the assumption that there is no effect without cause, and there is an orderly relation between cause and effect. More specifically, there is not any characteristic in the realm of effect which has not existed first in the realm of cause.

The universe including man is in the realm of effect. God is the causal being. We can thus know God through examining the universe, as the attributes of the effect can tell us about the attributes of the Cause, the characteristics of God. We can say that there is nothing in the universe, the effect, which does not come from the original image of God.

In the early days of Christianity, St. Paul travelled to Rome and taught that there is one God who is transcendent of the physical universe. The Romans honored a pantheon full of gods. Each god served a particular purpose, and each one had a shape and form. The Romans could not understand how anyone could believe in one invisible God. St. Paul settled this question once and for all and that answer is recorded in the Bible:

> For what can be known about God is plain because God has shown it to them. Ever since the creation of the world His invisible nature, namely, His eternal power and deity, has been clearly perceived in the things that have been made. So they are without excuse.
>
> Rom. 1:19-20

This passage clearly shows that by learning about the created world, we can also learn about the Creator — His characteristics, laws and principles.

God created all things and mankind. The universe may be called the indirect image of God, while human beings are created in God's direct image. Men and women are the

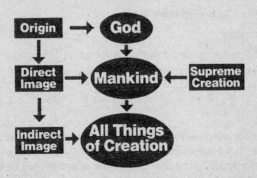

supreme creations of God. By observing the universe, and human beings in particular, we can learn about the characteristics of God. [3]

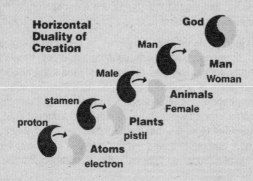

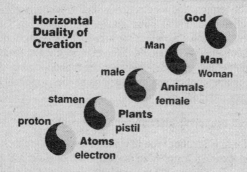

Horizontal polarity: positive and negative

In all levels of the creation, from human beings to animals, plants, minerals and even on the level of physico-chemical material, we observe the polarity of positivity and negativity. (The words positive and negative here mean merely that there is a relationship between two parts, and do not in any sense imply the qualities of goodness/evil, superiority/inferiority, or sufficiency/deficiency.)

On the level of human beings, there are two sexes, man and woman. In animals there are male and female. In plants, generally, there are male and female parts called stamen and pistil. On the level of physico-chemical material, there is always a positive and negative part. (Even the neutron, a neutral particle, can be divided to give a proton and an electron.)

We find these two attributes in relationship on every level. If we encounter this polarity on every level of the universe, we can say that the image of God must also exhibit the attributes of positive/negative, or masculine/feminine. That is, we observe in the creation a continuous and increasingly complete expression of the masculine and feminine aspects of the image of God. All things are created as the manifestation of God's complete image, which includes male and female, positive and negative. This we call horizontal polarity in God's image.

The proton and electron express to some degree the polar attributes of the First Cause, but there is a further progression such that when we arrive at the level of human beings, we encounter marked differences in physical structure, personality and emotions between men and women. All of these characteristics are expressions of the personality and character of God.

Vertical polarity: internal and external

There is another type of polarity, that of internal character and external form. Man is composed of mind and body. Mind does not refer only to the mental processes of a person, but rather to all of his internal aspects and personality. The body expresses this internal character. One's face, for example, reveals one's emotions. We may try to conceal our feelings, but those who study body language assure us that the body is continuously expressing, consciously or not, the emotions and feelings of the mind.

A similar situation holds for the animal realm. An animal has an instinctive mind, which expresses itself in the form and behavior of its body. With respect to a plant, we can also

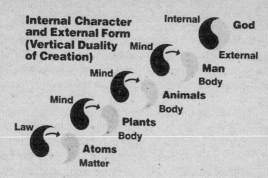

Internal Character and External Form (Vertical Duality of Creation)

Law → Atoms (Matter) → Plants (Body) → Animals (Body) → Man (Body) → God

Mind, Mind, Mind; Internal, External

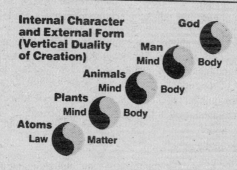

Internal Character and External Form (Vertical Duality of Creation)

Atoms (Law / Matter) → Plants (Mind / Body) → Animals (Mind / Body) → Man (Mind / Body) → God (Body)

talk about a type of "mind" which organizes the cells to form the body of the plant. This plant "mind" directs the growth of the plant and determines its form, height, shape of leaves, etc. This "mind" also guides the leaves towards the sun, and the root toward the water.

Even on the level of minerals and physico-chemical constituents we find the same polar attributes. Material is organized according to an inherent directive nature which causes energy to take a form, a "body." That is, an atom is the manifestation of some character; atoms obey laws. A proton always makes a "date" with an electron, never with another proton. Sodium atoms always react with chlorine atoms to form salt, following a series of laws which constitutes one aspect of the inherent directive nature of the material.

In this way, we can make another generalization regarding God. If all things of the universe have "mind" and "body," then the cause of the universe, God, must have within Himself the qualities of internal character and external form.

This would be completely in accord with what we have discussed regarding the scientific view of the universe. We know that the universe is made of fields of energy, but there must be an internal character which is organizing the energy. The internal character of God is the source of the internal character of the universe, and the external form of God is the source of energy itself, of which the universe is made. [4]

God's invisible nature or character manifested in reality — this is the creation. Therefore the character of each creation resembles God's own character. The creation is like a mirror which reflects God's image, and men and women are the children who reflect the parents' characteristics. Creation is the manifestation of the invisible image of God.

6. Summary

God is one unified Being having the characteristics of masculine and feminine as well as internal character and external form. God is transcendent, but He has projected himself into substantial form: men and the universe. Therefore, we find all things are existing as male and female, plus and minus, positive and negative. Furthermore, all things have an invisible internal character and external visible body or substance.

From this law we come to an understanding that everything in this universe comes in a pair system. God created nothing "solo." He created everything in pairs, so that the pairs would complement each other. Furthermore, God designed man to live a "pair" of lives, not just a "solo" life. We have not only our life in the physical world, but also another life which is the eternal spiritual life.

The family: building block of the ideal world

Men and women are the creations which have the potential of completely reflecting the image of God. They are the supreme creations of God. We emphasize, however, that an individual man or woman cannot fully represent God. In order to make the fullest expression of God, man and woman must be perfectly united as husband and wife in love. This would be the perfect expression of God.

Men and women both have mind and body which reflect God's internal character and external form, and man and woman united as a couple represent the unity of male and female character. The couple united by love is the culmination of God's creative work. From the loving couple, multiplication can occur. In the CAUSA view, the family is an eternal institution designed by God and the building block of the ideal society.

C. Conclusion: the theory of evolution

At the present time, there is a great deal of controversy concerning the correct view of the origin and development of the universe. This controversy has generally been cast in terms of the "creationist" vs the "evolutionary" views. We feel, however, that this controversy is unnecessary, and frequently misses the essential question involved.

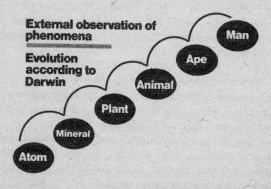

External observation of phenomena

Evolution according to Darwin

Man
Ape
Animal
Plant
Mineral
Atom

The essential question is that of purpose. Is the universe the result of God's purposeful creation or not? Our answer to that question is a decisive yes. The precise mechanism of creation is secondary.

Darwin's theory of evolution is based on an examination of our contemporary world, as well as certain evidence from the geologic record. We do not dispute these scientific findings, but we feel that Darwin's theory, if it is correct, is only an external description of God's process of creation. God may have utilized evolutionary mechanisms in creating the form (body) of men, but the entire process required emotion, intelligence and will.

Furthermore, there is a tremendous difference between human beings and even the most intelligent of animals, such as the apes or the various sea mammals. The essential difference is that men and women are the children of God, and God has given them eternal spiritual life. Monkeys and porpoises are animals. They are created for the joy of man. Men and women are created for the joy of God. Men and women are the children of God, created to be sensitive to His love and to share His love with all animals and all the universe.

A visitor to an airplane museum might see an old World War I plane and try to apply Darwin's theory of evolution to explain how the Boeing 747 descended from that plane. Did the old plane evolve into the 747 through random mutation? Of course not.

By the same token, an ape will never evolve into a human being through random mutation. The ape represents a stage or step in God's process of creation, but an ape will not become a man, no matter how many millions of years may pass. God had to accomplish each stage of creation and then add new creative energy according to His original plan to achieve each new creation. Compared to the ape, man is a new design, a new and unique creation.

Man is a child of God. The ape is an animal. Man has a spirit. The ape does not. Man is given the blessing of dominion over all of the creation. The ape is not even aware of most of the creation. He relates to a few objects which he needs to live. Man creates a culture. The ape does not.

Engels based his view of the origin of man on the theory of Jean Lamarck: tools produce intelligence; labor makes man. That process must be going on today. Yet, the gorilla in the zoo, even with all the tools in the world, will never become like John Wayne. After all the years of evolution, there are no ape species which have become "nearly human." The ape is still the ape, and man is still man.

Evolution and the design of the universe

We normally find a pattern in the work of an artist. After a certain period of time, we can even recognize that a painting is the work of Degas, Van Gogh or Cezanne. Throughout the universe, we also find patterns. We have just discussed the occurrence of polarity throughout the universe. Does not the consistency of patterns such as polarity throughout nature suggest that all things come from the same Creator?

The consistency of this pattern causes us to challenge the concept of a chance process in evolutionary development. Darwin argued that nature had advanced through a process of natural selection. He said that random mutations occurred and allowed nature to advance. Nevertheless, we must ask whether such "mutations" were in fact "random" or whether there was some providential design to them. As we have noted, as scientists continue their study of nature, they come more and more to feel that the world was created for the sake of human beings. How could this result from a random process?

CAUSA recognizes a design in nature and, therefore, also recognizes the necessity of a designer. That designer is none other than God.

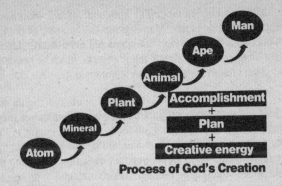

Amazingly, Marx's view of man is at a far lower level of sophistication even than Darwin's. In the *Dialectics of Nature*, Engels based his view of evolution on Lamarck. This view has been shown to be antiquated and without validity. The Marxist-Leninists still choose to cling to this view as is shown in even recent Marxist publications such as Afanasyev's 1980 version of *Marxist Philosophy*.

CAUSA Worldview III
Counterproposal to the Law of Dialectics

The CAUSA Worldview III offers a counterproposal to the laws of the dialectic, which were presented in the section on dialectical and historical materialism. According to dialectical materialism, the universe is made up of matter, which is in constant motion. This motion is supposedly maintained through the dialectical process.

A. Counterproposal to the law of dialectics

The laws of the dialectic are a substantial part of dialectical materialism. They comprise one of the four fundamentals of communism. They are supposedly laws which are governing nature and society. Therefore, for Marxists, they are the laws of progress guiding human history.

It is the position of CAUSA that progress and development do not occur through the confrontation of thesis and antithesis, resulting in a synthesis.

According to the law of dialectics, progress occurs

through conflict. A standard Marxist philosophy book from the Soviet Union reads, "Conflict alone is the source, the driving force of development."[5]

In contrast to this, the CAUSA Worldview maintains that development and progress occur through cooperation. If we can show this to be true, then clearly the law of dialectics would be exposed as false doctrine.

Here we will elaborate on CAUSA's view, but first, we must ask how Marx derived his view of relationships. When did people start to think that development occurs through conflict? In general, the belief that conflict is the norm in nature and human society is a result of taking imperfect or sinful man (man separated from God) as the norm for human life.

As a consequence of this separation from God, contradiction and conflict pervade human life. There is a basic split within each person between spirit and body. There is conflict between husband and wife. There is conflict between races. There is conflict between nations. We cannot deny that these conflicts occur.

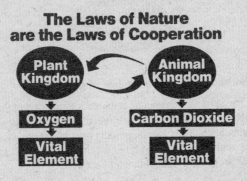

The Laws of Nature are the Laws of Cooperation

However, Marx began to maintain that such conflict was the norm. Marxists look at the conflict and contradiction found in sinful society, and then generalize it as a law of nature. They proclaim that conflict is nature's most basic dynamic.

The law of nature and human progress is the law of cooperation

Contradiction and conflict are not the means by which progress and development occur in nature. Certainly we find conflict in some elements of nature, but as a secondary phenomenon.

Nature exists and multiplies not on the basis of conflict but through cooperation. For example, between the plant kingdom and the animal kingdom, we have a clear example of cooperation. Plants exhale oxygen, and that oxygen can be used by animals. Animals exhale carbon dioxide, which, in turn, is valuable for plants. Through such cooperation, life is maintained.

Everywhere around us we find the same kind of cooperative process as nature's basic relationship. We find that even on a sub-microscopic level between protons and electrons or nuclei and electrons, there is a harmonious interaction of forces which allows for matter to exist. We find this same relationship existing on a cosmic level, between the sun and the planets.

In human society, fruitful relationships are also founded upon cooperation and reciprocity. Between parents and children, teachers and students, employers and employees and consumers and businessmen, the essence of a healthy relationship is cooperation. Unfairness or exploitation creates mistrust. For CAUSA, mistreatment of one's fellow man results from man's separation from God.

B. The law of life and progress: give and take action

We can say that such cooperative relationships are relationships based upon a principle of give and take. Let us consider how give and take occurs.

There are two preconditions which must be satisfied before give and take can take place. These are (1) the possibility of mutual benefit and (2) the positions of subject and object.

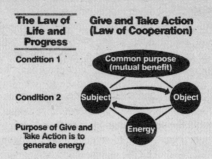

The Law of Life and Progress	Give and Take Action (Law of Cooperation)
Condition 1	
Condition 2	
Purpose of Give and Take Action is to generate energy	

Condition 1: Mutual benefit (common purpose)

In order to have real give and take action, there must, first of all, be a common purpose. Different parties come together when such a relationship will serve their mutual benefit.

Condition 2: Subject and object

Between complementary elements, there must be a relationship of subject and object. The subject is the element which initiates the action of giving. The object in turn responds to the initiative.

It is important to stress that position does not affect value. That is, subject does not have greater value than object nor vice-versa. In addition, these positions are generally interchangeable. For example, when person A is speaking and person B is listening, then person A is subject and person B is object. Later, while person B is speaking, person A becomes object. There is a constant changing of roles according to whether one is giving or receiving.

Whenever these two preconditions are met, give and take action can take place. Through give and take action, energy is generated. Energy is necessary for all existence, action and multiplication.

We experience this constantly in our daily lives. We may have an inspiring conversation with a friend, for example. Afterwards we feel refreshed or uplifted because such give and take produces energy. On every level, energy is what enables life or activity to continue. Energy is responsible for promoting multiplication, action, and progress. What is the dynamic which produces energy in any situation? It is giving and receiving in a subject-object relationship.

Universal prime energy

What is the cause of all subject-object relationships? Who designed the original dynamic? It is God. In CAUSA we speak of a primary or initiating energy which is the cause of all give and take action, and we refer to this energy as Universal Prime Energy. Give and take action is the method by which every being can tap into Universal Prime Energy and thereby draw energy to exist, act and multiply.

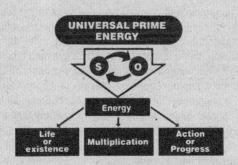

C. Practical examples of give and take action

Mind and body

Within each person there are two dimensions that are meant to function together in harmony. These are the psychic and somatic dimensions. That is, we each have a mind and a body. The relationship between mind and body determines the character of an individual.

Ideally, there must be a harmonious exchange between mind and body. For example, if every single day for ten years, a person sits in front of his television, and says, "I ought to do something for the poor," does that make him a good person? No, because it remains on the level of mind. There has to be a relationship between mind and body and between thoughts and deeds. For development to take place, the body should act on the wishes of the mind. A harmonious exchange between the spirit, or mind, and the body, is what determines the character of a human being.

Mind and body may also work together in an evil way. It is possible to have evil thoughts and to put those evil thoughts into action. For good or evil, give and take action operates within all human beings.

Husband and wife

The principle of give and take operates within the family. A God-centered family is a family in which there is a harmonious relationship between husband and wife. In such a relationship, there is a perfect circuit of give and take of love. Out of the harmonious relationship between husband and wife comes unity, and new creative energy comes from God. The result is happiness and the blessing of children. This happy couple is able to provide an excellent environment in which children can grow and develop.

Government and people

The same principle is true in politics. There is a government and there is a people. Who is the subject and who is the object? In a democracy, the people are subject. The role of the government is that of servant of the people. In a dictatorship, however, the government takes the role of subject. Frequently in this case, human rights are suppressed and people become the slaves of the rulers.

A real, God-centered concern on the part of the government and the people can serve as the basis upon which the well-being of a nation can be assured.

Lenin applied God's law of give and take

It is amazing that even Lenin, in order to bring about the Bolshevik Revolution, had to apply the law of cooperation. He did not gather his followers and say, "Let's fight among ourselves." Lenin, as subject, constantly pleaded with his followers (in the position of object) to unite with his direction, until finally he could build a core group of supporters. This was a cooperative relationship. There was a common purpose: to make the revolution. Lenin was the subject, while his followers were the object. Their cooperation resulted in the success of the Bolshevik Revolution.

Of course, as a devoted Marxist, we find that Lenin did make use of the dialectic. Whenever possible, he divided opposition groups one against another, to leave him free to advance. He used God's law, the law of cooperation, to advance himself, and he used the law of dialectics to destroy his opponents.

Other examples

The sciences of physics and chemistry attest to the validity of subject and object relationships. The atom, for example, contains a positively charged nucleus of relatively large mass, and a field of negatively charged electrons of very small mass. The nucleus, then, is in the subject position and the electrons in object position. The interactions of these particles produce energy, known to the physicist as "binding energy."

Biological systems are also systems of subject-object interaction. A cell contains a nucleus (subject) and surrounding cytoplasm (object). An animal has a nervous system (subject) and other organ systems (object). The interaction of these allows the animal to live. As long as this give and take action continues, the animal is able to metabolize and sustain itself. If this relationship is destroyed, the animal dies.

The solar system

If we examine our solar system, we find that God has established the same principle there. Between the sun and the planets we find a harmonious subject-object relationship. This serves to establish a certain order within the solar system.

Centering upon God, we find subject-object, harmonious relationships throughout the universe. The relationship between man and woman produces a child. The relationship between stamen and pistil produces seeds. The relationship between proton and electron produces an atom. In each case, it is the action of giving and receiving which allows for existence, action and multiplication. Through the union of two complementary elements, rather than through the dialectic, a new creation is formed.

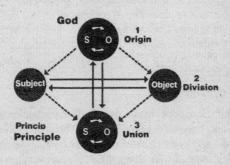

D. The principle of origin-division-union (O-D-U)

From these examples we can understand the principle of origin-division-union operating in our universe. In the process of creation, God, the invisible subject being, contains within him the essence of all subjects and objects, constantly engaged in give and take action. This is the point of origin. He then creates substantial subject and object beings. This represents division. When the substantiated subject and object perform give and take action, they are united into one entity, the union. That union is in perfect resemblance to the origin which is God, and that union becomes the object to God. Then the give and take action of the origin and union takes place. The union receives the necessary energy from God to live, multiply and develop.

The important thing to note is that subject and object are compatible. That is, they can form a circuit of reciprocal relationship that allows for give and take action. This is because they originate from the harmonized being of God.

This ODU principle operates on every level of nature and society. Therefore, God is clearly omnipresent.

In the give and take relationship, the subject must give one hundred percent of itself for the sake of the object. The object must give one hundred percent of itself for the sake of the subject. A relationship of total giving is the way in which creation occurs.

Selfishness violates the principle of total giving. Naturally, there does not exist a selfish proton, electron, stamen, or pistil. Selfishness only exists in human beings. Selfishness makes it difficult for us to be able to give of ourselves completely. And yet human beings are created to give. What is the real source of joy? It is when we can be able to give of ourselves 100 percent for the sake of a spouse or other loved ones.

We can conduct a very simple experiment to prove that we were created to give to others. Everyone has a face, but who is that face for? When you are with people, there is only one person who cannot see your face. That is you. Obviously, your face exists for others to see. The same is true of your voice. The reality is that we have never heard and will never hear our own voice as others hear it. This is clear to us when we listen to ourselves through a tape recorder.

We are created for others. We do not find joy by just centering on ourselves. We find joy when we give of ourselves to others. If we think of the most precious moments in our lives, they were times we spent with family and friends.

Giving and receiving is a principle which exists throughout our universe, and ultimately it is especially a principle for mankind.

E. The law of repulsion — secondary and auxiliary to the law of give and take action

In conjunction with the law of give and take action, another secondary, auxiliary law is in operation which we call the law of repulsion. We observe the phenomenon in our universe in the behavior of electricity and magnets. Plus and plus repel as do minus and minus. Engels interpreted this as an example of the operation of the laws of the dialectic in nature.

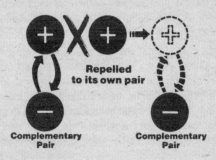

As we already noted, to have harmonious give and take action take place there must first be common purpose or mutual benefit. Furthermore, the subject must have give and take with an object, not another subject. There is no mutual benefit between two minuses or two pluses, and therefore, they repel each other. The law of repulsion is necessary, and it is not designed to be destructive. It is designed to augment and facilitate give and take action.

When two plus charges repel, each is able to find its own minus. Only in this way can each one form a reciprocal relationship and support the perfection of the universe. In other words, give and take action is primary. When a relationship cannot bring about give and take action, there is repulsion and the two parts are pushed apart. Then each one can seek a partner to form its own productive relationship.

The repulsion between two protons allows each proton to attract an electron and form an atom. In a herd of deer, two stags will battle over an available female and a section of territory. They do not destroy each other however. One will dominate and chase the other away. Then they can both find a female and breed.

Labor-management relations

Marxists are frequently concerned with labor-management relations, and they claim that the dialectic is naturally operating in these relations. However, we can show that applying the dialectic in labor-management relations is destructive and brings no benefit to either party. The law of cooperation must be applied for labor-management relations to be successful.

In labor-management relations, both the primary phenomenon of cooperative relationship as well as the secondary phenomenon of repulsion are occurring. Labor and management recognize fundamentally that they have a mutual dependence and they seek after mutual benefit. Extermination and total destruction of one party by the other is not the goal.

The recognition of self benefit is fundamental to the recognition of mutual dependence. In other words, it is not in the interest of labor to destroy management or vice versa. However if labor feels that it is being treated unfairly, then there is a repulsion against management in the form of demands for an adjustment of labor relations, such as wages, benefits, working conditions, etc. Mistreatment of labor will never bring harmonious give and take action. If, however, labor is making such excessive demands that business is collapsing, it may choose to sacrifice its own benefit for the survival of the business. Again, this is to insure smooth and harmonious give and take action which produces constructive results.

It would be nonsense to say that labor-management relations should follow the dialectic, and therefore one party should struggle to destroy the other. The goal here is not destruction, but fairness. Fairness alone will insure harmony and result in productive give and take action.

This has occurred recently in the United States in such corporations as the ailing Pan American Airlines or the Chrysler Corporation. The laborers reduced benefits and wages voluntarily so that the business could survive and prosper.

God vs. Communism

In our world, God is the subject and mankind is the object. Man is supposed to experience the love of God as his parent and subject. Yet, today there is a great confusion. This confusion has occurred because another subject has challenged the position of God. This subject is communism.

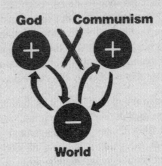

Clearly, communism is a God-denying ideology which today is being used by the adversaries of God and religion in an attempt to dominate the world. God and communism are not compatible. God must repel communism. There can be no other subject in the sight of God. The false ideology must be destroyed and the communists must be restored to the position of objects of God, along with the other people of the world. There should be one subject in the universe, God, and one object, mankind.

F. Conclusion

Our conclusion is simple. There is the law of cooperation, and there is the Marxist law of dialectics. The dialectic was used as a means to negate the need for a Creator, but today we see that Marx's dialectic is false. The law of cooperation is true and this law originates in the cause of cooperation, which we know as God.

The law of give and take is simple, yet very profound. If the Marxists can grasp it, then they can understand clearly that revolution and conflict are not the way to bring about constructive change. Constructive change can only occur through a cooperative process, the action of giving and receiving.

CAUSA Worldview IV
Counterproposal to Historical Materialism

The third fundamental area of Marxism maintains that history advances toward communism in accord with the dialectic. This is why Nikita Khrushchev confidently proclaimed in 1958. "We will bury you" and "History is on our side."

For communists, all societies are inevitably heading towards communism. We can contrast Marx's theory of history with the view of God-accepting people, which maintains that God governs history by His providence. However, many doubt the validity of this statement. In our problem-ridden world today, more and more people feel that God does not exist. He seems to be dead, or He seems to be helpless, in terms of human affairs.

A. Two crucial questions

We have seen clearly that God's purpose is to create a good world, but instead we have an evil world. In the Bible, we find assurances that God will restore this evil world to

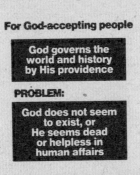

For God-accepting people

> God governs the
> world and history
> by His providence

PROBLEM:

> God does not seem
> to exist, or
> He seems dead
> or helpless in
> human affairs

Two questions:
1. How did God's good world become evil?
2. When restoration is His providence, why does it take so long?

goodness. Still, there are two crucial questions that demand answers. One of those questions is: How is it that God's good world became evil? This has challenged many people. Bertrand Russell, Albert Camus and others observed the world around them and saw so much suffering, so much evil, and so much wrongdoing, that they came to the conclusion that there could not be a God. If a good God existed, how could He allow the continuation of such suffering? How could He have allowed this world to become evil in the first place? This dilemma has led some to conclude that God does not exist.

There is also another question which we have to answer. If God does exist and does want to stop human suffering and restore the world to goodness, why does it take Him so long? People have become tired of waiting.

In an attempt to solve this confusion, various explanations have been put forth. One of these is the "God is dead" theology. This view emerged very strongly in the 1960 s through theologians such as Thomas Altizer and William Hamilton. According to this view, the traditional understanding of God had to be re-evaluated. This view particularly challenged the role of God as a parent and "problem solver." For them, God had given man freedom and dominion over the earth. It is man's role to accept responsibility for our lives and the world.

Likewise, other radical positions such as Liberation Theology and Christian Marxism have challenged the traditional view of God and emphasized that man plays the pivotal role in bringing about social change.

In the case of Russia, it was communism which took God's place. Communism seemingly solves the dilemma of human suffering. Belief in God, according to communist ideology, prevents us from understanding the real source of evil — division of labor by class. Once class relations are ended, communists claim that evil will disappear. For communism there is no God. History moves according to the laws of nature, which are dialectical. This is the view of historical materialism.

Although historical materialism has been critiqued very well by Free World thinkers, it nevertheless continues to gain new adherents. The CAUSA Worldview approaches the problem from the ground floor. Historical materialism is based on dialectical materialism, which is based on the denial of God. The foundation is false. Historical materialism is like a castle built on sand, which will be washed away by the flood.

Nevertheless, a critique of historical materialism alone is not sufficient. A view of history must be set forth which convincingly explains the patterns of history from a God-affirming point of view. CAUSA presents this view.

B. Free will and responsibility

Traditionally, Christianity has taught that God endowed man with free will. Frequently, however, we do not consider fully the implications of this belief.

In the opening passages of the Bible, it is written that God told Adam and Eve, "You may freely eat of every tree in the garden, but of the Tree of the Knowledge of Good and Evil, you shall not eat, for in the day that you eat of it, you shall die." (Gen 2:17)

This passage, whether one takes it literally or not, has profound meaning. God gives a commandment, and He warns

His children that if they fail to abide by it, the consequence shall be death. The first option is obedience — obedience to God's word. By inference, we can conclude that through obedience, Adam and Eve shall have life. The second option is disobedience to God's commandment. And the consequence of that disobedience is separation from God, spiritual death. That would be the opposite of God's will.

What determines whether man would go the way of good or the way of evil? Ultimately it is man himself. Man is given the right to make decisions which will affect his eternal life. This is a tremendous freedom. Obviously, when the first ancestors disobeyed God, the result was spiritual death. Freedom is a privilege which carries with it a great responsibility. The abuse of freedom brings the destruction of life.

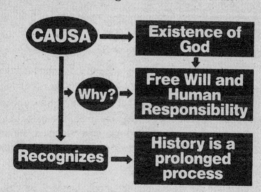

In the Bible there are many passages which clearly show that history is not shaped by God alone. For example, Genesis 6:6 reads, "And the Lord was sorry that he had made man on the earth, and it grieved him to his heart." Clearly man is responsible for things which happen against God's will. In Exodus 32:7-14, we find that God declares His intention to have His wrath "burn hot against" the Israelites for building the golden calf. Moses pleads with God, however, and finally we read that "the Lord repented of the evil which he thought to do his people." In Isaiah 38, we find that God announces through Isaiah that he will take the life of King Hezekiah, but after Hezekiah's prayer, God says, "I have heard thy prayer, I have seen thy fears, behold I will add unto thy days fifteen years." (Isa 38:5) These and other biblical examples attest that history is shaped by the interplay between God's will and man's free response to God.[6]

Unlike all other creatures, God created man with free will. Man's responsibility, then, is to cooperate with God to achieve his own growth and maturity, as well as the perfection of the universe.

The tragedy of history is that man has failed to cooperate with God. Man violated the law and went against the will of God and unwittingly took the road of spiritual "death." Thus, tragedy occurred in human history and tragic consequences have been continuously suffered by all of humankind.

Why did God give man free will?

At this point, the most significant and vital question for us to ask God is this, "Mr. God, why didn't you save yourself a great deal of trouble? You actually invited the problem. If you had made man like any other creature, incapable of violating your principle, you would not have suffered the consequences of the human fall. Giving man free will has caused all of your problems."

This is a very powerful question. Could it be that God was unaware of this possibility? No, He knew that if He gave man free will, there would be a possibility of man's fall. Then why was he obliged to give man free will? There must be some compelling reason why God must give man free will.

C. Three reasons for God to grant man free will

The reason can be understood in this way. God is a being of love, and He created man for love. Man therefore could not be created as a robot or a machine. A person has a mind and is not programmed. A person has a spirit. A person is capable of virtue, love, and creativity. These are qualities which stem from freedom and allow us to be God-like. God can only find real joy in a being that responds freely by personal volition.

God has a choice in creation. He can either create a free human being, or he can create something else which lacks free will, like a robot. Clearly, God wanted to create free men and women, not robots. It is free will which distinguishes man from a robot and from any other aspect of creation. It would be pointless to create human beings without giving them free will.

God is love and He created man for love

Man is not created as a robot or machine

1. Man is a Co-Creator
(Creativity of Man)

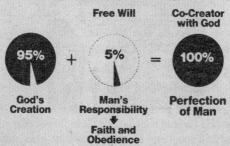

Free Will   Co-Creator with God

95%   +   5%   =   100%

God's Creation   Man's Responsibility   Perfection of Man

Faith and Obedience

Specifically, we may list three reasons why God would choose to give man free will.

1. God wanted man to be a co-creator

God did not want to have man be just an animal or a robot. The loving heart of God longed for children. God therefore wanted men and women to be like Himself as his total image. Certainly the power of creativity is among the greatest characteristics of God. God wanted man to share this power of creation and to become a co-creator with God. God made man with the potential for perfection rather than as a finished product. He completed 95 percent (figuratively), and then gave man 5 percent responsibility to create himself. The 100 percent represents the perfection of man. When perfection is achieved by this formula, the result is a joint effort of both God and man. God created 95 percent, and man must create 5 percent of himself. In this respect, man is elevated to the creator level.

In order to become a co-creator with God, man's 5 percent responsibility must be fulfilled by his own free will. Otherwise, the purpose of creation will be left unfulfilled.

Let us illustrate with an analogy. Let us say that God is building a wall, and there are 100 bricks to lay to complete it.

God has layed 95 bricks and asks his son to lay the last 5 bricks to finish the wall. Man responds to God and lays the last 5 bricks to perfection. A beautiful wall is completed and God turns to His son and pats Him on the shoulder, giving him praise by saying "My son, it is a job well done. This wall is a joint venture between you and me. You and I are both creators of this wall."

God wants to give this kind of credit to man. He wants to see the honor of co-creatorship bestowed upon man so that man, as the child of God, can share in the creativity of God.

What has happened is that man has dropped the bricks and has not finished the wall. God is certainly capable of saying to His son, "My son, you are having some difficulty, so let Me do it." If God did that, at that moment, man would lose his potential to be a co-creator and could no longer be a child of God reflecting His perfect image.

That is why God cannot take over man's duty but is instead always urging man to fulfill his responsibility in history.

God is like the greatest high school football coach. The coach will do everything possible to teach and inspire his players. He will push them, give them pep talks, scold them, etc. The only thing that the coach cannot do is go onto the field and play the game for them. If he does, they are no longer the players. The coach becomes the player and the game is meaningless. Similarly, God can do so much, but he cannot take over man's duty without taking away man's free will, and that would nullify man's unique position as God's child, turning him into a machine or robot.

Tragically, human history has been a record of the many failures of man. It was not God who failed; it has always been man who failed God. Still God must be patient and wait until one day when man will fulfill his responsibility. Man always has the final word, because faith must be exercised voluntarily. In this way we can understand the anguish of God. He is still waiting for man to come forward and carry the ball into the end zone. It might take tens of thousands of years, but God always has hope, because once the game is won, it can never be reversed. Once man reaches perfection, he would remain perfected forever. It is a worthwhile wait.

When someone is ignorant of this law, it is very easy for him to deny God. Communism could only come into being because of ignorance of man's portion of responsibility. Communist doctrine says there is no God, but ironically it is only because God has given freedom to man that communism is possible.

There is only one way to end communism. That is when man fully understands God's principles and laws and fulfills His desires by totally fulfilling his 5 percent responsibility. The full potential of man is realized by uniting completely with God and making the living God triumphant and real in every man's heart. This is our sacred responsibility.

2. Man is the Child of God

2. Man is the child of God

God is a free being, and He is our Father. We are created in the image of God. Clearly, a child should reflect the total image of his parent. God, the Father, has free will, therefore his sons and daughters must also have free will. God has responsibility, therefore men and women must share the responsibility.

In the ideal of God's creation, every person would live as a child of God. The nature and characteristics of these children must be identical with those of God. God is a free being, therefore man must be free. Endowed with the remarkable gifts of free will and creativity, men and women may be called the "second selves" of God.

3. To enable man to love
Love must be voluntary

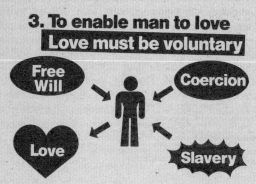

3. Love must be voluntary

The third important reason God gave man free will is that God wants to achieve His purpose of creation in the voluntary give and take of love with man.

You cannot force someone to love you. Love must be exercised in freedom. Love by coercion is no longer love, it is slavery. That is an essential characteristic of love. Only by experiencing voluntary love coming freely from his children can God achieve joy and satisfaction.

Let us take an example. Most of us wear a watch. You may be very fond of your watch, especially if it keeps good time. Yet, your appreciation for the watch is limited. You take it for granted that the watch will keep good time. It is set to keep time and has no free will to do otherwise. The watch performs according to the program of the watchmaker. No one says thank you every day to their watch.

On the other hand, the relationship between parents and

their children is totally different. There is no limit to the depth of love and appreciation in this relationship. If the parents come back from a trip and their child is waiting at the airport, how do they feel? What if the child has even saved his allowance without buying candy and bought flowers to give them? They will be overjoyed. They undoubtedly will kiss their child and they may even shed tears. Why? It is a little deed of love and comes from the exercise of free will by the child.

By the same token, God is giving His entire love to man through His free will. God in turn longs for man to freely return his love to God. That love alone can give God joy and satisfaction. God does not want to receive love any other way, and for this reason God created man with total free will. Our human responsibility is to understand God and freely respond to His love.

Chained "patriotism"

Dr. Pak often illustrates this by telling a story about one of his experiences during the Korean War. Dr. Pak spent most of the Korean War on the front line. Once there was a hill which was being fiercely defended by the enemy, and which seemed impossible to occupy. The enemy was strongly entrenched in bunkers. They seemed absolutely committed to hold on no matter what. The United Nations forces attacked with mortars, and by air, employing various tactics. Dr. Pak's company was given the mission to occupy the hill, and the fighting was terrible. Every inch up the hill was bought with blood.

Dr. Pak says that he was amazed at those North Korean enemy soldiers because they just would not stop fighting. They were being hit by artillery; they were being hit from the air; they were assaulted by infantry; but they just would not stop. They seemed determined to defend that hill.

Finally, in order to conquer the hill, every single North Korean soldier had to be killed. Dr. Pak said that when he entered the bunker, he felt that he needed to salute those men for their valor. He was ready to do so when suddenly he saw something which absolutely appalled him.

When he looked at the soldiers, he noticed that every single one of them had his foot chained to the concrete floor of the bunker. They were not heroes; they were slaves who had been programmed to die. It was a chained patriotism.

Love must be free. Love of nation, love of parents, love of the world, love of God. It must be free. Otherwise it is not love, it is only coercion.

D. Human failure prolongs restoration history

In creation, God takes 95 percent responsibility, and He delivers on His share. He then calls upon man to have faith and obedience to His word. This is man's 5 percent responsibility. If that had been accomplished, God's ideal could have been realized. God's responsibility was fulfilled, but man's responsibility was not. Thus, the end result was a failure. In other words, God can do all kinds of things, but until man responds to God's will, God's ideal cannot be accomplished.

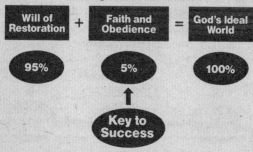

History of Restoration

Will of Restoration	+	Faith and Obedience	=	God's Ideal World
95%		5%		100%

Key to Success

The CAUSA Worldview responds to the objections of Russell, Camus, and others. Why is there suffering in the world? Because of man's failure to respond to God. Why does

God not force man to respond? Because at that moment, man would no longer be man. Man would be a robot. There would be no basis for human dignity. Time and again in history, God has sent individuals to try to reach out and alleviate mankind's suffering. God has reached out, but it is up to man to respond.

Man's responsibility in restoration

The same reasoning can be applied to the course of history. Human failure began an evil history. We did not fulfill our responsibility to God. All of history since that time has been a history of restoration. God has a will to restore this world (95 percent), but it can only be restored through man's response to God (5 percent). Man's free will and human responsibility are the key to a successful consummation of the process of restoration.

The central truth of the Judeo-Christian tradition is that God loves the world and will send the Messiah to save it. God sending His son, the Christ, represents His 95 percent responsibility. Man, in turn, must receive Christ and believe in Him, thus fulfilling his 5 percent responsibility. This is expressed in the New Testament: "For God so loved the world that he gave His only Son, that whoever believes in him should not perish but have eternal life." (John 3:16) The word

"whoever" implies that man has a choice. Refusal to believe means no salvation.

In a very famous passage of the Bible it is written that a blind man came to Jesus hoping to have his sight restored. Everyone scoffed. They maintained that it was impossible to be able to heal that man. Jesus took dirt, and spat upon the dirt, and made a paste and put it on the man's eyes and asked him to go and wash his eyes in the waters of Siloam. (John 9:1-7)

For the blind man, it was a test. He must demonstrate his 5 percent responsibility, that is, his faith and obedience in the words of Jesus. If the blind man would have only a worldly viewpoint, Jesus' words would seem completely absurd. Somebody had just spit and put mud on his face.

The blind man believed. He went to the waters, washed his eyes, and he could see. God does everything He can do (95 percent), but man must respond (5 percent), just as the blind man did.

In the case of the Exodus, the opposite occurred. God reached out but the Israelites did not respond. When they did not respond, the times became more difficult.

It is not that God fails: the point is that man fails, and

God never fails.
Man fails to respond to God's will

Prolongation of the goal of human history

about this God can do nothing. If God intervened, then He would violate free will, the very basis upon which man is different from all the rest of creation. Every time that man fails to respond, there is a delay of the providential history. When can we build a God-centered world, a just world? Man's response to God will answer that question.

E. Conclusion

There are three steps in the process of restoring God's ideal. First of all, men must find God — not only intellectually and philosophically, but in their hearts. Secondly, men must know God's will. Thirdly, men must have faith and obedience to God's will. All of this is the human responsibility.

Without the fulfillment of these three steps, the fulfillment of the history of restoration is impossible. God is waiting in anguish for man's faithful and obedient response to Him. And yet, most men and women are unaware of God's painful situation.

"God proposes, and man disposes." We must come to know and appreciate the suffering heart of God. Like the father in the parable of the prodigal son, God is suffering because of His children. He wants to give them His total love. In order to receive the love of God, men and women must genuinely assume the position of the children of God out of their own free will.

3 Steps to Restoration

1. **Man must find God**
2. **Man must know His will**
3. **Man must have faith and obedience to His will**

CAUSA Worldview V
CAUSA Worldview on Man

The behavior of every society is determined by its view of man. Nazism, for example, had a certain view of man. Social Darwinism has a certain view of man. Communism has a certain view of man. In this section, we will discuss the CAUSA view of man.

A. Rebuttal of the communist view

Let us examine the role of man in communist ideology. Essentially, the communist world view maintains that man is a product of his environment. *Homo sapiens,* in other words, is a species which emerged as a result of environmental pressures. In addition, individual men and women are what they are in accord with environmental factors. In response to environmental factors, a person will develop a certain type of character.

This gives rise to Marxist "ethics." A person is good or evil in accord with his or her economic formation. That is why, for example, when Vietnam fell into communism, one of the first things the new rulers did was to gather the soldiers who had been allied with the former South Vietnamese government, and force them into labor camps. They believed that through the environment of the labor camp, the character of the people could be changed.

In accord with the Marxist world view, economic alienation is the essence of evil. In other words, private property is the cause of evil, and when the economic system is changed, a regeneration of man can occur. The ideal society will be realized when, finally, private property has been completely eliminated. The way to build a truly just and moral society, then, is by changing the external system. If you change the external system, then naturally the internal character of man will be changed.

In the CAUSA view, the economic system is largely the creation of society. That is, it is a product of the members of society. You cannot change the cause by making changes in the effect. Changes must first be made in the realm of cause. This is a self-evident principle assumed by science. Change must therefore come in the realm of human character before human environment.

In light of this, Marx's claim that his view was "scientific" while others were "utopian" seems foolish. The Marxist view turns out to be totally unscientific. The regeneration of man's character cannot be affected by changing his external conditions.

This is borne out by the failure of Marxism as we discussed in Chapter 2. One violent Marxist-Leninist revolution after another has failed to bring the promised ideal society. The Soviet Union, the first Marxist state, is plagued with corruption, rather than regeneration of the human character.

The communist view of man

The communist view of man is as follows:

(1) Man is an advanced animal.

In the communist view, man is an ape-like animal which has undergone a unique process of development according to the theory of Lamarckism. Specifically, man is the being which began to use tools and perform social labor. The use of tools created the necessity for language, and this stimulated the nervous system and reasoning power developed. For this reason, Engels said that it was labor, not God, which created man.

If this is how the human being developed, then there is no foundation for human dignity. Man is an advanced animal, no different from other species. The ape may be a little more

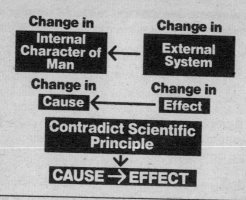

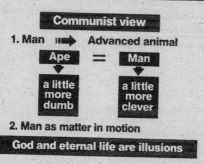

dumb, and man may be a little more clever, but both are animals and there is nothing to set them apart. Between a Volkswagen and a Cadillac, what is the difference? One is small and simple, the other is big and luxurious, but both of them are automobiles.

(2) Man is matter in motion.

Communism says man is matter in motion, nothing more. Man is a body. A body is just a machine. God and eternal life are illusions. We are totally describable in terms of our material constituents and the laws of chemistry and physics. We are a portion of the animal kingdom, without soul, without spirit, without significant individual value, and subject to improvement, modification and change by the laws already successfully applied by other members of the animal kingdom.

According to Marx, what we think, what we believe, and what we feel are products of our experiences within our economic environment. We are the product of our economic environment.

If we are the product of our environment, then it follows as night follows day that a specific environment can create a specific character, a specific set of ideas. It should then be possible to conceive of an environment that will create perfect characters and perfect ideas. This becomes the justification for an allegedly scientific program for the regeneration and perfection of mankind. The ultimate objective of communism is just that — the regeneration of man, the perfection of man. The first step in that program is to put the communists into power, because it is they who understand the laws of history. It is they who can create the proper environment for the regeneration of man.

It is an attractive vision. This is what attracts people — the wealthy, the intellectuals — this vision of perfecting and regenerating mankind. They have a chance to be one of history's elite and carry out this tremendous task.

There are, of course, certain unpleasant features which are not immediately apparent. The United States is made up of people who have had many experiences. Their ideas and concepts are already formed. If the communists have a successful revolution and conquer the United States, what will they do with these people? The communists are quite clear about this.

Karl Marx wrote in the *Communist Manifesto*, "You must confess that by individual you mean no other person than the bourgeois, than the middle class owner of property. This person must indeed be swept out of the way and made impossible." As you would clear away the wilderness to build a road, the communist elite identifies and clears away the contaminated members of the human species.

The practice of communism: a crime against humanity

When people believe this, they practice it. We saw in the country of Cambodia where a group of communists who had learned their communism in France — the Khmer Rouge and Pol Pot — came to power believing what Karl Marx taught them. They set out to apply it.

Karl Marx taught them that capitalism degenerates, that the city is the focus of capitalism, and that physical labor regenerates. Now they believed they had the historical responsibility to regenerate mankind. They set out to do it with a terrible consistency that staggers the mind. They said, "Out of the city!" And in one day they drove the people of Phnom Penh — 1,500,000 people — out of the city without a trace of bourgeois sentimentality or brotherly kindness.

In his text, *Murder of a Gentle Land*, John Barron writes:

Troops stormed into the hospital, Phnom Penh's largest and oldest, and shouted at physicians, patients and nurses alike, "Out! Everybody out!" They made no distinction between bed-ridden and ambulatory patients, between the convalescent and the dying, between those awaiting surgery and those who had just undergone surgery. Hundreds of men, women and children in pajamas limped, struggled and hobbled out of the hospital into the streets where in the hot sun the temperature was well over 100 degrees F. Relatives or friends pushed the beds of patients too wounded or enfeebled to walk. Some carried the bottles dripping plasma or serum into the bodies of loved ones. One man carried his son, whose legs had just been amputated. The bandages on both legs were red with blood, and the son, who appeared to be about 22, was screaming, "You cannot leave me like this! Kill me!"

Now what would the communists do if they conquered the United States? There would be no restraining their power. The communists have always been restrained to date because there exists in the world a force strong enough to destroy them if it decided to do so and was provoked beyond measure. But there would be no such force if they conquered the United States, and they would be free to apply their theory in practice with a consistency that would approach that of Pol Pot and the communists of Cambodia. Communist strategists have even speculated that two-thirds of the United States population would have to be destroyed, because the capitalist mentality is so deeply entrenched here.

Communism is the literal fulfillment of Psalm 14: "The fool hath said in his heart, 'There is no God.' They are corrupt. They have done abominable things. There is none that doeth good, no not one. Have all the workers of iniquity no knowledge; they eat up my children as they eat bread."

Violations of human rights and freedoms

When we consider that within communist doctrine, there is no philosophical basis for human rights, it seems very ironic that Marxist groups are always at the forefront of militancy in favor of human rights. Such demonstrations of concern, however, are consistent with Leninism, which teaches that it is necessary to adopt any position whatsoever in order to gain practical advantage over your opponent.

Marx foresaw the realization of freedom through the application of his theories, but the reality has been starkly different. Communism has no room for the variation from the norm which freedom brings, and there is no room for creativity. Soviet workers complain that they are treated like machines. Most important of all, there is no room for love. All emotion must be denied for the sake of the state.

Communism achieves this to such a degree that we may call the process "robotization." The system makes a man into a machine. The process is more degrading than slavery. A slave will still maintain some human character. A robot does not. For this reason, the march of communism is the funeral march of humanity.

Vyacheslav Syosoyev is a Russian artist who cartooned the Soviet robotization of workers. He is now being held in a KGB prison pending an official investigation of his "sanity." One cartoon in particular characterizes the nature of Soviet man. The man is without expression. As soon as some expression emerges, "boom!" The expression disappears. Everyone is uniform. Everyone is the same. The introduction of individuality would rob the system of efficiency. A robot worker is most desirable from the point of view of the Soviet rulers, because he is easiest to manage.

Confronted with such a system, we must clarify our view of human life. Our pursuit of truth must never falter. With this in mind, we introduce the CAUSA view of man.

B. The CAUSA view of man

In the CAUSA Worldview, man is not just an animal. Man is not just a body. Man is a divine being. That is, man is a creation of God. Furthermore, man is a being with divine value. Man is a manifestation of God's divine character and holiness. Man is the substantial creation made in the image of God.

Man **is** a spirit
and **has** a body

Man has more than biological life

The Bible speaks of life in a special sense. "For as the Father has life in himself, so he has granted the Son also to have life in himself." (John 5:26) Clearly, this concept of life refers to something other than biological life. Life in this sense refers to man's unique ability to commune with God. The real life of man is the spiritual life. The body is merely the vehicle for the spirit. Man is a spirit, and that spirit has a body.

This is the meaning of man as a divine being. The purpose of man is transcendent of this world, because man's spirit comes from God, and man's destiny is to leave this world and dwell with God for all of eternity. It is only here that we find the philosophical foundation for human rights and human dignity. Each person is a child of God. A crime against any human being is a crime against God.

Certainly this is the best possible critique which can be made against the exploitation of workers by capitalists, or the exploitation of the Third World by imperialists. Marx decried exploitation, but what is exploitation if we accept the Marxist view of man? It is merely one animal in the jungle surviving at the expense of another. Why is that a crime?

When we know the reality of men and women being the

children of God, we can no longer tolerate the mistreatment of one human being by another. It is truly sad that today many idealistic persons, disillusioned by hypocrisy in the West, are supporting the Marxist critique, which denigrates man. We must make every effort to encourage the practice of God's truth, which elevates man to the highest possible level of dignity and esteem while strongly condemning injustice and exploitation.

The purpose of life

Man is created for a definite purpose. When we are fulfilling that purpose, we experience the feeling of happiness. We cannot be happy unless we are fulfilling that purpose. Let us make an analogy. The purpose of a violin is to produce beautiful music. If you use a violin as a spanking rod, you abuse the purpose of the violin. You will not produce music, and you will destroy the violin.

What is the purpose of a human being? Man is created to love God, and to give joy and satisfaction to Him. When we are able to commune with God and to give genuine joy to Him, we experience the true happiness described by the saints and great spiritual teachers.

These same teachers have consistently taught that the most important way of showing our love for God is by loving

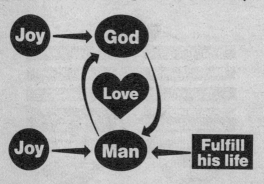

our brothers and sisters, the children of God. By loving God and our fellowman, we are able to fulfill the purpose of our lives. This is like a violin giving the most beautiful music.

Happiness is like a rainbow

Today, many people are desperately trying to experience happiness, but frequently, the more they try to be happy, the more unhappy they become. This is because of the nature of happiness itself. Happiness cannot be approached as a goal. Happiness must be seen as a reward bestowed upon us when we fulfill the commitments which we make in life. In that way, happiness is like a rainbow. You cannot deliberately cause rainbows to appear, and it does no good to chase after them. When the atmospheric conditions are correct, the rainbow automatically appears.

The aspects of man

We have already spoken about God's characteristics of internal character and external form as well as masculine and feminine. These characteristics are most fully manifested in human life, where we find man and woman as well as mind and body. In addition, we find that every human being has spiritual and physical aspects.

The physical aspect is subject to certain physical laws,

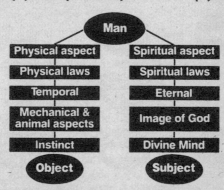

and the spiritual aspect is subject to certain spiritual laws. The physical aspect is temporal and the spiritual aspect is eternal. Physically we have certain mechanical or animal aspects; spiritually, we are in the image of God. Physically we are subject to instinct, spiritually every human being has a divine mind. What part is object? The physical aspect. What part is subject or primordial? It is the spiritual aspect.

If we are to develop a solution to the human problem, we must consider the "whole person." That is, we must consider both the spiritual and physical aspects of man.

The causal dimension in human life is the spiritual dimension, and yet it is this dimension which is too frequently ignored or de-emphasized. Marxism, for example, treats the spiritual aspect as a product or function of the physical. They try to deal with human history and human problems in exclusively material terms. By doing so, they invite failure.

C. The CAUSA Worldview on man

Let us summarize and enlarge on what we have said so far.

1. Man is in the image of God.

God created man in His own image. Man is like a mirror reflecting the image of God. When God sees man, He sees Himself just as parents see themselves in their children.

2. Man is the visible manifestation of the invisible God.

The creation of God is the manifestation of His invisible self into a visible, substantial form. Therefore, every creation is a visible manifestation of the invisible God. Among all creations, man is supreme. God projected Himself into a being capable of responding to the entire range of His emotion. God has given men and women unlimited potential for dignity and value. For this reason, men and women are the "second selves" of God. In the words of the Bible, "Ye are God."

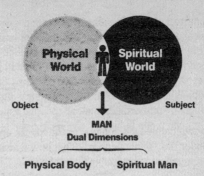

3. Men and women are the sons and daughters of God.

The most intimate and closest relationship in the universe is the relationship between parent and child — the relationship between a father and mother and their sons and daughters. God created men and women in this most intimate and closest relationship with Him. All humankind is created in the position of sons and daughters to God, and the relationship between God and His children is one of love.

Since all humankind comes under one Father, we must love one another as brothers and sisters. All men are one family of man, and the parent of that family is God. Our identity as God's children transcends race, nationality and culture.

Man cannot look for or achieve any greater or more permanent title than the title of son or daughter of God. You cannot honor any fellow man in any better way than to respect him as a son of God. This is the foundation of true peace and harmony among men. This is where human rights and dignity originate. When you look at someone as a child of God and give him his due respect you have done your best duty as a fellow man. You cannot do better than to love someone as a child of God. Certainly you cannot harm him, lie to him, extort him or exploit him. You cannot do any evil to your fellow man when you look at that man or woman as a son or daughter of God.

CAUSA Worldview On Man

1. Image of God
2. Visible Manifestation of Invisible God
3. Son (Daughter) of God
4. Eternal Being
5. Three stages of life

4. Man is an eternal being.

Man is created as an eternal being just as God is eternal. As the laws of creation explain, God created man with two dimensions, one is the physical self and the other is the spiritual self. At the same time, God also created the world in two dimensions, one is the physical world and the other is the spiritual world. Man alone lives in both worlds.

Often we encounter great misunderstanding with regard to the term eternal life. Some people believe that man is supposed to live on earth forever. This view holds that because of the fall, death came about. However, we must recognize that there is a great deal of evidence with regard to the existence of a spiritual world. Some of this evidence was reviewed in Chapter 2 of this text in the discussion of Marx's view of man.

If God intended man to live on earth forever, He would have no need to create a spiritual world. Furthermore, science has found no physical being capable of living forever.

We believe that man lives in two worlds. He lives with his physical body here on earth in the physical world, and with his spiritual self in the spiritual world forever. The spiritual body and spiritual world are made from spiritual elements. Between the two worlds - the spiritual and physical - the spiritual world is the subject and the physical world is the object, much as mind is subject and body is object. The two worlds are identical except that the spirit world is more "real" than the physical world, because it is the world of eternal existence. For this reason, the Bible refers to the physical world as a "copy and shadow of the heavenly sanctuary." (Hebrews 8:5)

Today the greatest source of problems in our society is that men and women do not realize that the spiritual world exists and that they will go on to live forever. They do not understand that during their lives on earth, they must prepare themselves for the next and ultimate stage of life.

5. Three stages of life.

Every person must pass through three stages of life:
    a) the embryonic stage in the mother's womb
    b) the physical lifetime on earth
    c) the eternal spiritual life in the spiritual world

The Three Stages of Life

Embryonic
Stage
(Liquid)

Terrestrial
Stage
(Air)

Spiritual
Stage
(Love)

a. Embryonic stage

During the nine month period in the mother's womb, the baby prepares himself for the earthly life. Living in a liquid atmosphere, he receives nourishment and oxygen through the umbilical cord. During this time, the most critical process taking place for the baby is preparation for the life that is forthcoming. The digestive organs are made ready for food, and the lungs must be prepared to be able to breathe air.

b. Physical life on earth

At the time of birth, the baby must leave the familiar and secure environment of the womb and emerge into a totally new world. Birth is at the same time both the "death" of the embryonic stage of life, and the dramatic beginning of earthly life. A baby in the comfort of his mother's womb has no idea that a world is existing outside, and he would have no desire to go through the experience of birth, because it is as unknown to him as death is to us.

Perhaps when a baby cries out at the time of birth, he is mourning his old mode of life. If the preparation is complete, however, there is no need to mourn. His lungs will function to breathe the air and his stomach will take in food. If it should happen, however, that his lungs do not fully develop, then he will be unable to breathe air, and a stillbirth is the result.

A human being is designed to live on earth for only a limited time. That is to say, the second stage of life is limited like the embryonic stage. Instead of nine months, however, the physical life could be one hundred years. The purpose of this one hundred years of earthly life is preparation for a higher third stage — the spiritual stage. The entire physical universe is like a great womb where nature provides us with food to eat and air to breathe.

The moment must come when we terminate our life on earth, but death is actually a second birth process into the spiritual world. The day of physical death is the day of spiritual birth. This dramatic experience awaits every living person.

c. Spiritual life in spirit world

In the same way that we leave the liquid atmosphere of the mother's womb to enter the air atmosphere on earth, at the time of physical death, we are thrust into another atmosphere in the spiritual world. What kind of atmosphere is it? It could not be material such as liquid or air. The atmosphere of the spiritual world is filled with love and with the spirit of

God. A strong pair of "love lungs" is needed to breathe that "air."

As much as we prepared our air lungs when we were in our mother's womb, we must prepare our "love lungs" while we are alive on earth. Without those love lungs, we would be stillborn into the spiritual world. This stillbirth into the spiritual world represents a far more serious type of death than the loss of physical life. It is real death, death in the sight of God.

Obviously, the question of how to prepare ourselves on earth for the next stage of life is extremely important. Experiencing the love of God and loving our fellow men here on earth is the most important and critical preparation we must make. As the baby prepares in the mother's womb to emerge into the physical world, we must prepare our spirit here on earth to pass on to the eternal spiritual world. We are a living spirit from the time we are born, but we will only develop when we receive the love of God and practice the truth of God by loving our fellow man. We need to learn how to love here. If we wait until the next world, it is too late to develop.

For that reason, God has established a perfect institution on earth in which we can learn and experience love — the family.

FAMILY

School of

Love

The family is the school of love

The family is where the essence of the love of God can be experienced and practiced. It is the God-given school of love.

The essential nature of the love of God is threefold:

1) parental love
2) filial love (child's love)
3) conjugal love

All of these three loves can be learned and experienced within the relationships of the human family.

Parental love is the love which parents give to their children. It is the most pure and sacrificial love of all. Children's

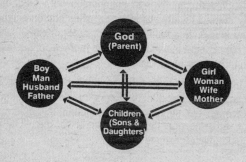

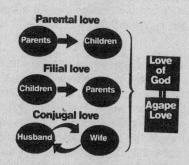

love is the love which children return to their parents. Conjugal love is the love experienced between husband and wife in marriage. These three types of love are the most profound experiences of love in human life. By having these experiences of love on earth, each person is able to experience and practice the love of God, which has been called agape love — totally unselfish love. When the love of God is practiced in the family, that practice can be expanded throughout the society, nation and world. By practicing the love of God, a person brings about the growth of his spiritual self.

The experience and practice of love must be centered upon God so that through every stage of human life man can be in communion with God, and man can feel the love of God directly. When man lives in communion with God, he has already started his eternal life even while still on earth. In a spiritual sense, this man will never suffer "death," and the end of his physical life will just be the moment of his transformation into eternal spiritual life.

The family is thus an indispensable God-given institution. In the process of spiritual development, each person should pass through the stages of son or daughter, adult man or woman, husband or wife, and father or mother. These are man's God-given, permanent titles.

Man lives forever, yet one's life here on earth is the only opportunity during which he can prepare for his eternal life. Man should live his earthly life fully aware of his eternal future.

On the other hand, the person who lives on earth with only a materialistic outlook, completely denying his spiritual life by living a selfish and greedy life, will be totally unprepared for birth into the spiritual world. This is the greatest tragedy imaginable — to enter the spiritual world without having developed the sensitivity to God's love which enables us to live happily in that world. The pain and regret of that situation are intense and long lasting, and very difficult to remedy. Eternal spiritual life without having developed the ability to commune freely with God is called "hell," while eternal life in love with God is called "heaven." In either case, no human being is able to extinguish his spiritual existence. Whether or not man perfects himself, his existence goes on forever.

Men of wisdom must realize this ultimate truth and utilize every second of their earthly lives toward the well-being of their eternal lives. To do that, one must recognize God, receive His truth and practice God-centered, unselfish love toward his family and toward his fellow man.

D. The two dimensions of human life: the physical self and the spiritual self

We already explained that man exists in two dimensions. One is man's physical self and the other is man's spiritual self. Man lives in the two worlds, physical and spiritual.

Strictly speaking, we do not pass into the spiritual world at the time of physical death. Rather we are continuously living in both realms — spiritual and physical — throughout the course of our physical lives. One's spiritual self is joined with the physical body until such time that the physical body separates itself from the spiritual self at the time of physical death. From that point on, the spiritual self becomes independent and lives on in the spiritual world for eternity.

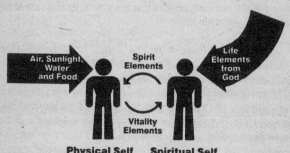

Growth of the spiritual self

It has already been stated that man's earthly life is the primary opportunity for his spiritual self to grow to maturity or perfection. But what is the mechanism of this spiritual growth? To learn something about the principles of spiritual growth, we will first consider the process of physical growth.

The physical body of man, like the physical body of any other living thing, requires a period of growth to reach maturity. During this growth period, certain elements are consumed by the body. These include air and sunlight from above, as well as food and water from below.

In the same way, the spiritual self also must pass through a growth period in order to achieve maturity. We must know what sort of "elements" are necessary for spiritual growth to take place. In general, we can say that an individual must receive truth and love from his parent, God. These would correspond to air and sunlight in the physical growth process. That is, they are given freely from outside the individual. We call these spiritual elements "life elements." God is the ultimate source of all life elements, and we receive them through our parents and other parental figures.

Just as physical food is essential for the growth of the physical body, the development of the spirit also requires a spiritual "food." This is called the "vitality element." It is generated by our own physical bodies when we practice truth and love in our daily lives.

In other words, the spiritual self must have give and take with God by receiving God's truth and love, and must pass on those elements of inspiration to the physical body. The physical body receives the message and obeys it, and practices the truth and love of God in real life. In this way, the physical self can return abundant vitality elements to his spiritual self, by which the spiritual self can grow.

Men must receive God's truth and love while on earth and practice it. In this way, man becomes an embodiment of the truth and love of God. That is the only way one's spiritual self can grow to full maturity. Man must practice God's greatest commandment to love God and his fellow man. This alone can provide for the eternal well-being of an individual. This is the important purpose of the physical stage of life.

It is important to realize that the material well-being of the physical body is of secondary importance compared to our proper spiritual development. When a man is totally blind to the reality of God and His truth and love, and lives a selfish and greedy life on earth, he has completely denied the growth of his spiritual self. In the words of Jesus, "What will it profit a man if he gains the whole world and loses his soul?"

In the CAUSA Worldview, every action of man has eternal impact. What we do has an eternal effect on our spiritual well-being. We can say that man reaps what he sows. Whatever situation a person may find himself in, it does no good to blame others. Man has no one to blame but himself, and each person must take responsibility to live a good and moral life.

E. Communism destroys family and religion

What then of communism? On the surface, it appears to be asking people to sacrifice themselves for an unselfish ideal. It would then seem to be spiritually beneficial to man. This, however, is extremely misleading. In reality, communism sti-

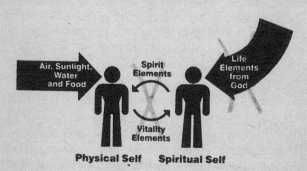

Air, Sunlight, Water and Food

Spirit Elements

Life Elements from God

Vitality Elements

Physical Self   Spiritual Self

fles human spiritual development. It denies the existence of God, and denies His truth and love. The greatest injury done by communism is that it totally blocks out man's spiritual life by teaching that there is no God and no eternal spirit. Instead of love and sacrifice, the essence of life becomes hate and resentment. If you study Marxist literature, it becomes clear that at the very core of Marxism is resentment. In order to promote the dialectic, Marxism must promote hatred. This hate withers and destroys the human spirit.

Here again, a strong contrast can be made with the communist view. Communism denies the most sacred institution of all — the family, thus denying man the experience of the practice of love. By breaking apart families and encouraging children to betray their own parents, they have engendered such hatred and animosity that millions of men have come to deny their eternal life, and be "stillborn" into the eternal world of love. This is the worst crime which the God-denying ideology of communism commits against humanity.

Communism destroys the family. This is a point which Marx declared very clearly in the *Communist Manifesto*. Bright children are routinely separated from parents. They are taught that the party and the state are more important than their parents. Prosecuting one's parents for "ideological crimes" is regarded as an heroic action in communist states such as North Korea.

It is interesting to consider the words of Richard Wurmbrandt. He spent 17 years in a prison in Rumania, and he said, "I came to understand the power of evil when I spent the time in prison. I began to see that there must be a Devil, because it would impossible for men to treat other men the way that I saw people treat people in that prison in Rumania."

Something happens when people are taught to hate in that way. They become capable of doing anything to advance their cause. State interest becomes the moral justification for their crimes. Ultimately, the love of God is cut off, and actions, instead of being motivated by love, by concern, or by ethical ideals, become motivated by hatred. The result is spiritual death.

In the words of Jesus, "Do not fear those who kill the body, but cannot kill the soul. Rather fear him who can destroy both soul and body in hell." (Matt 10:28) This is what communism does. This blanket denial of spirituality can be compared to a "blackout." Communism represents a spiritual blackout which today affects billions of lives. It denies the eternal well-being of people. Besides the physical atrocities which have actually destroyed millions of people, communism has ruined the eternal lives of billions more. This is why communism is the worst crime ever perpetrated against humanity.

Here we find the reason why, in the name of God and in the name of humanity, communism must be stopped. This is CAUSA's fundamental concern. When we see that there is a philosophy today which is destroying the spiritual dimension of the human being, then we have to stand up, we have to oppose it, we have to stop it.

We cannot be satisfied with saying, "Well, we're going to stay where we are. They can have their part of the world, we can have our part of the world, we don't worry about it." If we have real compassion, if we really feel that all the people on this earth are our brothers and sisters, and if we really feel that we have an eternal life, we cannot allow millions of people to die spiritually because of a false ideology. Compassion calls us to action.

F. Conclusion

About 45 years ago there were many people who were fleeing from Nazi Germany. And in the midst of all of those people, there was one German who was living in New York and teaching at the Union Theological Seminary, and he said, "I have to go back to Germany. I know everyone else is running, I know I'm well here in America, but I have to go back to Germany. I can't stay here." And the reason that he went back is that he felt God's call. He said that there are two kinds of grace. There is cheap grace, the kind of grace that invites us to say, "I'm well; I don't have to worry about others." But he said that through his prayers and efforts he had found another kind of grace which he referred to as costly grace, and he spoke about the cost of discipleship, the cost of real belief in God. He said that it was this belief which mandated that he return to Germany, even at the cost of his life, and do everything in his power to stop Nazism. That man's name was Dietrich Bonhoeffer. Shortly before the fall of Adolf Hitler in 1945, he was executed because of his opposition to the Nazi government.

In the name of God and the name of humanity

COMMUNISM MUST BE STOPPED!

Bonhoeffer's life is an example for us. He recognized that the real value is the eternal spiritual value. His earthly life has ended, as each person's must, but he lives on in the eternal spiritual world in a greater capacity, and in the hearts of all those who admire his actions. In the eyes of God, he is not dead at all; his noble life goes on forever.

Today, we must think about liberation of the communist world. When Reverend Moon came to America in 1973, he announced that he wanted to have a rally in Washington, D.C. to awaken the American people to the danger of communism. And in 1976 he had that rally. Then he said, "Now I want to have a freedom rally in Moscow." That is the spirit behind CAUSA. We want to bring liberation to the communist world.

CAUSA Worldview VI
Overall Conclusion

We will now summarize and conclude our presentation of the CAUSA Worldview.

A. CAUSA stands for change

It is the CAUSA position that a profound change must come to our world. We are not among those who advocate the mantainance of the status quo. However, in contrast to communism, CAUSA proposes a fundamental change. This is not a change in a system, but a change in man. Systems are created by men. A change in man, then, is a change in the realm of cause. This change will bring about changes in the realm of effect. The economic system, the social structure and the method of government are in the realm of effect. CAUSA upholds the principle that unless man changes, nothing changes. Structures are made by men, men must change, and men cannot change without God.

CAUSA PROPOSES FUNDAMENTAL CHANGE

```
        Change
          │
          ▼
        Cause ─────────►  Effect
          │                 ▼
          ▼              System
       Internal  ──────► Society
        man               Nation
                          World
```

1. Alienation: a point of agreement with Karl Marx

The CAUSA Worldview agrees with Marxism in one point only. That is, human alienation has occurred, and therefore a solution is needed. From this point on, however, Marxism and the CAUSA Worldview are as different as night and day.

First of all, Marx saw human alienation as an economic event. Perhaps because he saw human alienation manifested clearly in man's economic activity, he believed that the root of the problem was there. He therefore believed that the solution must be the abolition of private property.

CAUSA

Alienation occured →	**Solution is needed (no status quo)**
Spiritual Alienation (not economic) →	**Spiritual Solution Value Awakening**
Separation from God →	**Union with God and His moral principles**

In fact, as we have seen, abuses in the economic arena are but one symptom of the fundamental human problem. Marxism deals with symptoms, not with the disease.

The root of the human problem is man's separation from God, called "spiritual alienation." Spiritual alienation requires a spiritual solution. In religious terms, human beings need salvation. Human salvation is not something abstract. Neither is it a sensation or some sort of emotional experience. Salvation means that the relationship between God as Father and mankind as children is completely restored.

2. Where must we begin?

The union of each person with God is our ultimate goal.

As we have said, God is working to bring each person into unity with Him by stimulating the human conscience. Our conscience guides each one of us toward moral value. Our journey to God is therefore the journey to a higher perspective of moral value.

How is our perspective of value raised up? Only the truth is able to elevate our perspective of value and lift us up to a higher viewing point. The process of raising our perspective of value in response to truth can be called a spiritual awakening. We begin our journey to the highest perspective of value by searching for a new expression of truth. This is the point of departure for CAUSA.

3. The journey of mankind toward God

Human history is the journey of mankind toward God. Certainly at the outset of creation, God endowed men and women with the power to know Him. His desire was not only that they know Him, but that they dwell with Him and share every day with Him in love. Men and women are intended to live with the constant awareness of God. This would not require any extraordinary effort, such as prayer and fasting, but would be as easy as feeling the warmth of the sun or recognizing our own parents.

Where must it begin?

Goal:

Spiritual Awakening

New Moral Values

The fall of man, the separation of man from God, deprived God and man of that closeness. Whatever particular interpretation one may take of the biblical description of the fall, the results of man's separation from God are clear. Knowledge of God was lost, and darkness fell over the human mind. From that moment, man's long journey in search of God began.

This journey is not completed in a single step. In fact, mankind has made many steps ranging over many thousand years. Each step takes us closer to the day when we can emerge gradually from darkness and see the shining sun, God.

The time of Abraham and the birth of Hebraism

The Bible describes distinctive steps in the process of man knowing God. In ancient times, for example, human understanding of God was very primitive. Men worshipped idols, and the concept of a monotheistic God was strange to them. Abraham, the son of Terah, an idol maker, was inspired by God to begin a new religious tradition. That tradition is the Hebrew faith. Abraham rejected his father's idols and prayed to the one God.

The story of Abraham is one of the great stories of human faith. Ultimately, Abraham was asked to sacrifice that which was most precious to him, his son Isaac, born to him at the age of 100 years. Abraham demonstrated absolute faith and obedience to God. He was even willing to kill Isaac on Mount Moriah. At that moment, God stopped Abraham, saying, "Now I know that you fear the Lord."

At this early stage of human history, then, God was seen as an object of fear, and the way people related to Him was through offerings. This was the extent to which God could teach about Himself at that time.

The time of Moses

Later, we find in the Bible the story of Moses. How did God relate to His people in Moses' time? We can compare it to the way a parent would relate to a young child. Just as a parent would guide a child by prescribing what the child should and should not do, God guided His people by giving them the Mosaic Law.

This age might be called the age of law. By telling His people what to do and what not to do, God hoped to guide them along the path to Him. In this age, God reigned over man as the "Lord of the hosts of heaven," with mankind in the position of servant.

The time of Jesus

Christ came 16 biblical centuries after Moses. In contrast to the Mosaic Law, we can say that the teachings of Jesus bring religion to the stage of faith and love. When asked which is the greatest commandment, Jesus replied, "You shall love your God with all your heart, and with all your soul, and with all your mind. This is the great and first commandment. And a second is like it, You shall love your neighbor as yourself. On these two commandments depend all the law and the prophets." (Matt. 22:37-40)

We could say that through Christ, God was treating men and women as a loving parent would treat his adolescent children. Rather than simply prescribe what they should do, He respects that they have reached a certain degree of maturity and He challenges them to show their faith and love for Him by loving one another. Jesus Christ emphasized the profound truth that God is our Father, and men and women are His children.

The present age

In the 2000 years that have elapsed since the birth of Jesus Christ, human civilization has achieved a phenomenal level. Men have walked upon the moon, and the space-shuttle is regularly circling our planet. Human intellectual capacity has developed far beyond what anyone could have imagined.

Along with this, man's capacity to learn and understand the truth of God has progressed. How will God reveal Himself to modern men and women? What stage have we now reached along the road of knowing God?

CAUSA's view is very clear on this point. God wants each of us to take the final steps in the path back to God. This can be achieved when we come to know God intimately and profoundly. The present age is the age of the actualization of sainthood. Each one of us is called to be a child of God, to be a temple of God, to be a saint. This was the goal for man from the very beginning. Now all the trends of historical development indicate that this goal will soon be achieved.

When men and women become what they originally should have become, the commandments of religion will be unnecessary. When someone becomes an embodiment of the truth, every action is naturally pleasing to God, and the extra-ordinary demands of religious life would no longer be necessary. It is the will of God that all men and women become like Christ. All men and women are destined to achieve sainthood. When this is the case, what kind of society would be created? This could only be called the ideal society. Certainly the dwelling of God would be with all men.

B. CAUSA: the process of change in men, society and the world

1. Godism

The process of change within men begins with the understanding of a new expression of truth. Truth is eternal and unchanging. Nevertheless, the expression of truth which men of a given age are able to understand is continuously changing. Recognizing this, CAUSA starts with a new and clear expression of truth. This expression of truth is able to improve our understanding of God, and the relation of God to mankind. St. Paul predicted that as time went on, we would no longer "see in a mirror dimly, but then face to face." (1 Cor. 13:12) CAUSA feels that time has come.

Certainly with the advances which humanity has made in all realms of knowledge and understanding, it is appropriate at this time that God would inspire us to formulate clearly our God-affirming principles into a coherent, inspiring and convincing world view. This is the purpose of Godism.

2. A spiritual awakening

The new understanding of God engendered by this new expression of truth is able to quickly elevate the individual's perspective or point of view. We call this a spiritual awakening. This process takes the age-old blindfold from our eyes and allows us to see the whole reality.

3. Change in priority of values

There are basically two kinds of values, material and spiritual values. Material values are temporal, while spiritual values are eternal. God created both values to be good, and they are essential to human well-being. It is important to realize, however, that material values are secondary while spiritual values are primary.

At the present time, there is confusion regarding the importance of spiritual values. The spiritual awakening which the CAUSA Worldview kindles will bring about a change and clarification of the priority of values.

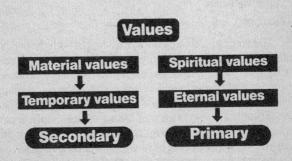

4. Revolution of man

At this point we might ask the question, What is the greatest obstacle preventing this process from happening? In other words, what is the worst enemy of humankind? We have been saying all along that the worst enemy of God and man is communism. At this point we should make clear that communism itself is only a manifestation of the fundamental human problem of evil. Communism is the external enemy of man, while selfishness is the internal enemy.

If tomorrow morning, all the communists in the world renounced Marxism-Leninism as a false dogma, would we then have all heaven and all happiness? Sadly, we know that we would not. We still would have to win the internal battle against selfishness.

A quiet yet intense revolution from selfishness to unselfishness must take place within the human heart. This is the revolution of man.

What is selfishness?

Selfishness does not refer to the natural desire of every person to better himself. We have a natural ambition to secure greater well-being and a drive to achieve higher values. These are not selfishness. These are all aspects of the God-given original nature of man. Selfishness refers to the narrow misapplication of man's desires or ambitions. This narrowness gives rise to greed, jealousy and vanity, and these are poison to the spiritual life of man.

Selfishness is a perversion of man's original nature. It comes from blindness towards spiritual realities. Life presents us with an endless series of choices, and blindness to spiritual realities leads people to make the wrong choices.

Selfishness can be compared to going shopping and mak-

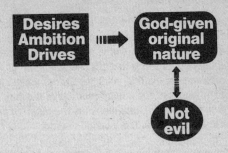

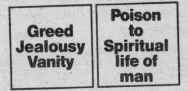

ing a wrong choice because of lack of information. You feel cheated later when you find out the truth. Whoever lives a selfish life will feel cheated after death when they realize what a bad choice they have made. This is the result of blindness to spiritual reality.

Selfishness is like a drug

Drug abuse is a serious problem in the United States and other Western countries today. Drug abuse is like selfishness. Drugs produce an immediate artificial "high," but in the process they cause permanent damage to mental and physical health.

Selfishness comes when people do not see spiritual reality

In the same way, people who are ignorant of spiritual reality and are seeking immediate material well-being frequently behave in a selfish way, often hurting and abusing others. Men and women cheat on their spouses. Children deceive their parents. People steal from each other and violate one another. In this way, they may enjoy some momentary pleasure or short term material satisfaction, but they suffer eternal spiritual harm.

Unselfishness, on the other hand, may require the postponement of immediate gratification, but the reward is always a deeper form of satisfaction. Ultimately, when everyone practices an unselfish lifestyle, life on earth becomes a time of greatest pleasure and joy, and life in the spiritual world is the continuation of that joy eternally.

Material values and material well-being are not evil. Quite the contrary, these things are good things created by God. Material things, however, are best used as a means to spiritual satisfaction. After all, no one can take even one penny with him on his eternal journey. The wise way of life, then, is to invest every material resource we have on earth for the sake of the spiritual well-being of oneself and all people.

New men and women

Communism is talking about the "regenerated man" and

the "new communist man," but this individual has never appeared in the communist world. The enlightened man and woman can only appear when one is touched by the truth of God, surely not by a change in the economic system.

We all can become new men and women when:

1) We are spiritually awakened to higher values.
2) We have new motivations and new goals in life.

When we have clear and inspiring goals in life, we are filled with vitality and enthusiasm.

The word "enthusiasm" comes from the Greek "entheos" meaning "God entered." Enthusiasm means "God entered into man." When God enters man, we have higher values, new vitality and enthusiasm.

6. Ideal society

Defeating communism is only an intermediate objective. Our final goal is to build a moral society. On that day we will realize the age-old human dream which is none other than the realization of the ideal of God. To achieve this, it is necessary that each one of us take seriously the call to sainthood, and the task of building a "society of saints."

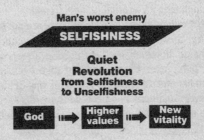

Man's worst enemy

SELFISHNESS

Quiet Revolution from Selfishness to Unselfishness

God ⟹ Higher values ⟹ New vitality

C. Summary of the CAUSA Worldview

The following is a brief summary of the CAUSA Worldview.

1. Godism vs. communism

We have been comparing and contrasting two world views: Godism and communism. Let us review the points which we have made. Godism advocates a change in man, while communism advocates a change in the economic system. Godism advocates an internal revolution within the human being, the change from selfishness to unselfishness. Communism advocates an external and violent revolution in line with its ideological perspective.

Godism aspires to deal directly with the fundamental moral corruption which pervades all systems. Communism deals only with the symptoms of these problems.

2. The importance of the individual

The key is the individual. On the individual level the deviation of man from God began. Likewise it is on this level where restoration must also begin. If individuals are changed, then naturally families will be changed. Then the communities, nations, and the entire world which these families live in will be transformed.

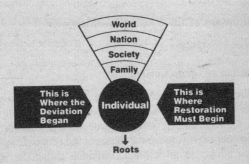

3. God or no God?

Godism maintains that there is a God; communism postulates that there is not. Godism maintains that life is eternal; communism states that man is a temporal being. Godism believes that there are absolute values; communism is based upon relative values. Godism espouses cooperation in human relations centered upon love; communism emphasizes the dialectic centered upon hatred. Godism recognizes that there are many struggles in human life, but in essence, these are between good and evil, selfishness and unselfishness. Communism identifies the basic form of struggle as class struggle.

Ultimately it can all be reduced to a single belief. Godism

maintains that there is a God; communism denies this. Only one of these beliefs can be true. We find the answer in the living reality of God.

D. Five points of the CAUSA Worldview

The following five points are the succinct expression of the CAUSA Worldview. We feel that these five points are broad enough to encompass the beliefs of all God-accepting people as well as people of conscience. At the same time, these five points are specific enough to exclude all communistic and atheistic ideas.

If you can accept these five principles, or even one of them, we would like you to work with CAUSA. These are the five points CAUSA feels all religious people and people of conscience can accept and unite upon. We are confident that a communist is not able to accept even one of the following principles, which represent the foundation of CAUSA.

The CAUSA Worldview maintains that:

1. God is the Creator.
2. Man is the child of God.
3. Man is created free to love and take responsibility.
4. Man lives an eternal life.
5. Selfless love is the supreme value.

CAUSA WORLDVIEW

1. **God is the Creator**
2. **Man is the child of God**
3. **Man is created free so that he can love and take responsibility**
4. **Man lives an eternal life**
5. **Selfless love is the supreme value**

E. Parallels between the CAUSA Worldview and beliefs of the American Founding Fathers

These five points run closely parallel with the principles affirmed several hundred years ago by the Founding Fathers of America. Dr. Cleon Skousen, founder of the National Center for Constitutional Studies and a leading expert on the U.S. Constitution, in his text *The Five Thousand Year Leap,* explains that the United States of America accomplished in little more than a hundred years what required thousands of years to bring about in other parts of the world. The reason, according to Dr. Skousen, is that the Founding Fathers placed a high priority on religion and moral values.

Founding Fathers' thought

Religion is the foundation of morality and essential to good government

This priority is very evident when we consider that the same Congress which approved the United States Constitution also passed the Northwest Ordinance of 1787. Article 3 of this ordinance states: "Religion, morality, and knowledge being necessary to good government and the happiness of mankind, schools and the means of education shall forever be encouraged."

Formal education was to include the teaching of three points:

1. Religion	**No**
2. Morality	**No**
3. Knowledge	**Yes**

The Founding Fathers believed that education should include not only the teaching of knowledge, but religion and morality as well. Today, however, the U.S. public school system devotes little effort to the education of moral values. Religious teaching in the schools has often been replaced with secular humanist principles which are, in essence, atheistic. While many oppose the re-inclusion of religious principles in the American public school curriculum because they do not want their children to be indoctrinated in the beliefs of a particular denomination, the fact is that the Founding Fathers set out from the beginning to make the teaching of religion a unifying cultural factor in education and to exclude any emphasis on a particular creed or doctrine. They sought a universal religious code that would be acceptable to people of all faiths.

Benjamin Franklin offered one expression of this universal code when he expressed the following articles of faith:

Here is my creed: I believe in One God, the Creator of the universe. That He governs it by His Providence.

That He ought to be worshipped. That the most acceptable service we render to Him is in doing good to His other children. That the soul of man is immortal and will be treated with justice in another life respecting its conduct in this. These I take to be the fundamental points in all sound religion.

When we summarize it we arrive at the following five points:

1. One God, the Creator of the universe, is to be worshipped.
2. He governs the world by His Providence.
3. Men can glorify God by loving His children.
4. The soul of man is immortal.
5. In the next life, the soul of man is judged by his conduct in this world.

This formulation, or something closely resembling it, seems to have commanded the widespread respect of the Founding Fathers. Samuel Adams, commenting on these points, said, "This group of basic beliefs which constitute the religion of America is the religion of all mankind."

CAUSA believes that the fact that the American Founding Fathers were thinking not only of America, but of all mankind, is quite significant. God's will is ultimately to unite all mankind into one world family of God.

We would like to express the contrast and similarity between the Founding Fathers' "universal religious code" and the CAUSA Worldview in a little more detail. The Founding Fathers expressed the belief that God is the Creator and is to be worshipped. It is not CAUSA's intention to promote any particular form of worship or doctrine of salvation. That is the mission of the various churches. Therefore we say "God is the Creator."

To the Founding Fathers' article of faith, "He governs the world by His Providence," CAUSA adds that "man is created free so that he can love and take responsibility," thus emphasizing that man must take part in God's providence by exerting his free will. "The soul of man is immortal" and "man lives an eternal life," are, of course, identical in content. Finally, the Founding Fathers believed that "the soul of man is judged by his conduct in this world." The fifth point of the CAUSA Worldview, which states that "selfless love is the supreme value," underlines the standard for the judgement of man's earthly life and the main criterion for the growth of the human spirit. When man has successfully practiced a life of selfless love here on earth, his spirit will be free to commune with God and enjoy fellowship with all people in the eternal hereafter.

F. CAUSA pursues traditional values

The parallel between the CAUSA Worldview and the above-mentioned points of faith of the Founding Fathers is not coincidental. Just as the Founding Fathers of America believed that religious life was going to be vital for the survival of America, so CAUSA sees it as being crucial for the survival of the Free World. And as the hope of the Free World today lies with America, CAUSA urges America to return to its founding spirit. It is the fervent hope of CAUSA that these presentations will engender a new strength of religious zeal, and that each CAUSA participant, whatever his or her

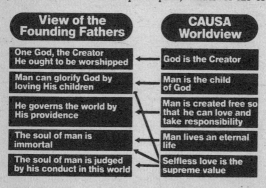

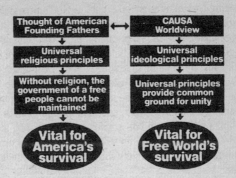

Thought of American Founding Fathers	⟷	CAUSA Worldview
↓		↓
Universal religious principles		Universal ideological principles
↓		↓
Without religion, the government of a free people cannot be maintained		Universal principles provide common ground for unity
↓		↓
Vital for America's survival		**Vital for Free World's survival**

religion may be, will be inspired to a new energy of dedication to God and mankind.

In CAUSA there is hope. For the first time, we see hope of reversing the tide in our deadly struggle between freedom and communist tyranny. For the first time we see real hope for America and for the world. CAUSA brings a new day of hope.

CAUSA Worldview VII
Practical Applications of the CAUSA Worldview

The great failing of the West to date has not been a scarcity of great truths, but rather the inability to put these truths into practice. It is not our intention to introduce the CAUSA Worldview as a teaching without implication in daily life. On the contrary, the origins of the CAUSA Worldview are in the intimate experience of man with God and the realities of life. Clearly this truth is capable of tremendous impact on the real life of man in society.

The CAUSA Worldview leads directly to a particular lifestyle, the God-centered way of life. When God becomes the center of each individual's life, all religious people and people of conscience are drawn together into unity. For this to happen, the CAUSA Worldview must be actively applied in a program of character building.

A. Three pillars of a good society

In the CAUSA view, a good society must rest on three pillars. These are:

1) God
2) Family
3) Unselfish love

These three themes are constantly interwoven in the CAUSA Worldview.

1. God

God is the bedrock foundation of a good society, and belief in God is the basis of the CAUSA Worldview. God is the ultimate source of the power of life. It is essential, then, that

CAUSA Worldview:
The Three Pillars
of a
Good Society

each person must know God in order to fulfill himself as an individual, and in order to contribute to the fulfillment of his family, community, nation, and finally, world.

2. Family

The family is one institution which God designed as part of His original plan for creation. The family, which begins with the unity of husband and wife, is the basic unit in the sight of God, because it is here that His ideal can be realized. Within the family, love can blossom and reach fulfillment, and that is the very purpose of creation. Furthermore, the family is the school of love, and the community, nation and world are the extension of the family.

3. Unselfish love

> If I speak in the tongues of men and of angels, but have not love, I am a noisy gong or a clanging cymbal. And if I have prophetic powers, and understand all mysteries and all knowledge, and if I have all faith, so as to remove mountains, but have not love, I am nothing. If I give away all I have, and if I deliver my body to be burned, but have not love, I gain nothing.
>
> I Cor 13:1-3

Love is the essence of life. Through love, God can fulfill the purpose of His creation, and man can fulfill the purpose of his life. The real evil of communist philosophy is the substitution of hate for love. Although Marx protested against the dehumanization of the worker, there is no greater dehumanization than robbing the human heart of sentiments of love and in their place inflaming grievances and resentments. Hate isolates man from God. As the Bible says, "He who does not love does not know God, for God is love." (I John 4:8)

Yet in our world we find many kinds of love. How can we distinguish God's love from other forms of love? God's love is unselfish love. God is the pure and loving parent. He seeks only the well-being and happiness of His children. He constantly sacrifices Himself for the sake of the children. This is genuine love. While selfish love will draw man away from God, unselfish love will always seek to unite everyone with God. Selfish love is the source of evil and the root of the human problem.

The CAUSA Worldview promotes unselfish love, pure love, God's love. This alone can unite man with God and give man fulfillment and joy.

A good society can never come about unless it rests on the three pillars of God, family and unselfish love.

B. The goal of life: eternal joy with God

It is pointless to begin a great undertaking without a clear goal. When you take a trip, you have your destination clear. Our own life is certainly the greatest personal undertaking which we can imagine, and yet many persons live without clearly understanding their goals in life. Other people formulate goals, but these goals may not be the same as the purpose which God has for them. In either case, the individual is headed for frustration in his life.

The purpose for which God created men and women is to receive God's love and to return love to God. That purpose must be our life's goal. We are created to fulfill the love of God as the children of God. When we do that, we satisfy God and we are satisfied. For this reason, the religious question has always been, "What is the will of God for me?" When we have answered this, we have identified our goal in life.

We can make three recommendations:

1. To become a child of God

The first step, simple as it may seem, is to realize our identity as the children of God. There is no one who is closer to the parents than the children. Certainly the servants, neighbors, or friends of the parents do not share the same intimate relationship of love as the children do. Children who do not recognize their identity are a source of great concern to the parent. Therefore, the profound realization that we are the children of God is the first step towards giving God joy.

2. To obtain "eternal life"

"Eternal life" means the attainment of the highest stage of spiritual development. Our goal must be to secure eternal life. This can only be achieved by the diligent application of God-centered principles here on earth. These principles are outlined in the CAUSA Worldview.

3. To achieve fulfillment in life

We want to be happy. God wants us to be happy. The purpose of creation is that we be happy. And yet human life is plagued by unhappiness. The reason is because we do not live with the dramatic awareness that we are the children of God destined to live an eternal life with Him.

God has invested vast potential for genius in each person. He has given us every imaginable gift. When we are able to understand our true identity, this potential will become realized in our lives. When one has fully developed his God-given potential he feels happy. He has achieved fulfillment in life.

CAUSA is committed to a

strong, God-centered America

strong, united global movement

**One Fatherhood of God
and
One Brotherhood of Man**

C. The commitment of CAUSA

CAUSA is committed to two things: winning over communism and creating a moral world. Godism, a God-centered world view, is essential to achieve these goals. Both are achieved when we take Godism and apply it in our lives.

The spiritual way of fighting communism

This can be called the spiritual or ideological way of fighting communism. There has been a constant attempt to "contain" communism militarily, economically and politically for the past 150 years. Still the Free World is losing ground. There is no easy way, no cheap way, that we can stop communism. We must first change our way of life. We must apply Godism and live God-centered lives. At that point, the tide, which has been running against us, will turn.

A strong America

Furthermore, communism cannot be defeated unless America is strong. America was created to be "one nation under God." However, God's ideal is "one world under God." This will be the fulfillment of "one brotherhood of man under the fatherhood of God." This can happen when God becomes real to all people.

A global movement

Communism cannot be defeated and a new moral world cannot be brought about without a strong, united global movement. Communism is global, and does not recognize national boundaries. Furthermore, communism has a global strategy. Without responding with a global strategy, we cannot win.

D. The practice of unselfish love

What can we do to assure that our love is unselfish love? How can we identify unselfish love?

Unselfish Love

Honesty	Trust
Purity	Fidelity
Compassion	Harmony
Service	Joy

1. Honesty

Unselfish love starts from honesty. The history of selfish love is the history of dishonesty. According to the biblical account of the fall of man, the human fall is associated with dishonesty. The woman listened to the lie of the serpent rather than the truth of God. Regardless of how we interpret this story, there is a profound truth expressed here. Dishonesty destroys love and breeds mistrust.

If you love someone, you must first be honest with them. Honesty brings trust and an environment where love can flourish.

2. Purity

Unselfish love is pure. An unselfish person must preserve purity of heart towards his or her spouse. This requires complete fidelity, tragically lacking in many marriages today. The loss of purity brought about by immoral conduct is poison to the marriage relationship, which is the center of family life.

In the same way, we must maintain purity of heart in all of our relationships. The patriot is the man who keeps a pure heart of devotion to his country. The saint and true child of God is the man who keeps purity of heart towards God.

3. Compassion

Unselfish love is compassionate. The compassionate heart is generous and forgiving. This type of attitude naturally creates harmony and unity, while cold-heartedness causes separation and friction. No one wants to be treated without feeling. We are not computers; our value cannot be measured by our efficiency.

The greatest expressions of human compassion are sincere tears shed out of love for one another. This is the most beautiful thing in the world.

You have loved your spouse
family
country
world
God

4. Service

Unselfish love is expressed in service. The final test of unselfishness is willingness to serve. That service brings joy. Service is an act of giving. We give our knowledge, talent, time, effort and heart when we serve others. Only when we serve someone are we able to understand them.

These are the tests of unselfish love. When we are honest, pure, compassionate and serving to others, then we are loving them unselfishly. When we extend honesty, purity, compassion and service to our spouse and family, we know that we are loving them unselfishly. The same is true for our country, the world, and ultimately, God.

Am I honest with God? Do I have purity of heart towards God? Am I compassionate and serving towards God? When we can answer yes, we are loving God unselfishly.

CAUSA Worldview VIII
CAUSA Outreach

The overall CAUSA strategy is to change society by changing individuals. The change in the individual may be called a spiritual change, and this is naturally expressed in a political change in society.

We do not recommend specific political measures, not because they are not important, but because that is not our way of working. We want to inspire individuals to commit themselves to basic principles. These individuals can then apply their ideas, as well as their talents and creativity, to translate principles into political and social programs.

CAUSA strongly supports the democratic progress as it is applied in representational government. This democratic process, however, is based on and assumes a morally strong and healthy society. This can only exist when each individual has a healthy relationship with God.

CAUSA seeks

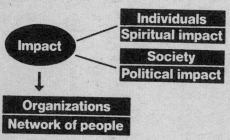

In order to carry out our educational work and influence society, we need to create a network of people. This task requires teamwork. Individual heroes are fine, but structure, organization and teamwork are most important to our success.

Building
CAUSA networks
1. Chain-reaction principle
2. Affiliated organization network

A. A network of people

In order to reach out to as many people as possible as quickly as possible, we need to apply the chain reaction principle used in the atomic bomb. We need to construct a spiritual atomic bomb, not to destroy but to build. In the chain reaction, as each atom is split it sends out particles which split more and more atoms. In other words, the chain reaction starts out slowly, but it becomes large very quickly.

In 32 weeks, what can happen:

1 1 x2	12 2,048 x2	23 4,194,304 x2
2 2 x2	13 4,096 x2	24 8,388,608 x2
3 4 x2	14 8,192 x2	25 16,777,216 x2
4 8 x2	15 16,384 x2	26 33,554,432 x2
5 16 x2	16 32,768 x2	27 67,108,864 x2
6 32 x2	17 65,536 x2	28 134,217,728 x2
7 64 x2	18 131,072 x2	29 268,435,456 x2
8 128 x2	19 262,144 x2	30 536,870,912 x2
9 256 x2	20 524,288 x2	31 1,073,741,824 x2
10 512 x2	21 1,048,576 x2	32 2,147,483,648 x2
11 1,024 x2	22 2,097,152 x2	4,294,967,296
2,048	4,194,304	**4.3 billion**

If we apply this to our outreach, so that every person reaches out to two more, two to four, four to eight, we can reach over 4 billion people in just 32 weeks. This process will be even faster if every person reaches out to two people every week. We then have the multi-dimensional view.

Certainly no one is going to work just the first week and then stand idle. Working every week, in 32 weeks one person could start 32 different "family trees."

It is also possible for one CAUSA volunteer to reach out to 12 people, just as Jesus Christ did. Then these 12 can reach out to 12 more to make 144. In this way, a whole community is quickly reached.

2. CAUSA affiliated organization network

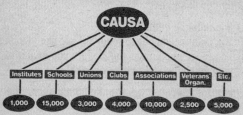

B. A network of organizations

There are many organizations now in existence which share the goals of CAUSA. These include schools, unions, clubs, associations, veterans' groups and other patriotic groups. We hope to be a catalyst to encourage their work and bring them into relationship with one another.

This can be done by working with the leadership and teaching them the CAUSA Worldview. They in turn can teach their own people and spread the ideas.

This network is now being constructed, and in this way the message of CAUSA has already reached millions of people.

Success depends upon "I"

1. "I" must be totally committed
2. "I" must multiply "myself" (sign of spiritual health)
3. "I" must make sure my "second self" also multiplies

C. The secret of success

The most important secret of success is you. Without you, nothing will succeed.

1) You must be committed.
2) You must reach out to other people like yourself.
3) You must encourage the people you reach to follow your example and reach out to others.

When this happens, we are already changing the world. And who will benefit most from that? You will. By helping and educating others, you are uplifted and inspired, and you become spiritually healthy. Your spiritual growth will be phenomenal.

The CAUSA conclusion is optimism

Although we have described many painful realities of our society as well as the danger of communism, we are filled with optimism. This is because of our confidence in God. We are confident that God is on our side, because we are on His side. And God and we make a majority.

When we are convinced that we can do the job, then we have won half the battle. "A good beginning is already half the way there."

CAUSA is you

What is CAUSA? Who is CAUSA? CAUSA is not an organizational structure; CAUSA is you. CAUSA is dependent on what you do with CAUSA. If you feel that CAUSA is your mission, CAUSA becomes yours. When should you make your commitment? Today, because tomorrow will never come. Tomorrow always remains a day away. The hour of decision must be today and now.

What is CAUSA?

One participant at a recent CAUSA conference felt this very deeply. She wrote, "God bless CAUSA. I must say that God has sent me to this seminar to learn and understand that this is the best way to combat our greatest modern-day enemy — international communism. Today I place CAUSA at

"More powerful than an invading army, is an idea whose time has come."

Victor Hugo

May God Bless You!

the center of my life. This seminar has also taught me love, unselfishness and a stronger desire to help those next to me. I will spread this gospel now that I have the tools."

When you feel as she felt, then indeed CAUSA is you.

Victor Hugo wrote, "More powerful than an invading army is an idea whose time has come." We believe that CAUSA is an idea whose time has come.

May God bless you as you put the truth into action in your life.

CHAPTER SEVEN NOTES

1. Aristotelian and Thomistic argumentation on the existence of God leads to the conclusion that there must exist a First Cause (prime mover in Aristotle) which is God. (Aristotle: *Metaphysics XII; Physics VII-VIII.* Thomas Aquinas: *Summa Theologiae I,* q.2; *Contra Gentiles I,* 13-16,44; *II,* 15; *III,* 44.)

2. Robert Jastrow, *God and the Astronomers,* New York, Warner Books, 1980, p.29.

3. Roman Catholic thought relies heavily on the analogy of being *(analogia entis).* By carefully studying the nature of the world, we discover a great deal about the nature of God.

    Because our world contains gradations of goodness, truth, etc., there must be a *summum bonum* which is the cause of all goodness, truth, etc. This we call God.

4. The CAUSA view of the constitution of beings basically differentiates its ontology from the Aristotelian; nevertheless, it does not contradict it. Aristotle advanced the concepts of substance and accident which are different entities of the same object, whereas the CAUSA view presents the same object as relational, namely,

that the same object or being has its invisible and visible characteristics. The novelty of the CAUSA position consists here in departing from Aristotle's concepts of potency and act *(Metaphysics XII*, 4-5) and building its ontology on relationship.

5. Afanasayev, p. 83.

6. For an interesting review of scriptural passages supporting the view that man has free will, see *Did God Know?*, Howard R. Elseth, Calvary United Church, Inc., St. Paul, Minnesota, 1977.